P9-CEL-039

WINNING
BY
NEGOTIATION

Winning by Negotiation

Tessa Albert Warschaw

McGRAW-HILL BOOK COMPANY
New York   St. Louis   San Francisco
Düsseldorf   Mexico   Toronto

Copyright © 1980 by Tessa Albert Warschaw
All rights reserved. Printed in the United States of America. No part of this
publication may be reproduced, stored in a retrieval system, or transmitted, in
any form or by any means, electronic, mechanical, photocopying, recording,
or otherwise, without the prior written permission of the publisher.

1 2 3 4 5 6 7 8 9   DODO   8 7 6 5 4 3 2 1 0

LIBRARY OF CONGRESS CATALOGING IN PUBLICATION DATA

Warschaw, Tessa Albert.
Winning by negotiation.
Includes index.
1. Negotiation. 2. Success. I. Title.
BF637.N4W37   158'.1   80-14535
ISBN 0-07-000780-2

Book design by Stanley Drate

For My Mother
and
The Memory of My Father

ACKNOWLEDGMENT

My deep appreciation goes to Elizabeth Dickie-Pellett, who patiently, lovingly, and supportively guided my journey. She is the model for the Win-Win Negotiator described in this book.

I am most grateful to my family: the Alberts, the Resnicks, and the Millers, for feathering my nest and keeping it warm during my flights of fancy.

I am indebted to Harriet Dezen, Viva Knight, and Susan Spiegel for unconditionally and unselfishly allowing me to brainpick and brainstorm. Their encouragement and invaluable contributions helped this book come to life.

Irv Weiman shared his profound and voluminous business expertise and consistently gave wise counsel.

Appreciation goes to Michael Laurence for not going bananas in Beverly Hills.

A special thanks to my agent, Aaron Priest, whose consistent belief in *Winning by Negotiation* never faltered.

My professional friends and colleagues—Connell Cowan, Eleanor Haspel-Portner, Elsie Giorgi, Ron Mann, Adelle Scheele, and Trudy Sternlicht—generously shared their ideas and their expertise.

To the persistent web of encouragers Dotty Gagliano, Peter Sykes, Terry Collins, Lisa Van Nieulande, Nicole Szumacher, Lee Ann Miller, and Ed, Anna Marie, and E. P. Horner, thank you all.

I am grateful to those anonymous negotiators who shared their personal and professional negotiations. Without this sharing this book would not have been possible.

I also stand in great debt to the many men and women

who are and have been my clients. They too have been my teachers.

There is no way I can adequately express my gratitude to Gladys Justin Carr for her brilliance, her wit and wisdom, and words that shall forever ring in my ears, "Less is more."

Contents

WINNING
BY
NEGOTIATION

Opening
Ceremonies

There is one question I invariably ask each of the executives, professional homemakers, doctors, stockbrokers, and other successful but dissatisfied people who bring their marital, family, and child-raising problems to my counseling office: "Has it ever occurred to you to negotiate?" And just as invariably, the answer is some form of "no"—a blank stare, a puzzled frown, or, "What do you mean, 'negotiate?' "—even though many of these men and women have vast experience as negotiators in their business life. Nor, it develops, have the spouses and children of my clients attempted to negotiate their differences with them. "Negotiation?" one wife asked. "Oh, you mean 'compromise.' I've been doing that for years."

What I've been doing for years—with my clients and seminar students, and in my lectures to corporate and men's and women's groups—is to show people how to bring the techniques of business negotiating to bear on the problems of everyday life: how to negotiate for power and money, for sex, love, and romance, with family and friends, and with all those professional and service people with whom they're obliged to deal so often and with such unsatisfying results. My methods are based on an intensive study I've made of the strategies of successful business negotiators, men and women whose persistence, awareness, sensitivity, skills of observation, genius for timing, willingness to seek help, capacity to listen, and sheer zest for the game have made them what I call "Win-Win Negotiators."

I've studied the losers as well—relatively healthy people who came to me because they weren't clicking as they wanted to or thought they should, people I eventually learned to categorize as Dictators, Jungle Fighters, Silhouettes, Big Daddies and Big Mammas, and Soothers, according to the negotiating style they displayed. I've urged my clients and students and audiences to try the tools and tactics of the winners, and to learn to recognize and deal with the characteristics of the losers—whether they identified those characteristics in others or themselves.

Watching many of the people with whom I've worked evolve from losers to Win-Win Negotiators—able to get the love, recognition, money, or power they so long coveted—has been the most gratifying experience of my life.

Those winning strategies are the subject of this book.

There are, in most of us, certain kinds of emotional problems that require professional help. But many of the problems that we experience in our dealings with others, many of the emotional binds in which we find ourselves, don't require long-term therapy and the expense of hundreds of hours and thousands of dollars in order to be resolved. They could be solved through the simple process of negotiation.

Yet most people, I've found, feel an incredible paralysis in attempting to deal with others. They fear to negotiate because they think they don't know how. They think of negotiating as something that high-powered executives do in spacious conference rooms, smoking fat cigars. They would rather do almost anything than have the kind of confrontation they assume a negotiation implies. They associate the process with conflict, and associate conflict with stress and the prospect of loss. Conflict, to them, implies dominance and coercion. In this association, unfortunately, they have been encouraged no end by trendy books and articles advocating ruthlessness and intimidation as the strategies of success. In certain circles today, debasing others is actually chic.

I find these developments tragic, lacking not only in awareness of the changing nature of values in our society but in the psychological forces that determine human conduct. Winning through intimidation does gain short-run "victories," but it leaves such a residue of human destruction that nothing is gained in the long run.

Every day, we receive fresh indications that the old behavior patterns that once governed American life—force and fear on the one hand, acquiescence and appeasement on the other— are increasingly suspect. Many young people are unwilling to take the kind of personal abuse their parents often had to suffer in order to get ahead. Many people of influence today who are trying to deal with others using the same techniques they endured as they struggled to the top are wondering why the old methods aren't working any longer.

The reason they aren't is that objectives have altered appreciably over the last ten years. Where previous generations often accepted without question the virtue of unlimited striving in order to "get to the top," today's generation isn't as concerned with running corporations as it is with expressing itself in a rich variety of ways and living a balanced life.

The change in behavior patterns is most noticeable, perhaps, in the home. The days when most of a family's decisions were made primarily to further the husband's career are all but gone. It is not simply a consequence of the women's movement and the rise of feminine consciousness; it is that more and more households include a working female whose needs for attention and support may be every bit as vital as her mate's.

Many men are simply unprepared to cope with this challenge to the dominance they had always taken for granted. They had signed up for working and risking on the outside, and resting and being cared for at home. Women signed up for just the opposite. Now they must deal not only with the anxieties any new adventure creates but also with the strains their new identities impose on their relationships with men.

As a consequence of this revolution of roles, both men and women find themselves caught in a double bind. Men who persist in their old competitive roles find themselves typed as chauvinists. Yet when they seek new expression through sensitivity, caring, and responsiveness, they find themselves typed as weak. Women who remain traditionally submissive and passive feel they've sold themselves short. Yet when they seek new expression through assertion and strong decision-making roles, they are typed as bitchy and unfeminine.

To make the transition between old and new roles, men and women must learn how to negotiate the inevitable strains that develop between them and also within themselves. Clearly, what has passed for negotiation in the past will never do.

We need a new way to come together—a way to anticipate, neutralize, and resolve our conflicts. Negotiation is the way to do that, but a kind of negotiating very different from the intimidating methods that have created so much social malaise.

Negotiators can be categorized as to the kinds of outcomes they seek. Basically, there are four—"Win-Lose," "Lose-Win," "Lose-Lose," and "Win-Win."

Win-Lose Negotiators want to take home all the bacon. In order to do so, they must dominate the other person, be that person a colleague, rival, spouse, or child. What happens to the other person doesn't bother them; in fact, the consequences of their destructive acts may not even occur to them. Their minds are totally fixed on victory.

Lose-Win Negotiators gain what they want by losing. They are passive negotiators, and the last thing they want is to dominate. The prospect of finishing first terrifies them.

Lose-Lose Negotiators can't stand the thought of the other person's winning, but they don't want to win, either. So after making certain that the other person loses, they sabotage their own victory.

Win-Win Negotiators want both parties to the negotiation to walk away winning, each with enough to show for his efforts for them still to be friends or partners. There is no anger or frustration or confusion when the negotiation is finished. Each party is willing to give up a certain amount in order to achieve this result—especially since the chances are that they will meet again.

Win-Win negotiating involves an appreciation of differences and an acknowledgment of other viewpoints. It applies to all aspects of life. Whether you are in the boardroom or the bedroom, you are aware of your own needs, feelings, desires, history, and goals, but aware of the other person's, too.

Win-Win negotiating is nothing if not practical, because as a practical matter, you can't get what you want from another person—except by coercion—unless that person is getting what he or she wants from you.

Most of us were raised by parents for whom winning was the only thing. In a sense, they had no real choice in the matter: it was the attitude the culture rewarded. Today, the win-lose philosophy—"I win, you lose"—no longer has the adherents it once did. We still want to win, for the most part, but we are in the process of redefining what that means. Where before winning meant total victory without regard to one's adversary, we know today that it's no longer appropriate for one person to walk away with *all* the rewards and love and self-esteem.

And no longer effective—the most pragmatic test of all.

I lecture frequently to corporate groups on the subject of Win-Win negotiating. After one recent lecture, the president of a major oil company came up to me and said, "The kind of man we're putting into key positions today is exactly the kind we devalued ten years ago."

"What kind of man is that?" I asked.

"The kind who makes sure that everyone gets something. We find now that you just can't win it all."

The most vivid proof of this I have, perhaps, is the kind of people who are enlisting in my seminars on negotiation. Increasingly, they are people who have found that the win-it-all manner in which they had always functioned isn't working for them any longer. They're scared. They believe they're on their way out. One man in his early sixties who had joined my seminar after reading about my work confessed to his bewilderment at the increasing problems he'd been having in his real estate business. "I've always gotten along fine in this business," he said. "I'm very successful. I'd be terrific if I didn't have to deal with anyone else." After probing a little, I discovered that he was having the same problems at home. His wife had grown distant, and his children no longer came to visit. They had taken all they could of his dictatorial manner.

Win-Win negotiating is so new that it is still something of a rarity, but negotiating itself is something we do every day of our lives. In virtually every activity, we must deal or bargain with another, or others, in order to get what we want. "You wash, I'll dry"—that's a negotiation. Where we live, how we live, with whom we live, none of these is accomplished without give and take. You're going to discover how to do that now in the Win-Win way.

You'll discover how to resolve your conflicts and differences with your spouse, lover, children, parents, employer, doctor, or agent. You'll learn how to do this, moreover, without distressing them. To the contrary, you'll all walk away from your negotiation feeling that you've won.

You'll find out how to handle the ten most common negotiating problems—time, money, family, sex, in-laws, independence, intimidation, communication, power, and recognition.

You'll discover how to anticipate conflicts so that they can be resolved in their earliest stages, before bitterness sets in. And because negotiation is not a method devoted exclusively to disputes, you'll find out how to use it to resolve conflicts in values—time together versus time to make money, spending versus saving, going to work versus going to the ball game, having versus not having children, and so forth.

You'll try out the tools of the trade: opening ceremonies, hidden agendas, warm-ups, probes, mid-course corrections, trade-offs, whammies, bottom lines, closing ceremonies, and many others—every one of them taken from the world of business and adapted for personal use.

You'll discover how to develop and pull on your support network—your web of human relationships—in ways that will strengthen and enrich you, and help you to gain your objectives.

You'll see that every person with whom you deal, in both your public and private life, can be classified according to the *style* of negotiation he or she displays. Is your spouse, lover, child, parent, friend, or boss:

A Jungle Fighter?
A Dictator?
A Silhouette?
A Big Daddy or Big Mamma?
A Soother?
A Win/Win Negotiator?

Or various blends of the above? You'll discover how to recognize every one of these negotiators, and the special tactics for dealing with each of them.

You'll discover, above all, how to identify your own negotiating profile, and how to transform yourself into a Win-Win Negotiator with the seemingly magical knack of satisfying everyone, yourself included.

It may be that you'll find win-win negotiating more an ideal than a practical objective. But as you grow and seek to change, the win-win style will provide you with a model toward which you can move in stages. By adopting those parts of win-win that fit with your own style, the transition can be a gradual one, moving your style towards the ideal.

To become a Win-Win Negotiator, either in whole or in part, you must learn, before anything, how to recognize your present negotiating style, as well as the styles of those with whom you deal. So let's begin with "style" itself.

PART ONE

Styles

Style:
What It Is,
Where It Comes From,
What It Says About You

Style is what fascinates. It is what is memorable. It is what is left when you walk out of the room. It's the expression of your essence, as individual as your signature or thumbprint.

We all have style. It is our uniqueness, our essence. There are those whose fear of revealing their essence makes their style bland or negative. There are others who rejoice in expressing their style, and they captivate us.

Who can forget the Kennedy charisma, the Kissinger shuttle, the Muhammad Ali rhetoric, the Marx Brothers, Eleanor Roosevelt, the Beatles, Barbara Walters, Walter Cronkite, Mickey Mouse? We do not forget them because each of them broadcast style that could be imitated but never duplicated.

Onto this essence that we imprint on others' minds each one of us has superimposed an image. Image can be a part of style, but isn't necessarily. Some people do project an image that accurately reflects their essence. Others veil themselves in deceptions, placing themselves in settings as carefully staged as those found in a first-rank Broadway show.

Imagine:

You walk into a room and see a chrome desk and a glass table and artifacts from Africa and a beautifully coiffed woman

11

in a kaftan who floats toward you, takes your hand firmly in hers, smiles graciously, and says in a warm and mellow voice, "Sit down. Let me pour you some coffee." You say to yourself, "She's charming. This will be easy." And before you've finished your coffee, you know you're up against the toughest negotiator you've ever met in your life.

You walk into another room—and would immediately like to leave. There, in the midst of his clutter and destruction, stands a certifiable "killer," critical, blaming, aggressive, his twisted scowl a preview of the worst half hour you'll probably ever spend. Ten minutes later, you've made an acceptable bargain by trading consideration and respect.

Each of us is a combination of both *image and style,* but they are not necessarily joined. When I see you walking down a hallway or entering a room or sitting at a negotiating table, it's your image I'm meeting. Your physical bearing, your look, your smile or frown, your handshake, your voice, your dress, your grooming—I categorize all of these as aspects of your image only, until and unless you show me through further contact and disclosure that they are truly indicative of you. Then, and only then, do I know for certain that it's your negotiating style I'm seeing. A friendly salutation may be nothing more than a gracious opening to a very tough negotiation in which you alternately stun me with silence and maim me with words.

Only when you begin to negotiate with me will I be able to separate image from style, and know for certain what kind of negotiator—and person—you really are, whether you are competitive or collaborative, responsive or distant, positive or negative. Only then will I know if what I'm seeing is the real you, or just surface wrappings. Your actions will tell me all I need to know—just as mine will tell you about me.

If our image is an act, the keen, attentive observer will see right through it just as surely as we ourselves, when we're alert, can see through the images of others and take in their essence.

Once the negotiation proper begins, the air is filled with clues.

Do you occupy more than your share of the couch, or otherwise seem to take over the room? Do you interrupt a lot, cutting off others midway in the development of their ideas in order to express your own? Do you deal with issues in a logical way, or intrude gossip and emotional history? And your language: is it direct and calm, or do you shout to make your points, use obscure or meaningless words, send double messages, speak to impress rather than inform? What about your nonverbal "language"—your eye contact, body stance, hand movements, facial expressions? Is it strong or weak, open or covert, low-keyed or frenzied? And, finally, your timing. Do you deal with matters smoothly and logically, or haphazardly and abruptly? Do you make the rest of us feel pressed and pushed and harried? Or are we soothed and satisfied when the negotiation has ended?

These are the clues I need to inform myself as to how and when to move. And yet even these clues are not enough if I expect to hold my own in my negotiation with you. I have to relate the style I'm seeing to a host of other factors.

Your style will vary depending on the *arena* you're in and the *person* you're with. A Soother in the office may be a Big Daddy to his son and a Jungle Fighter to his wife. Women who have made it big in the commercial world may never have outgrown childhood dependencies. Not long ago, I met an overpowering businesswoman who had started her own company and caused it to succeed by sheer force of will. Yet she is still so totally in her father's thrall that she will not buy an automobile without his approval.

Your style changes as your situation changes and different objectives are sought. It changes in terms of the *time of life* you're experiencing and your *needs of the moment.* Your feelings of being loved and appreciated or not, your health, even your financial well-being—these and many other factors influence your behavior. If you're broke, you're going to be a much different person than when you're "flush," not just because you have no money but because you don't have control over your life.

To complicate matters, styles don't always exhibit themselves in their purest form. A Dictator may have Big Daddy elements in him. A Silhouette may also be a Dictator. A Soother may be a closet Big Mamma. Even a Win-Win Negotiator may incorporate Big Mamma or Big Daddy characteristics. The styles of these amalgams will vary depending on the problem of each negotiation. Your own style may vary in terms of your perception of the immediate need.

Styles can be as different as the people they symbolize. Quiet elegance, calm tranquillity, dramatic flair, self-assured competence, unhesitating acceptance—all of these are personal styles, and all of them can be effective. Beaten and cowed, depressingly blue, boringly bland—these are personal styles, too, all of them ineffective.

Style, in sum, is a statement of who you are. It's your style that impacts on other people—whether you light up a room or turn off the sun, provoke laughter or snuff it out, strain to speak first or wait to be heard, move to the center or sit in a corner. It's your confidence or lack of it, your willingness to risk or your desire for safety, your ability to say no or your haste to comply.

Image and appearance get you through the door. The effectiveness and integrity of your negotiating style keep you in the room.

Style: Where It Comes From

Four categories of forces help to shape people's style— their basic emotional needs, their economic needs, the persons on whom they model themselves, and the values on which they settle.

Emotional needs arise in the earliest years of life. Love, affection, approval, security, self-esteem—all of these are nurtured, or not nurtured, in the home.

Most styles emerge from an economy of emotional abundance or scarcity. Persons nurtured on an abundance of security and love know not only that they have a lot to begin with, but that there's more where the supply came from and that it can be readily replenished. These people seem more able to give love and emotional sustenance to others. But persons raised on a scarcity of security and love may hang on to every scrap they can get. And not just those commodities, but money and power as well. Many are so fearful of losing what they have that sharing it with others is unthinkable.

Individuals who have experienced an abundance of constructive love and affection have a base from which to develop a positive self-concept, i.e., self-esteem. Without such a background, the development of self-esteem becomes infinitely more difficult. This is not to say that those who come from emotionally barren homes never develop self-esteem; among those I've interviewed over the years, I have found some persons, deprived of emotional support as children, who did develop good self-concepts through competence, skill, and talents. But it's just that much harder.

Economic need: A child who grows up poor may spend his or her life making certain that he or she will never be hungry again. How deeply such imprints are made, and how they determine decisions many years after the fact, can be appreciated by this recollection of a child of the Great Depression: "One winter day, as a kid of eleven, I walked across New York with a pair of skates that I sold for ten cents so that my family could buy some oatmeal. But the oatmeal turned out to be so spoiled that we couldn't even eat it. That was how we lived, every day a variation on that same theme. Then, thirty years later, you suddenly see hundreds of thousands of dollars dangled in front of you, and how do you react? You sell out, even though you know that the big corporation that's taking you over won't be faithful to your private vision. You do it in the time it takes to snap your fingers. Poverty warps you for life."

Modeling: Children begin by imitating parents, teachers, and friends. In time, almost everyone chooses to model on one or more persons in his or her life, to be as much like—or unlike—those persons as possible. Whether the modeling is positive or negative, it is powerful, effective, and fast.

Modeling isn't confined to childhood. All of us know someone who found mentors later in life and styled himself or herself on them. "I learned about this business from a tough negotiator," one executive I interviewed recalled. "Boy, was he tough. He made me sweat. I'd be up all night working on proposals, and then he might not use them. But he expected me to be perfect in every way and to anticipate his needs. I'll never forget him." He surely won't. He has become that which he imitated, to the point that those with whom he works now describe him exactly as he described his mentor.

Values: As you mature, you are drawn to certain modes of conduct. You "value" one kind of response over another. Out of these choices your style emerges.

Here, for example, are ten different ways you could choose to be in any negotiation:

Competitive	or	Cooperative
Ignoring	or	Accepting
Loving	or	Rejecting
Controlling	or	Permissive
Participating	or	Withdrawing
Accommodating	or	Resisting
Nurturing	or	Patronizing
Resolving	or	Deadlocking
Talking	or	Silent
Kinetic	or	Passive

Your choices, together, would constitute a profile. Some values would be central and critical, others peripheral. Choices change, depending on the situation; if so, your style changes, too.

Values emerge from the economy of abundance or scarcity in which you were raised, your religious commitments, your norms of right and wrong. Fortitude, or lack of it, derives directly from your antecedents, which conditioned you to accept yourself as a person of value or to diminish yourself as worthless or nearly so. Were your feelings acknowledged or not acknowledged? Were you appreciated or not appreciated? Have you experienced life in a peaceful way, or do you feel overwhelmed? Each of these alternatives has had a bearing on the style you presently bring to your interactions with others.

Needs, modeling, values, and the feedbacks they produce combine in your life experience to develop your *central tendency.* And that, in effect is you—your predictable behavior pattern, your familiar way of being, your *style.*

When you negotiate, you want to look for the central tendency in others, to be alert to when it comes most clearly on display, and with whom, and what provoked it. You need to recognize it in all its permutations, understanding that the arena, the need, the people present, and the time of life may dictate a change in another person's style, but that his or her central tendency is always there. And as conscious as you become of others' central tendencies, you must be no less mindful that your own is also on display.

Style: What It Says about You

Your style radiates either positive or negative energy. It indicates whether you are in love with life or terrified of it, whether you are willing to draw near to others and to new experiences or prefer to keep them at a distance.

Your style informs those persons with whom you negotiate whether you view yourself with confidence or don't, whether you feel accepted or rejected, ignored or appreciated.

Your style reveals whether you are free or compromised, dependent or independent, secure or insecure, courageous or afraid, hanging on to whatever you have out of fear that you might lose it or willing to take a chance in the hope of enriching your life.

Your style signals how you deal with conflict—whether you recognize it as the inevitable accompaniment to progress or prefer to deny its existence even when you're threatened. Do you face negotiations with obvious zest for the challenge of the encounter, or do you panic?

Your style, in short, is a giveaway—even if it's your style to hide.

Further on, we're going to identify your style. Before we do that, let's look at the styles themselves—Jungle Fighters, Dictators, Silhouettes, Big Daddies and Big Mammas, Soothers, and Win-Win Negotiators.

Jungle Fighters

You couldn't miss them if you tried. They are a razzle-dazzle, brassy lot, enraptured with their own theatrics, flaunting an extravagance of dress and manner that draws the attention they crave. Their volume is turned high, resonating through office, house, or restaurant, accompanied by big and busy gestures. On the jogging paths they wear the flashiest suits, at the office or at social gatherings, expensive yet far from conservative clothes. They can be, and often are, extremely charming, with a library of mesmerizing stories they deliver like accomplished actors. They dare—to be different, to create. They have vision. They have force, of such magnitude that when they leave a meeting the atmosphere collapses as though the air had been expelled from the room. They are electric and optimistic, embodying fire, talent, tenacity, and verve. They appear to exert a compelling magic over everything they touch. *Beware.* Jungle Fighters are the most dangerous negotiators of all.

To them, negotiation falls somewhere between a game and a war. They love it all—the intrigue, the strategizing, the deployment of forces, and above all, the combat. Gains like money and security are almost incidentals. What Jungle Fighters crave is the hunt, the chase, the conquest, the notoriety, and the accompanying intoxication—that surge of adrenaline, rush of blood, and extra flow of their juices. If there is no conflict, they will create it. However small the battle or stakes or issue, they must win and you must lose. They will use deceit, pull any kind of shrewd or ruthless negotiating tactic they can. No price is too high to pay if total victory results.

Jungle Fighters—christened by Michael Maccoby in *The Gamesman*—are extremely bright. It's the manner in which they often use their brain power that most distinguishes them. Their creativity and talent are enlisted almost entirely in the service of their ambitions. They demean others into submission. They send double messages, use circumventing monologues, try to talk circles around you, or change their strategy from one second to the next, anything to catch you off guard or anesthetize your senses. They force issues and take over agendas. They interrupt, cut you off, use sarcasm, toss off flip remarks— whatever it takes to win. To Jungle Fighters, charm is simply another tactic. "My last associate was a Jungle Fighter, only I called him a Street Fighter," a New York attorney told me. "That's the way he made it. He lied and blew things out of proportion and couldn't back up half of what he did, but he made his case with such charisma and authority that people believed him."

Jungle Fighters understand human nature well enough to know that they must make promises in order to keep people interested in their objectives. Delivering on those promises is another matter, regardless of how much damage their failure causes. They are the most consummate of "con artists."

Life at Full Throttle

Jungle Fighters work, play, and love hard—everything at full throttle. Play, in particular, is a "hats and horns" experience. "We began with Tequila Shooters at seven A.M.," a Jungle Fighter's companion recalled with awe following a marathon day together. "After a round of golf, it was three martinis at lunch, then two sets of tennis. Cocktails at six, wine with dinner, then some highballs, and a brandy at four A.M. At seven o'clock, he was ready to start over." In the office, Jungle Fighters act so quickly that decisions are taken almost before you've had a chance to think. That's exactly what they want. They even move faster than other kinds of people. Walking down the corridor to the boss's office, they'll invariably beat you to the door. They seem to be always pushed and busy; if interrupted, they'll turn on secretaries and spouses.

The Jungle Fighters' challenging eyes sweep over you, probing for weaknesses and strengths that will tell them how aggressively and creatively they will need to manipulate you. They don't miss a thing, and they know in an instant if you're fair game. They are always out to get you, and they usually find people who allow that sort of thing to happen—who, for their own reasons, seek the victim's lot. Jungle Fighters invariably pick people for subordinate roles who are less confident than they are, whether as spouses, lovers, secretaries, or partners. It's their insurance against loss of power. And power is their raison d'être.

Jungle Fighters are win-lose negotiators. They keep the losers off balance with lies, false promises, or whatever else it takes, even if it means demeaning them in public. Rather than tell you privately that you've been drinking a little too much, they'll offer you the same advice in front of the company president. Rather than telling their mate in private that she's been putting on a little weight, they'll do it in front of friends.

Jungle Fighters function in every field of human endeavor, especially in the fields of entertainment, law, and medicine, but also in advertising, communications, academia, merchandising, and even sports. They seem to gravitate to the fields that are most competitive, particularly where visibility is a fruit of success. Some Jungle Fighters need visibility so desperately that they will do anything, use anyone and anything to get it. If you are working for a Jungle Fighter and you take your thoughtful, well-written report in to him, the chances are overwhelming that the next time you see the report—or film or book or whatever—it will have his name on it.

Some years back a free-lance magazine writer I know took an extensive outline for a story up to an editor at *Life*. A week later, he learned with jubilation that the magazine had bought his idea and would let him produce the story. When he arrived at a conference called to discuss the project, however, he found that his shooting script had been altered in two small but significant ways. One ten-word sentence had been put at the top of the script. And his name had been removed and the editor's name substituted. The free-lance writer was so aghast—

and so in need of the assignment—that he did nothing, which was exactly what the Jungle Fighter had counted on.

With service people, Jungle Fighters add imperiousness to thoughtlessness. They hate to be kept waiting for an appointment, they're the drivers honking in a traffic jam, the patients pacing in the doctor's waiting room.

The Hazards of Jungle Life

Given their total dedication to connivance and their propensity for full-throttle living, it should come as no surprise that Jungle Fighters function, in the main, under conditions of extreme stress. Stress is their major medical hazard, a fact of which they are well aware, either because they know it intuitively or because they've been warned by their doctor. They also know that heart attacks and early death are risks that come with the territory. As a consequence, they almost always take superb care of themselves, jogging, playing tennis, skiing, working out in a gym. They generally demonstrate extraordinary stamina, working twelve to fifteen hours a day, getting by with little sleep. They tolerate illness, pain, and problems extremely well. The only time they'll give you any indication of the emotional load they're operating under is when they can achieve something by doing so.

Not all Jungle Fighters are killers. There are Jungle Fighters known as Snipers, who manipulate and control in an undercover way, using others to fight their battles. And then there are the Fencers, who merely enjoy the parrying and reserve their thrusts for use only if and when the game turns against them. "I used to see a dynamic woman with whom I always enjoyed trading verbal parries," one shocked victim recalls. "Then one day, I accidently nicked her—and I was suddenly skewered."

Not all Jungle Fighters are in competitive fields or act in abnormally competitive ways. Some are trend setters—distinguished men and women, gifted diplomats for the most part, who come out of the closet only under intense provocation.

Not all Jungle Fighters are vicious in all places. Even killer Jungle Fighters will not always be as destructive in the home as they are in the office—unless, of course, there is a threat to their power base. They will use any means available. They want you to be thoroughly overwhelmed by their power—real or illusionary. Even if they know it's a sham.

Not all Jungle Fighters are invincible, either. They are expendable; they can be had. Somewhere in the downstream thickets lurks an even sharper shooter waiting to pick them off as they round the bend.

Love, Jungle Style

Jungle Fighters want to be loved, like everyone else. They just don't know how to go about it. They don't really trust it. What they trust is strength and toughness and relentlessness—in themselves alone, of course; they retreat from others who share their characteristics. What they need, however, is what all human beings need eventually, no matter how tough their exteriors. They need to belong. It is their lack of "belongingness" that propels Jungle Fighters into personal relationships—in which their suitors, alas, are more like their prey.

It would seem that no one could live with Jungle Fighters, but that's not the case. Many people are willing to put up with them precisely because they do win, they do succeed, they do make money, they do become visible—achievements that, however dubious, their families and associates share.

One Midwest manufacturer talks about the "high trade-offs" he got by working with his Jungle Fighter partner. The partner had already established a successful business and, in the time they were together, had demonstrated his ability to go after new business and get it. A San Francisco woman spoke of the "enormous challenge" of living with her successful husband; life was never dull, and they were always "where things were happening." Said a Phoenix woman of her ten years with a Jungle Fighter: "It was my future, and my son's. It was living in a million-dollar home and never having to worry another day. It was my pot at the end of the rainbow."

Inevitably, the costs exceed the benefits.

"I was married for six years to a Jungle Fighter—a top corporate litigator who could not leave the judge and jury in the courtroom," one Los Angeles business person recounts.

"The trade-offs for me for the six years were prestige, money, glamour, and excitement. The negative trade-offs were that my personal development and career were stifled at every turn. There never seemed to be any room for negotiation at home because his excuse was that he was doing battle all day long and didn't want to do battle at home. As long as everything was going his way, we had a terrific life together. I finally gave up, needing to get my identity back and my own life on the road to success again."

Hard Times for Predators

These are not good days, generally, for Jungle Fighters. A lot of people are giving up on them. I know of five bright, articulate, competent Jungle Fighters, all of whom have made impressive money for their corporations, every one of whom has been passed over for a key promotion within the last two years. ". . . Such abrasive personalities are probably the single most frequent cause for the failure of bright men and women in executive ranks . . ." psychologist Harry Levenson told the American Psychological Association at its 1977 conference. It's too costly to tolerate them in the organization. They can't be kept where they are because they alienate people. They can't be promoted because nobody wants to work under them. According to Levenson, more abrasive people are sent to professionals—therapists and encounter group leaders—than any other kind of person in the organization.

Ambition is a healthy trait. But if, in the service of ambition, other people get trampled, the trampler will ultimately pay the piper. Human beings are resilient and adaptable; they will pick themselves off the floor and joyfully learn to sabotage the Jungle Fighter—using, if necessary, the same tricks he's used in the past to manipulate them.

The disaffection of their peers and families is not the Jungle Fighters' only problem these days. Both males and females of the species are having extreme difficulties in relating to the changing roles of men and women. Male Jungle Fighters simply don't know what to make of the new assertive women—whom they usually refer to as "aggressive broads"—or how to deal with them. In the past, women always served as their appendages or extensions. Now, for the first time, they are encountering women as competitors. It is not simply that they haven't developed a repertoire of behavior patterns with which to deal with such women, it is that they seem to be constitutionally incapable of acknowledging competitive women's strengths. As a consequence, the only tactic left to them is to put the women down as "loudmouths" or "bitches." But others have determined that these women are intelligent and effective; otherwise they wouldn't be meeting the Jungle Fighters in the executive suites. Result: male Jungle Fighters and their new colleagues are often unable to work together.

But it's just as often the women's fault. Many are new to the executive environment. They bring with them not just inexperience, but a conviction—based on literature, film, and television, for the most part—that jungle fighting is the norm in boardrooms. And so, many of them adopt these very tactics themselves, thereby alienating male colleagues who could become their allies.

Yet, for all their problems, Jungle Fighters—male and female—could be prime candidates for conversion to Win-Win Negotiators. They have many qualities that are the prerequisites of success—ambition, intelligence, drive, and above all, the kind of tenacity that comes only from self-confidence. I think of the young Jungle Fighter who, on being refused a loan by his banker, said, "Come on, I'm starting a business. Take a chance on me. What do you have to lose? I've made an investment with you. Make one in me." He got the loan.

They can be so compelling, these Jungle Fighters, so charming and inspiring. They have such fantastic energy and clarity of vision. What a pity these capacities are enlisted so often in the service of human destruction.

Jungle Fighters need to be persuaded that all issues are not life-and-death affairs, that every person isn't out to get them. But until you have overpowering proof of their conversion, assume that they're out to get *you*.

Jungle Fighters in Brief

ASSETS	LIABILITIES
creative	demeaning
ambitious	disruptive
charismatic	intrusive
tenacious	tumultuous
competitive	untrustworthy
entertaining	disloyal
attentive	aggressive
perceptive	combative

3

Dictators

Dictators are win-lose negotiators: they win, you lose. They are obsessed with the acquisition and retention of control. "Who negotiates?" said my friend the chairman of the board of a company with thirty-five subsidiaries. "I just tell them what to do and they do it."

While both Dictators and Jungle Fighters are tremendously aggressive negotiators, there are important differences between them. Dictators almost never exercise their temper in the extravagant ways that Jungle Fighters habitually do. Their explosions, when they come, are controlled and for effect, but they usually use their intellect before they use their fists. They parry and thrust, but rarely draw blood. They don't feel obliged to destroy you. On the contrary, they need you. What is a Dictator without subjects to rule?

Competence Is Their Calling Card

Dictators know how to organize—both themselves and others. For this reason alone, they make effective leaders. They pick their subordinates well. They are goal-oriented, always keep their objectives in focus, and almost never look away. They persevere, and don't let up until the objective is reached. If they begin a task, they will complete it, and in a given time.

Competency is the Dictators' calling card. Their brains

work overtime, gathering and weighing information. "I can build a case in seconds if I need to," a strong Dictator told me. "I can call forth a lot of information, and I know that I know what I'm talking about. So does everyone else." As his remark suggests, they are supremely confident. Says another Dictator: "Many, many times I've found that I was right where everybody else was wrong. I don't trust the herd decision at all." They are willing to enter power vacuums, whatever the financial or social risk. It is this quality of authority they lend to their every action that breeds such confidence in others. To business associates and family members alike, they are perceived as the source of prosperity and security—and their manner underscores this image.

Where Jungle Fighters are flamboyant, Dictators are restrained, low-keyed, spare, cool. Their dress is the uniform prescribed for success—whatever that may be. Their expressions are economical: a stare, a raised eyebrow, a set mouth, a small ripple of muscle in the cheek, an almost imperceptible thrust of the jaw. The head is tilted back ever so slightly, the better to scrutinize you as you talk, or else turned completely away so that you can only wonder what the Dictator is thinking, or whether he or she is even listening. The voice reveals nothing, not anger or approval. Talk is measured and calculated.

At a recent conference I attended, I observed a classic Dictator approach his wife who sat listening to a speaker. No word was passed between the two, but the communication was clear. He touched her shoulder, snapped his fingers and pointed to the door. As they moved silently out of the theater row she paced herself three steps behind him all the way to the door. He did not turn around once.

Dictators are gatekeepers of information; you learn only what they want you to know. Even the space in which they function is carefully guarded; entry is only by permission. You are expected to keep your distance, unless granted an audience. Any attempt by you to be personal, particularly in a business setting, is normally rebuffed; Dictators, as a rule, are discreet about their private lives; they maintain a closed communication system, giving directions and commands but no clues as to their feelings. At times it seems that they have set up a force field to keep you at a distance.

The Orchestration of Intimidation

Everything Dictators do is intended to underscore their power and increase your sense of intimidation. It's understood that they will be the first to enter a room or step into a car. The car is big and expensive; travel is always first class. The settings in which they function are contrived for drama and effect—large spaces, big desks, rich furnishings, chairs that set them higher than others, lighting that sometimes gives you the feeling you're getting the third degree. And always, there is that critical stare from those all-seeing eyes, looking you over for anything out of place or against the rules. They themselves never have spots on their clothing, and nothing in their world is ever out of place. It's as though chalk marks, invisible to everyone but them, set the location of everything and everyone. Time is just as precise. Life is performed, not experienced. The curtain rises and falls at unvarying moments. Everything in between—meals, conferences, even social engagements—must go according to schedule. As he leaves home in the morning, a Dictator may say, "I'll be home at five thirty. We'll have cocktails at six, and leave for the Cowans' at seven."

A Dictator often begins a meeting with a subordinate or family member by looking obviously at his watch. The message is, "State your case." The meeting is over when he decides it is, at which time he signals you to leave by looking at a paper on his desk or picking up his phone or simply flicking his hand.

Like Jungle Fighters, Dictators are often extraordinarily unrealistic about human capacity. They assume that others are just as driven as they are. As trying as this is, it does have its positive aspect. It makes others who might not otherwise do so stretch to higher standards.

Yet Dictators do show a calculated regard for subordinates and family members that Jungle Fighters rarely do. Whereas Jungle Fighters are explosive, Dictators seldom make snap decisions. You can appeal to their logic—not yours, theirs. They take their time, gathering the information they need to solve a problem, and then think through their decisions. Where Jungle Fighters never give you their full attention—part of their tactic of confusion—Dictators are completely absorbed in what you have to say. They must hear everything, believing they must know everything in order to stay on top. As one wise Dictator put it: "I know I'm a bit of a tyrant, but I know, too, that I must listen to be smart. I also know that I'll kill the creative process in my people if I'm too forceful."

Dictators do compile quantities of data in behalf of their case. They are articulate, persuasive communicators. But their "logic" seems designed to serve their viewpoint, their arguments to make sense only if you accept their premises. With Dictators, there is rarely an alternative. Even if you are right, they will prove you are wrong—and that you were mistaken to voice your thoughts in the first place. A dialogue with a Dictator is not a discussion; it is an interrogation, often accusatory in tone.

And, oh those expectations! Dictators' standards are outrageous in most cases. They have little tolerance for mistakes; if you make one, you can expect, at a minimum, a subtle message that you haven't come up to standard. Many of them are perfectionists, making impossible demands not only of others but of themselves. No impassioned pleas when you negotiate with Dictators; if they consider an item nonnegotiable, it is *not* negotiable.

Orders from the Command Post

Office Dictators are sometimes more flexible at home, but they tend to reign in both places, establishing priorities and standards, deciding on major and minor purchases down to the last soap dish, making all of the family decisions, withholding money, demanding perfection in school, setting up dating rules for sons and daughters. Living with a Dictator is like listening to orders from a command post—from the bathroom, kitchen, and bedroom. Spouse and children are viewed as subordinates—and tend to act that way. "If you have a dictatorial person in the house, you do anything not to arouse him," a Dictator's son reports. "So you keep quiet and give in. You know that if he controls, there won't be any trouble." All decisions are deferred to the Dictator, whose plans always come first, regardless of others' needs. "When you start making the money, you can decide how we spend it," a Dictator will tell his wife. His family, like his staff, is rated exclusively by the Dictator's measurements. Nothing is relevant that he doesn't deem relevant. As the lonely wife of a Dictator lamented, "All I wanted was a touch or a smile. What I got instead were facts and figures and three ways to solve the problem."

With their families, Dictators keep up a running interrogation: "Where did you go? With whom? Why? What time did you leave?" Their statements are sprinkled with "You shoulds" and "You should haves." With children, they are particularly tough. "Get your feet off the table. . . . Go to your room. . . . No discussion . . . you're wrong. . . . We'll do it my way, or not at all. . . . I'm not interested in your opinion. . . . There's no point in arguing. . . . Absolutely not."

Dictators, like Jungle Fighters, are fearful that if they so much as loosen their control or let up in any way, they will be upset or unseated or otherwise lose command. Their greatest fear, as Michael Maccoby points out in *The Gamesman,* is that they will be considered irrelevant or unimportant.

It's to these people, with their natural bent for authority, that we often hand over power. We give them the baton and say, "Here. You lead the band." And, of course, they do. It's handing over the baton that allows them to succeed on a grand scale. It's following the lead of these ambitious and bright individuals that allows them to impose their rules and controls on us. They create their own realms and are monarchs of those realms, while we are the submissive subjects.

Waving Their Batons

Dictators gravitate to those fields in which most people have little experience or knowledge, so that they can control others with their expertise and arcane language. Law, law enforcement, politics, business management, and medicine are especially appealing. The field of gynecology is loaded with Dictators. Many gynecologists punish their patients with disapproval—"Eight pounds in three weeks? You're going to be an elephant by the time you deliver"—and they position themselves in such a way that they're in charge of the entire pregnancy, almost as though the mother had nothing to do with it. "There are three kinds of women who go into the delivery room," a tall, imposing doctor said to the expectant mother who had had the temerity to ask him some questions. "First there are the young ones who go in with total faith in me. They're always okay. The second ones are those who ask a lot of questions, but they, too, know that I'm in charge of the situation. They're *usually* okay. The third are intellectual women. They don't trust me. They want to be in charge of themselves. But let a crisis arise in the delivery room, and they become hysterical." The doctor paused, and smiled. "Make your choice, and decide how you want it to be." The young woman made her choice. She got another doctor.

"Trust me," the Pygmalionesque Dictator tells his wife or girl friend, whereupon he guides and nurtures, putting her in the right clothes, enlarging her cultural vistas, and doing whatever else is necessary to make her a fitting extension of himself.

Dictators are concerned with only one thing—how you can gratify them. The only way you can do that is to facilitate their agendas through subordination and competent performance. The one thing you can count on is that they'll recognize your competence. Provided you do what they want in their way, you'll get your rewards.

Although Dictators do surround themselves with strong, creative people, they don't really trust anyone. They may have one confidant, whose loyalty has passed the most extreme tests. But should this person withhold one piece of vital information or cross his Dictator boss in any way, he can be fired in an instant, even though this is his first imperfection in twenty years of service.

Decline and Fall

For one who prides himself on his thoroughness, the Dictator makes surprisingly little effort to find out what his subordinates or his family think about him. Because his manner is often so forbidding, neither associates nor family volunteer such information. Says one Dictator's employee: "I tell him what he wants to hear, not the truth." Inevitably, the Dictator begins to hear only what he wishes to. He becomes what Ashley Montagu calls a "psychosclerotic," one who suffers from a hardening of the mind. He comes to believe that his way is the only way to do it. He tells himself, "What works for me must work for them." He announces, "It worked twenty years ago. It'll work today." It's just such rigidity that eventually leads to his downfall.

As long as Dictators continue to produce, they can usually retain the confidence of those who signed on with them, including their wives. There *are* women who enjoy life as privileged chattels. They assume no responsibility, make no decisions; there is no agonizing over choices. Everything material is provided. But there comes a time when the flattering reflection of their husband's power and achievement they see in the mirror is no longer enough to content them.

A male Dictator is positively bewildered when his wife suddenly leaves him. "How could she?" a confused and angry Dictator thundered to me one day. "I made her everything she is."

"But it all belongs to her now," I answered. "She's become whatever it is you mentored."

Dictators in Brief

ASSETS	LIABILITIES
assertive	rigid
organized	isolated
poised	obsessive
decisive	opinionated
shrewd	demanding
analytical	self-righteous
efficient	judgmental
	intimidating

Silhouettes

"Tell me what you love about me," the woman demanded. "My face? My hair? My figure? My voice? My mind? The way I make love?"

"I love that you leave me alone," her Silhouette husband said.

Silhouettes fear intimacy of any kind. They deal in an economy of scarcity—of money, enthusiasm, and love. They are emotional tightwads, blank faces, stone walls; gray, uptight people, unresponsive to life. Their energies are consecrated to keeping others from penetrating their defenses. Family members are just as unwelcome as business associates in their silent worlds.

Silhouettes are prototypic lose-lose negotiators, given to the most cryptic responses, of which denial is the most classic. The other person is cut off before a negotiation begins.

"Are you angry?"

"No."

"What are you feeling?"

"Nothing."

Silhouettes do anything and everything to ignore conflict and avoid exposing their feelings. To this end, they divert their gaze or look at the world with glazed and vacant eyes, a response that others find bewildering—exactly the Silhouettes' objective. Their clothes are neutral, offering no clues to their disposition, more concealing than revealing. If they were the kind who wore decal T-shirts, the message would say, "Out of Town." They stand apart from the group whenever possible, their bodies rigid, their heads scarcely moving, their stiff backs up against a wall. They speak in monotones, using short sentences and understatement, saying as little about themselves as they can get away with. If a turtle had a voice, it would be a Silhouette.

Silhouettes offer no measure by which others can gauge the effectiveness of their own efforts—no smile or frown or raised eyebrow, no vocal expression of approval or even disapproval. They are desperate not to be pushed; if and when they are, they become hostile and will say what it takes to relieve the pressure. "People often think I'm angry because I'm not chatty," a brilliant executive Silhouette says. "I just like to sit and observe and be quiet." But she was so tense as she spoke that her body quivered, and her voice had an edge like broken glass.

When Silhouettes do show anger, it's in a shrewd and calculated way, using their emotion like a bullfighter's cape to draw attention from the issue. Example: The wife of a Silhouette comes home one afternoon, upset by yet another breakdown of the family car. "We can afford a new one," she protests to her husband. Does he respond to the issue? Never. He responds to her anger—by becoming angrier than she is. The quarrel is then diverted to his anger, and the problem of the car is forgotten.

The Sound of Silence

But Silhouettes have a far more effective response to pressure than anger: silence.

Silence, in our culture, is perceived as strength—or, at a minimum, a cover for inner strength. Gary Cooper became a film hero by cultivating the image of a strong and silent man who could barely get a word out. Being silent means being in charge; the silence forces others to do the work, or come to you or try to anticipate your wishes. Being silent means that when the Silhouette finally speaks, his word is automatically valued because it's such a rare commodity. The rest of us become so frantic for a sign of feeling that we will accept almost anything.

While the closed-mouth attitude of Silhouettes derives essentially from a fear of exposing their thoughts and feelings to others, it is often adopted as deliberate strategy. Silhouettes are past masters at achieving power and control by means of minimal response. "If we had a discussion or argument, he would be silent for days," the former wife of a Silhouette recalls. "By the end of a few days, or one day or sometimes even an hour, I would be pleading for forgiveness, even though I was convinced that I'd been right." Says a veteran of some memorable negotiations with a Silhouette: "He'd use silence as a response. That used to unnerve me to the point that I would babble, and wind up telling him four times more about myself than I ever wanted to."

One woman married to a Silhouette tried to compensate for his silence by speaking out more and more. "What I was trying to do was force my husband to talk," she recalls. "So I would talk a lot just to see what kind of response I could get. But I realized I was talking to myself. When you live with this kind of person you become desperate. When you become desperate, you become nervous. When you become nervous, you talk more. And the more you talk the more guilty you feel. I got put in the role of the dominant talker when all I was attempting to do was get a response—any response!"

Silhouettes seize on one word in a conversation and use it as a red herring to divert attention from the problem, close off their feelings, or end the conversation. They have an arsenal of responses designed to cut you off: "I'll do it later . . . not now . . . maybe. We'll see. . . . We'll discuss it some other time . . . I'm busy right now. . . . I don't want to talk about it. . . . Talk to your father . . . I have other things on my mind. I can't deal with this right now."

Silhouettes perceive almost every overture by another person as an infringement on their time. Whatever form their cutoff takes, it is calculated to protect them against such infringements. So preoccupied are they with their thoughts that they scarcely respond to external stimuli and pay scant attention to their spiritual, emotional, or physical well-being.

Absentee parents, social isolates, they often live and die for their work.

And what driven perfectionists they are! Once they set their minds to a task, they become totally committed and rigid. If they say they will lose fifty pounds and won't eat whipped cream for six years, they will lose fifty pounds and not eat whipped cream for six years. Carried over into the business world, such dedication can be priceless. In addition, Silhouettes usually possess unquestioned integrity. Their loyalty and tenacity is unrivaled. They're on the job at all times. This kind of determination translates, during a negotiation, into an incredible strength of conviction. The intensity shows. They watch, closely and silently. They never seem to tire or to become ruffled or mussed; one Silhouette I know is so "cool" that after negotiating for hours in an overheated room, he doesn't even perspire. And they never give up. They never admit that something is impossible. They don't accept human limitations. They are directed by an almost inhuman inner force.

Sometimes these qualities blend into a successful mixture, but just as often they don't—not because tenacity, loyalty, integrity, indefatigability, et al., aren't marvelous characteristics, but because, to be of value, they must be applied. Application requires people. Fade out, Silhouettes.

Alone in Their "Inner Room"

Silhouettes choose careers that keep them as separate from people as possible—and if they didn't, they should because it's when they're alone that they do their most creative work. They love research, which is why so many of them become professors; as such, they publish so much that they never perish, but they are often extremely unpopular with students, with whom they are unable to share. (In spite of this psychological obstacle, some Silhouette professors are able to impart the passion they feel for their work.)

Silhouettes excel as inventors, mathematicians, librarians, architects, painters, and writers—especially of technical materials and criticism. They could be happy as forest rangers. While the solitude into which they withdraw is often perceived as antisocial, it does have its positive aspects. Creative people need solitude in order to create. Even when they are among others, they will often retreat to an "inner room" in order to commune with themselves; while it might appear that they've left you for the day, week, or month, they may simply be inside their own heads creating better mousetraps.

In a biography about Carson McCullers, she is quoted as saying that the artist's internal chemistry is so fragile it should never be touched by others. Silhouettes respect this need in one another. They admire and respect anyone whose own perspectives are clear; they just want reciprocal respect. And because they want privacy for themselves, they offer it to others. Whereas life with a Dictator or Jungle Fighter is to have one's space constantly and totally invaded, Silhouettes don't intrude. You can have your own life and friends. If they're not pressured, they may even want social contact, appearing when invited but never appearing when not.

Silhouettes, in sum, want to do their own thing, with minimal interference from the people in their lives. They don't want to owe anything to anyone. Rarely, if ever, will they ask for help, which means that they place extraordinary burdens on themselves. They will do almost anything for their friends, but they won't allow their friends to reciprocate. They want no debts of any kind that would encumber them, compromise their independence, or threaten their isolation. The friends of Silhouettes never seem to know what to give them.

Marriage, Singles Style

Marriage, for Silhouettes, is usually one of convenience. If you marry a Silhouette, you can expect to be viewed as a caretaker who will provide a setting and the necessities of existence, and protect him or her from other people. But marriage to Silhouettes can be convenient. Because they are so single-minded and driven, they very often succeed. With success comes money, status, and prestige. In addition, you have an abundance of private time and space. If you're equally driven, such a marriage could be ideal. Even if you're not driven, you could only be grateful to a spouse who tenders such respect to privacy. If you like to have your coffee before talking in the morning, have it with a Silhouette. Only the cup will rattle.

Silhouettes make a wonderful audience, if that is what you want. They are quiet and attentive while you talk. They appreciate your excitement more than any other style. Male Silhouettes, I found in my research, often marry vibrant, dynamic, articulate women who seem to represent their own unexpressed side. The women, in turn, say that there was an exciting mystique about their Silhouette mates. They wanted to find out what was going on behind that mysterious silence.

The Silhouette husband of a beautiful, creative, energetic but dependent woman with whom I worked once told her: "Do anything you want between nine and three. But at three o'clock I expect you to be home to start preparing my dinner." But when he came home, at day's end, he wouldn't talk to her. He would sip his cocktail and have his dinner and then watch television in silence, and if she tried to go to her room to read a book, he would say, "Don't go. I want you right here." One day, she left him for good.

There are some Silhouettes who enjoy their isolation. But most Silhouettes simply pretend they do—often even to themselves—until the emotions they've contained all their lives make them sick or drive them to a therapist's office.

Everyone needs to be touched, not just physically, but by some other person's acknowledgment that he or she exists, and is a worthy partner. Silhouettes are no different. The one certain way to reach them is to threaten to leave them. They are terrified of being left alone, which is not the contradiction it seems to be. It has taken enormous effort on their part to make this one human connection; they're not at all sure they could make the effort again, or succeed if they did. Herein, as we'll see further on, lies the clue for negotiating successfully with Silhouettes.

Silhouettes in Brief

ASSETS	LIABILITIES
motivated	reclusive
competent	uncommunicative
discreet	rigid
creative	insensitive
loyal	evasive
tenacious	bottled-up
self-sufficient	private
trustworthy	

Big Daddies and Big Mammas

They are dream merchants. They coax you into believing that your fantasies can come true. They offer comfort, listen intensely, and help you grow. They leave you breathless at your good fortune in being blessed with such generous mentors. They take a caring, nurturing interest in everyone in their lives. They are concerned about the future and committed to progress. They have fabulous stores of energy, which they dispense freely to one and all.

However . . .

Big Daddies and Big Mammas are probably the most manipulative of all negotiators. They use words to soothe, nurture, present their case, and usually convince you that it is for your own best interest—not theirs, but yours. They may seem to be working for you, but no project gets anywhere unless there are appreciable benefits for them. To a certain extent, this self-interest is normal, but Big Daddies and Big Mammas give it a special twist that puts them in a class by themselves. They do strive for your success—but then they claim its fruits. They are wonderful with words and lavish with praise, but you have to listen to the hidden message, the "what's-in-it-for-me?" question that underscores their every effort. Before you know it, you've been had. You've finished the project—and they're getting the promotion.

Good parenting is knowing when to let go. Big Daddies and Big Mammas rarely know how to do that. Instead of basking in the reflected glory or their child—or protégé—they move him or her out of the limelight and take the bows themselves.

Big Daddies and Mammas will help you to grow, but they must be in charge of that growth. They *are* concerned with the future, but only insofar as they can create and perpetuate a dynasty. They want to be remembered long after they are gone. Those congenial environments they create are calculated designs to increase productivity in their own behalf. That memorable candlelit dinner, those hours of good talk next to the fire, must eventually be paid for. Big Daddies and Mammas never hesitate to call back their markers.

Buckets of Compassion

Yet what Big Daddies and Mammas offer is tough to resist—love, acceptance, understanding, approval, praise, and tangible rewards. Oh, what a lovely presence they project! When you speak, they look at you as though you are the most important person in the world. Their eyes, brimming with compassion, never seem to waver. They follow your message with firm, supportive sounds—lots of "umms" and "aahs"—and their responses are verbal hugs and kisses: "Do you want to talk about it? . . . Are you sure you can manage? . . . Why don't you let me handle that? . . . What do you need? . . . With my help you can make it. . . . If you run into any trouble, just call me . . . I'll take care of it for you." All the while, their hands are busy, patting, stroking, caressing; one arm goes across your shoulders. In fact, they are always very close to you, their bodies leaning forward. But through the warm, loving haze in which they've enveloped you, you begin to see that they're a little too close for comfort, that there's a little too much stroking and nurturing, that their care and concern seem a trifle forced, that their interest is just a tad too patronizing. And those comments; you have to wonder why what they're saying seems to be exactly what you wanted to hear.

The moment you show the least sign of doubt that Big Daddies or Big Mammas know what's best for you, all of the approval mechanisms go into reverse. The "umms" turn to "tchs," the lips are compressed, the eyes tighten, the head moves from side to side, the body draws away. All that "good stuff" on which you've been nurtured is suddenly withheld; Big Daddy or Mamma doesn't call for a week or show up at your party, and you're asking yourself over and over, "What did I do wrong?"

What makes their act work is that they offer in abundance the one human commodity that is essential for growth—tender loving care. But they will do so only up to a point—the point at which their control over you is threatened.

A Democratic Facade

Like Dictators, Big Daddies and Mammas have to be in control at all times. They have to know everything that's going on. They will almost never grant you the power to handle an important situation alone. Stephanie, well trained and motivated and with a good background in finance, got a job as a secretary in a stock brokerage. She was immediately recognized by the office manager, a Big Daddy, for her quick mind and desire to learn. He promoted her, assigned her to an important account, and then worked closely with her, not only on the account but on her business manner and image. He even helped select her clothes. As long as Stephanie followed Big Daddy's game plan, everything went well. But the moment she began to propose ideas and make decisions on her own, Big Daddy was furious. It didn't matter that the ideas were good ones; what mattered was that they weren't his. Within a month, Stephanie was gone.

Many Big Daddies and Big Mammas are closet Dictators. They profess to operate democratically, but it's all a facade. I once worked for a Big Mamma, a school principal who prided herself on her "open" administration. Anyone who wished to help formulate the operating policies of the school could do so, she boasted. At staff meetings, she would listen to everyone who wished to be heard. When all of them had finished, she would announce, "Thank you very much for your input. This is how we're going to do it."

Once in a while, you're able to win a victory, but the win

is calculated to appease you. A Big Mamma may very well commend you publicly for the work you've done on a particular committee. But privately she'll tell you, "Of course you realize that I'll have to chair the committee."

The great danger in dealing with Big Daddies and Big Mammas is not that you won't find out you're being manipulated. It's that, because the strokes are so comforting and the rewards so good, you'll never gain the independence you require to reach maturity.

Big Daddies and Mammas tend to overfeed, and overwater their plants—which often die of root rot. Too much "feeding" of a plant, child, or protégé can often be psychologically fatal.

All people need mentors in their lives, particularly as they're developing. But no one wants to be smothered. Big Daddies and Big Mammas do everything they can to perpetuate your dependency. If you're their child, they'll lavish presents on you that they think you should have. As employers, they'll pay high salaries and give generous bonuses. The only thing they'll withhold is your freedom. Before you recognize that you're in a dependent relationship, you're hooked.

At some point, you want to assume responsibility for your own life. This Big Daddies and Mammas are unable to let you do. They seem to want nothing more than your success; in reality, they are threatened by your achievements.

The High Cost of Breaking Free

Big Daddies and Mammas must have people. They must have that flow of love going out and coming back in. Try to leave a Big Daddy's or Mamma's circle of "love" and you've got a fight on your hands. Leaving is equivalent to betrayal. Once they've been betrayed, you're finished and the Jungle Fighter in them emerges. One client who tried to break away from a Big Daddy therapist was told, "You can leave me if you want, but in my educated opinion, you'll fall flat on your face." Given that prognosis, the client, a highly insecure man, continued for another year in a totally unbeneficial therapy. Another Big Daddy, a Dictator in disguise, had managed to perpetuate his wife's childlike dependency for nearly thirty years. One day, at long last, she told him that she wanted to learn to drive.

"Drive?" he raged. "You'll hurt someone, or kill yourself. I wouldn't have a moment's peace with you on the road." It was months before she could bring herself to take driving lessons in secret.

Cross a Big Daddy or Mamma and you have bought big trouble. They'll withhold love and approval and fill you full of guilt. "My Big Daddy is always there to offer love, caring, and unlimited help," the object of his affection, a smothered woman in her mid-thirties, avers. " 'I'll do it for you, Mindy. I'll go for you, Mindy.' He never complains. If I'm having a problem, he'll tell me what to do. But if I then don't do it his way, it's like I've committed mortal sin."

Big Daddies and Mammas will never demean you in public like the Jungle Fighter does. They may be a little patronizing in front of others—but they'll save any wrist slapping for a time when you're alone. It's important for them to maintain their image of the kind, all-loving guru.

Often they succeed, but there are times when they don't, and on those occasions Big Daddies and Mammas reap a bitter harvest. Consider the young man who decided, after three years of college, that higher education was not for him. His mother, a Big Mamma, thought otherwise. She had quit school herself a year short of graduation; she was determined that her son should finish, and, to that end, began to bribe him with presents. First, she gave him a motor scooter on the condition that he continue. Then it was a car, and then a trip to Europe. The following year, he graduated. Returning from the ceremony, he handed his diploma to his mother. "Here," he said, his voice edged with contempt, "you wanted this more than I did."

Another witness—a woman so self-aware that she can see the changing seasons mirrored in her moods, but whose relationship with her father remains at an infantile level: "I can get anything I want out of my daddy as long as I approach him as a child. The few times in my life when I've tried to approach him as a woman, he's gotten very hostile and angry." She sighs. "How much easier life would be if I just let go, and let Big Daddy do it. That's an enormous temptation for me. The price is that I'd have to be six years old again."

"You're a Giant—Outside"

"The payoff is so big for Big Mammas," a woman in her foi ties recalls. "You're never alone, you're never disconnected. You don't ever have to face yourself because there are people who are only too happy to engage your heart and your soul at any given moment. The disadvantages are that you never for a moment can admit that you have a need, a fear, that you don't have an answer, or worse, that you don't care. You must always be available. That's the price you pay for Big Mamma-ing. It gives you a feeling of being a giant—outside."

Their preoccupation with others leaves Big Daddies and Mammas little time for their own agendas. Says one smothering mother: "One of the rewards of being a Big Mamma is to see your children succeed under your tutelage. The only thing you give up is your own success, because you're so busy nurturing that there's no time for self-nurturing. The thought that other people's successes are yours is a delusion. Success comes from expressing your own self." She paused for a moment. Then smiling ruefully, she said, "Underneath, I really feel a lot of resentment."

"I miss it a lot at times," says one reformed Big Daddy. "At other times, I think, 'How could I have ever done something so destructive to myself?' My phone doesn't ring twenty-four hours a day anymore. I have time to do my work, to read things I'm interested in, to take care of myself. Big Daddies never really take care of themselves. They haven't got the time."

Today, the Big Daddy/Big Mamma role is in a greater state of flux and redefinition than any other category of negotiating style. The underlying cause is the redefinition of male and female roles under way in society itself.

In the past, Big Daddies have often been irresistible to dependent women, and acculturation has, in the past, made many women dependent. Whereas boys learn early on that they must make the money, take care of the family, and support the government, girls learn that someone out there—Daddy, lover, husband, banker, stockbroker, Uncle Sam—will take care of them. Or so it has been until recent years. Today, a growing number of women have different expectations. They still want kindness and affection and even a certain amount of nurturing from men, but basically they want to make their own choices.

This change in values has put Big Daddies in a dilemma. All their lives, they've been conditioned to care for women, be the strongmen, make the decisions. Now, suddenly, the very actions for which they were once rewarded—however much the "rewards" covered up women's frustrations and anger— are now openly assailed. They ask themselves, "What do I do now? Where do I get something for myself?"

Not, surely, from women, in the ways they once expected. Women, conditioned to care for the family to the exclusion of other interests, if necessary, no longer want to be totally responsible for that Big Mamma nurturing role. They want time to grow, to experience life more fully, to use their minds in more creative ways. A growing number of women are no longer willing to predicate all their actions on approval from the Big Daddies in their lives.

Paradoxically, the ranks of Big Daddies are growing. Numbers of Dictators are adopting Big Daddy styles because they're discovering that their old authoritarian devices aren't working anymore. They're trying to achieve the domination they once enjoyed in a more subtle guise; to control by means of "love" is much more socially acceptable than to control by intimidation.

If you've been wondering why that Dictator boss of yours has recently mellowed out, there's your reason. Be careful; he's just as tough as ever.

Big Mammas and Big Daddies in Brief

ASSETS	LIABILITIES
caring	manipulative
nurturing	devious
supportive	non-revealing
energetic	threatening
attentive	over-protective
gracious	self-neglecting
calm	
expansive	

Soothers

These anxious, evasive stylists lose more often than any other negotiators. But to nourish their illusions, they must engage in prodigious feats of denial; effectively, they must avoid responsibility as they would avoid a plague. They either turn their backs on conflict or give in almost by reflex. In fact, their objective is to lose, whether they are conscious of it or not, because only by losing do they "win."

"Negotiation for me has always been a squeamish request for more," a Soother husband and father with whom I've worked confesses. "I anticipate the answer 'no.' When it's over, I realize it wasn't negotiation at all, but a settling for whatever the other party wanted to give me in the first place." A woman client lived with a man for forty years, believing him to be ungenerous and difficult. Yet she never felt she had the strength or skill to extract herself. "I'm not a skilled negotiator," she admitted. "Such negotiating as I did was just self-defense for survival. I found out early on what I would have to do to survive, and I did it."

Why So Many Women are Soothers

Soother women far outnumber Soother men, and with good reason. Whereas men were taught as little boys that if they wanted something they should go out and get it, women were encouraged to believe that someone would get what they wanted for them. Take the little boy who announces to his father that he'd like to have a bicycle. "That's fine, son," Father replies. "Now let's figure out how you can earn it." Together, they come up with a plan—a paper route, perhaps, or some Saturday morning chores. In the process of earning his bicycle, the little boy learns that he has a purpose in life and control over his destiny. But look what happens when the little boy's sister tells her father that she, too, would like a bicycle. "Honey," says Father, "I'll get it for you for your birthday." The little girl does *not* learn that she has purpose in life, that she controls her destiny, or that she has the opportunity to learn to solve problems. To the contrary, the lesson to her is that she is dependent upon others for the gratification of her needs.

A majority of the women with whom I work are Soothers—almost exact reflections of society's traditional image of who and what they should be: the server, the nice person, the one who won't aggress. For them, peace at any price—usually a stiff one. One Soother married to a Dictator gave me this account of what such a life produced:

"When I met my husband, I was seventeen, still a virgin, still in high school. He had traveled, he was in business, he was twenty-two. Two months later, I was no longer a virgin. We became engaged, and he took charge of my life. I wasn't so attracted to him as I was impressed by his credentials. And then I felt tremendous guilt because I was no longer a virgin. Why would anyone else want me? Remember, this was 1953. So I made the commitment, thinking, regardless, that this would be the perfect marriage, made in heaven. And I entered a world of total submissiveness. He enrolled me in college, chose my classes, ferried me to and from school. When I graduated college, he interviewed for my job, made all the decisions. I did everything he told me to, including having dinner ready at five thirty every night. I was the perfect wife."

Some Soothers spring from volatile households in which they receive psychological and sometimes physical abuse. Either or both could accentuate the tendency to passivity in many children. Several of my clients became Soothers because they learned that if they weren't compliant they would get slapped around. One young man I know was never hit himself, or even shouted at, but became a Soother anyway, and at a very early age, because he saw his older brother being scolded and threatened and, on occasion, even pummeled. He became perfect even before he knew what the word meant, because he had figured out that he would never be punished if he never did anything wrong.

I once read a poster that said: "If you don't want to be criticized, don't do anything, be anything, or say anything." That statement could serve as the Soothers' slogan.

Conformists to a Fault

Soothers learn, early on, to be as inconspicuous as possible. It is not simply that their dress is drab or their manner unobtrusive, it's that they don't make their presence felt. When you deal with Dictators, you feel their power; with Jungle Fighters, it's their electricity; with Big Daddies and Mammas, their warmth. Even with Silhouettes, you feel the intensity that drives them on. With Soothers, you feel little, except perhaps a wisp of cool air. They give you nothing to bounce off of.

Jungle Fighters are excited by challenges and want to make something happen. Soothers usually see challenges as threats. They will rarely place themselves out on a limb if they can possibly help it. If the Soother does go out on a limb, the Dictator is telling him how far out to go, and the Jungle Fighter is sawing it off.

Soothers allow others to choose for them. They put themselves down and exhibit an inordinately low sense of self-esteem—to such an extent, at times, that they don't feel worthy enough to occupy their own space. In such cases, they give others permission to preempt it.

Soothers are evasive and hard to pin down. Their statements are often indirect. Their opinions go unexpressed, their feelings unresolved. Often as not, their thoughts are incomplete, shut off by another person's power. Silence becomes their disguise. Dictators, Jungle Fighters, and Silhouettes rarely apologize. Soothers seem to be apologizing all the time—not only for themselves, but for others.

Soothers really know what they want, but they don't want to admit it lest you disapprove of their choice. They dance around interminably over the smallest of issues. "They won't take positions," one real estate developer recalls. "It just challenges one's ability to pin them. That's what you have to do, pin them down. You deal with somebody like that, you get as much of it in writing and as specific as you can."

Soothers are the permissive parents, rather than the enforcers. "Ask your father," a Soother mother will say. Father: "We'll have to check with your mother." And they will fish for your opinion before stating their own.

> YOU: What do you think of the movie?
> SOOTHER: What do *you* think?
> YOU: I don't like it.
> SOOTHER: Neither do I.

A predictable set of physical characteristics goes along with the Soothers' evasiveness. Their eyes are diverted or cast downward, sometimes even tearful. The message in them says, "Help!" Masklike features often cover their anguish. Their heads are down, the shoulders round. Hands may be clasped together. The Soothers' walk is almost a shuffle; they are usually a few paces behind the group. Their voices are low, their speech hesitant, its content indecisive and understated. "Is this all right? . . . What do you think? . . . Do you like this one on me? . . ." Soothers are conformists to a fault. They put tremendous amounts of energy into a quest for acceptance. They want more than anything to be part of the group because they are starved for any sign of approval that will increase their sense of self-esteem. Their greatest need is to be loved, and as a consequence, they'll do almost anything you ask of them and numerous things you don't.

Soothers are the most proficient self-saboteurs in the business. If they have talent, they don't practice. If they're to be tested, they don't prepare. If they're to be interviewed, they often "forget" to show up.

Why Soothers Are Losers

As you can imagine from the foregoing, Soothers pose some very special problems in a negotiation.

• They start off every negotiation expecting to lose.

- They won't tell you what they want.
- They'll seldom tell you the truth if the truth is likely to upset you. Instead, they'll tell you what they think you want to hear, which can be misleading and dangerous and get you in trouble.
- They won't voluntarily confront a problem. Either they'll pretend the problem doesn't exist, or else gloss over it. They'll seldom return phone calls, on the assumption that a call could mean a problem.
- Once the issue must be faced, they'll show none of the focusing power of Dictators or Silhouettes; such focusing as they do will be on trivia that could in no way solve the problem. If friction develops, they'll try to change the subject, usually from a business to a personal issue.
- They are often crippled by anxiety during high-stress negotiations.
- They won't say no, out of fear of losing your approval.
- They blame themselves too quickly and make confessions too early.

While lack of assertiveness is endemic among all Soothers, it is particularly acute in Soother women. There are thousands of women today who are trying to throw off the Soother's role, only to find themselves all but crippled by fear of reprisals— rejection, abuse, accusations that they are "unfeminine"—if they negotiate too strongly. "I'm absolutely at war with myself," a young woman in transition, newly appointed to the executive ranks of her corporation, exploded in my office one day. "Part of me says, 'Be nice, don't push.' The other part says, 'You jerk, you're sitting there like a blob. How are they going to know you're strong?' How *can* you be strong without looking nega-tively pushy as opposed to positively assertive?"

The passive, compliant person who rarely tells you what she needs, feels, wants, or thinks, who wants hassle-free rela-tionships, is the most prevalent breed of Soother, but not the only breed. There is another breed of Soother who employs the "tryanny of illness" to arrange life as she wants it. Her illness, as often as not feigned or imagined, takes command not only of her life but of the lives of all around her. Everyone must live as she does; she is completely absorbed in herself.

While she doesn't overtly show aggression, she is one of the most aggressive of the stylists. Whereas the Jungle Fighter will scream, shout and rage when he is angry, the Soother who uses the tyranny of illness remains verbally nonexpressive. Her style, according to one doctor, is "sneaky," and thus tougher to deal with.

I have a client who was a bright and promising executive at the outset of his career; he had to give up a promotion because his wife had arthritic problems that required them to move to a warmer climate. Several years later, he decided to leave his wife, only to be told that she had developed multiple sclerosis. "It turned out not to be multiple sclerosis at all," he recalled bitterly much later. "It was a 'shadow disease' embodying the same symptoms but neither the crippling nor the killing effect. Yet she had convinced herself that she had multiple sclerosis, and she convinced me. We lived her illness for twenty years."

Soothers may deceive their families or colleagues, but rarely themselves. They know they feel deficient and rejected. They know they're afraid to put their sound out—"I sat like a fish in that meeting," a woman Soother anguished after it was over—to let others know who they are and what they really want. They know they have storehouses of unresolved problems, unexpressed feelings, incomplete thoughts. And they keep it all inside, which often leads to what I call the "victim's disease," an ulcer.

How Soothers Survive

For all their "soothing," Soothers somehow manage to survive. They perpetuate marriages and relationships and hold on to their jobs. Some of them even rise to responsible positions, where they surround themselves with competent people who will do their work for them.

In the most superficial sense, Soothers make agreeable office colleagues. They pick up tabs at the bar, give parties for the staff, cultivate friendships, and even provide quantities of material for office gossip by discussing their private lives or letting others overhear their personal phone calls. They share themselves in this way in an effort to create feelings of intimacy between themselves and their colleagues; in effect, they are giving themselves away in the hope of getting something back.

Colleagues and family members learn never to go to a Soother for a decision, and some of them interpret the Soother's evasiveness as lying. And yet, Soothers often score high marks with their superiors, who find their slavish devotion and willingness to work particularly useful. The superiors are also comforted by the knowledge that Soothers will rarely fight them or threaten them or compete for their job.

Soothers do have their arsenal of weapons, and some of them are very effective. Hesitancy of speech is one of them. The Soother will "umm" and "ahh" long enough for someone else to step in and try to bring the matter and issue to a conclusion. Once that person has stated the problem and proposed solution, the Soother will reply, "Let's go ahead and do that." The idea—and the responsibility—now belong to someone else.

Socially as well as professionally, Soothers do have engaging traits, motives notwithstanding. They are great appreciators, almost alter egos, who make you feel marvelous with their praise. "You look gorgeous! Sensational!" one friend will tell another. Soothers are extremely pleasant company, fun, charming, eager for a good time. They are loyal friends and colleagues—one of their greatest strengths. When there is conflict, they are exceptional buffers, absorbing your own upset and anger, and they make a career out of helping people resolve their differences. They perceive the maintenance of peace and harmony as their greatest contribution. Because they have tremendous tolerance for others' handicaps, they are excellent in public service work, helping the physically handicapped or senior citizens, nursing or doing speech therapy. In fact, Soothers usually gravitate toward fields in which helping others is the theme: social workers, teachers, secretaries, nurses. Bureaucracies are filled with Soothers. Dictator doctors are often backed up by Soother helpers. Dictators who enjoy making decisions for others are always on the lookout for Soothers.

In certain respects, Soothers may be just what the doctor ordered—sweeteners to the often bitter medicine of life. The irony is that while Soothers work so hard to maintain harmony, they are often responsible for increased conflict. They can't, or won't, see that if all the kindness and sweetness in the world is used to sugarcoat problems, it will do nothing but produce more problems.

It is this essential ambiguity of Soothers that keeps them from unqualified success, and happiness, as well. Deep down, they know this; men Soothers have tremendous regrets for their years of passivity; women Soothers feel they have sold out. This knowledge, in turn, produces deep resentments, which can be expressed by what is known, in psychological terms, as passive-aggressive resistance. Suppose you're married to a Soother, and you're so overwhelmed with work at the moment that you ask him or her to pay the monthly bills, something you normally do. "No problem," your mate replies. "Happy to do it." Three months later, your utilities have been disconnected, you're getting nasty calls from American Express, and your credit is in jeopardy. Angrily, you confront your mate. "Oh, sorry," your spouse replies, "I forgot."

It's possible that your mate really did forget because Soothers are also busy—busy from overcommitting to others. But it's just as likely that he or she is fighting back, either deliberately or unconsciously. By forgetting—a form of indirect aggression—by being late, by burning the steak when your boss is coming to dinner, by leaving two important paragraphs out of your brief, the Soother evens the score a little—and drives you wild in the process.

Soothers in Brief

ASSETS	LIABILITIES
appreciative	cheerful to a fault
gracious	anxious
harmonious	unassertive
helpful	uncommitted
loyal	obsequious
attentive	sycophantic
available	undependable
willing	indecisive
	evasive

7

Win-Win Negotiators

They move into your life with fluid ease, then stand, centered and secure, their faces smooth, unlined by destructive emotions. They lean forward, offering a resolute handclasp. Their voices are firm and clear, their sentences direct and spontaneous, filled with words like "we . . . us . . . our . . . let's consider . . . what are your thoughts? . . . how can we resolve? . . . let's discuss . . . discover, share . . . redefine . . . negotiate." No translations of their statements are necessary, no allowances required for guile; they speak, like music, directly to the spirit. They are authentic; what you hear, see, feel, and experience is real. Like Jungle Fighters, they race hearts and turn heads and cause the skin to prickle—but for entirely different reasons. Where Jungle Fighters, with their scowls and barbs and snarls, shoot stabs of fear into your body, the amicable eyes of Win-Win Negotiators invite you to respond.

Win-Win Negotiators aren't Supermen and Wonder-women. They do get angry, rattled, impatient. But they know and you know it will pass. Their point of view doesn't come out of textbooks or crash courses in self-assurance. It has been amply tested in the marketplace. They have fought the conventional professional and social battles, seen the flow of blood, tossed through sleepless nights, and decided that no prize can be worth the cost of relentless tension and minimal joy. Survival, they have learned, depends on other people.

But mere survival is not their objective. They want a balanced life, the kind achieved only in community with other people, who believe as they do that caring and nurturing are reciprocal.

Win-Win Negotiators seek to achieve what their name describes. They win, and their adversaries and/or partners win. Each side walks away with something.

Make no mistake. Win-Win Negotiators want their share. If they are committed to mutuality, it's not primarily because they're charitable but because they're emphatically pragmatic. They've learned the hard way that, in the long run, winning and survival depend not just on themselves but on others.

During World War II, my uncle, a manufacturer of plumbing parts, kept numbers of small plumbing businesses from going into bankruptcy by extending them a long line of credit on merchandise and not pressing them when they were unable to pay—knowing that the war would end, as would their financial crisis, and that he would reap the bounty of his goodwill.

They Ask: "How Much Will the Loss Affect the Other Person?"

What makes Win-Win Negotiators important, both socially and historically, is that, in modifying their perception of what they need to win, they have redefined what winning means. They consider not just their own goal, but the other person's goal and the common goal. They know that negotiating is not solely a question of how much they will win, but *how much the loss will affect the other person.* They have no desire to live in an unstable environment of a few winners and a multitude of embittered losers. In short, they don't have to have it all; what's there can be shared.

Win-Win Negotiators don't always succeed. There are times when they lose, but they know they'll come out of the valley and climb the peak again. They know because they operate out of an "economy of abundance." They believe there are enough personal and universal resources for everyone to enjoy. They can't be duped into thinking that there's not enough to go around. They also understand that holding on tight creates tension and fear inside the self. They're more than willing to share. Contrast this attitude with that of the other five stylists—Jungle Fighters, Dictators, Silhouettes, Big Daddies and Mammas, and even Soothers—who operate from an "economy of scarcity," believing that there's not enough to go around and that the guiding principle, as a consequence, must be "Hold on Tight!"

Win-Win Negotiators are master observers of the human condition. They function with clarity about themselves—their purpose, needs, and goals—as well as clarity about you, be you opponent or partner. They aren't quick-change artists, manipulating you with one style and then another in order to achieve an objective. They don't turn into Dictators when, at three o'clock, they suddenly discover they're going to need a report by five. No sudden outpouring of Big Daddy or Mamma love is used to win you over; the regard they feel for you is consistent, regardless of the occasion. They rarely say one thing and do another. If they agree to do something, they'll do it. If they can't do it, they'll say, "That's something I'm not able to do at the present time." You always know exactly where they're coming from, particularly because they are not afraid to put their voices out, to say, "I want, I feel, I need."

Win-Win Negotiators don't dump their emotions on the first available victim. They know when something's going on within themselves, pay attention to those feelings, and take care of them without wreaking havoc on those within their range. A Win-Win high-school teacher came to work one morning filled with anxiety because his wife, well beyond the normal age for childbearing, was in labor with their first child. He might have taken his emotions out on his students. Instead, he told them about the problem—and they helped him get through the day.

Win-Win Negotiators won't humiliate you in public, as Jungle Fighters do. Public humiliation is not a Win-Win tactic. If they are unhappy with something you did or said, they'll take you aside after the meeting, review the episode, and say, "What do you suggest doing? How might we handle it differently?"

Win-Win Negotiators don't luxuriate in emotionalism. Jungle Fighters will explode for the sake of the theatrics; when a Win-Win Negotiator explodes—and he does—it is out of a sense of outrage. He is concerned with healing, not destructiveness. I recall a poster on the wall of a woman who had abandoned the corporate life in favor of her own business: "My human dignity is nonnegotiable."

Their regard for others is one of the Win-Win Negotiators' greatest strengths. They come into a negotiation thinking well of you. They trust the people with whom they surround themselves. They assume you'll be diligent and honorable and energetic until you prove otherwise, and only then will they take action.

Win-Win Negotiators stay focused on the objective. If their own progress is impeded by someone slower than they are, they don't waste time wishing that they could be left alone to run things; they say, "Hey, Joe, can I give you a hand?" The twenty minutes saved by helping Soother Joe can be used for fruitful discussion on an important issue.

An Insatiable Taste for Change

Unlike the Dictator, Win-Win Negotiators never say, "It has to be done this way." They say, "I think it's worth a try." Whereas the other stylists see each negotiation as another threat, the Win-Winners perceive it as a new game. "It is not possible to step twice into the same river," Heraclitus, the Greek philosopher, wrote 2500 years ago. Win-Winners understand that. They know that change can't be stopped, that even such a casual act as rubbing the fingers together removes scales from the skin and thereby changes the body. They waste neither time nor energy in trying to resolve conflicts in the same way over and over again. They make no assumptions about new acquaintances because they are women or men or blacks or Chicanos or children; their only assumption, and it is well tested, is that each new acquaintance will be full of surprises. They see each new situation as fresh, unblemished, and unpredictable, and they would have it no other way. They understand that change, not sameness, is natural to life, that out of the merging of your differences and their differences, something unique emerges. They want variety and growth, and they understand the profound connection between the two. The other styles want sameness because they know how to handle it. But Win-Win Negotiators know that out of sameness nothing comes but sameness.

But if Win-Win Negotiators are "riskers," their risks are calculated. They love to ride big waves, but if the red flag is up they won't go in the water. When they take a chance, they make plans against the prospect of failure. But once they make a decision, they don't waver. They give their plan a try.

Win-Win Negotiators don't try to outmuscle a combative force. That doesn't mean they tolerate it. To the contrary, they buffer and divert it until it's either neutralized or begins to work against itself.

Win-Win Negotiators don't feel that they need to be loved by everyone. They have enough self-regard not to need propping up by other people's praise. They understand that their point of view is one not yet appreciated or even understood by many others; if they're not totally approved of or accepted, they don't fault their point of view, they simply recognize that others haven't caught up with them. They believe serenely in the future of the win-win ideal.

This inner conviction translates well into negotiating strength. Because Win-Win Negotiators don't have undue hunger for approval, they don't have to concede issues too easily or quickly. If they make a mistake, they'll admit it without too much hesitation; their ego can stand it. And if they don't get promoted, they won't lose time sulking. Rather, they'll ask themselves, "What did I do or not do that cost me that promotion?" They're not all that troubled by criticism, especially that from themselves.

Win-Win Negotiators know that being open and honest doesn't mean they must say everything that is on their mind. They know the value of discretion. They are conscious of how much information and revelation others are able to absorb and tolerate at any one time, especially in personal relationships. They modulate their self-disclosures in reference to others' styles and capacities.

An Empathy for Others

Most important is the Win-Win Negotiators' empathy with the other person. They express their own point of view, but they also recognize their responsibility to explore the other person's point of view. They don't feel that they must constantly justify their position. They try to understand which issues are important to the other person.

Years ago, I taught first grade in a neighborhood so poor that the children came to school without having had breakfast. My objective was to teach those children how to read. But their objective was to eat. Had I concentrated on my objective without concerns for theirs, I might not have taught them anything. Instead, I geared all of the instruction to their preoccupation with being fed. We formed a juice committee, a cereal committee, a bacon and egg committee, a toast committee. Another committee wrote and delivered invitations to our breakfasts. The entire class visited local markets in order to learn how to read the names and prices of foodstuffs. The children "won"— they got their food. But I "won," too. They learned to read.

Win-Win Negotiators are not a new species. They've been around awhile. But the ideas they valued were not valued in turn, so they put themselves in areas of human activity where they did not have to live counter to their convictions. A decade or two ago, Win-Win Negotiators were found mostly in education and public service, where profit was not a motive. They were rarely in big business because their characteristics, at the time, were not respected by big business. Foremost among these characteristics is an antipathy for killing a business opponent.

Killers still abound in industry and business. One Win-Win Negotiator took my seminar precisely to learn how to deal with a Dictator boss who insisted he get more work out of people in his division. My student was convinced, for his part, that they were already working to their maximum, and that further demands on their time and energy would not only produce inferior work but damage them in the process. This he was unwilling to do—a point he was able to sustain only after learning how to dramatize the benefits for the Dictator of a better course of action.

Compassion, empathy, concern—such expressions of humanity were without dollar value in the eyes of the captains of industry. Today, the reports my colleagues and I are getting is that such qualities have a decided value now.

I talk to people everywhere, in restaurants, on airplanes,

in hotel lobbies. I'm always curious to know what they do. They're curious, in turn. It isn't long before we're talking about negotiating, because that's one activity we all have in common, whether we do it poorly or well. Once, an attorney said to me, "Tessa, if I talked the way you're suggesting, my colleagues would think I was crazy." But for every remark like that, I hear two others that are just the opposite, remarks like this: "The kind of man we're looking for today is the kind who realizes that when he wins everything in a negotiation, that negotiation has failed."

Today, Win-Win Negotiators can enter arenas formerly closed to them, or which they had previously shunned. The movie industry, merchandising, fashion, advertising—such highly competitive, big-buck businesses are still dominated by Jungle Fighters and Dictators. But even in these arenas Win-Win Negotiators are finding that they can function successfully without compromising their values. Because they're such good observers, they'll learn quickly about the needs of Jungle Fighters and Dictators, identify who really has the power and, finally, form a support system to help them achieve their own objectives.

Dictators, Jungle Fighters, Silhouettes, Big Daddies and Mammas, and Soothers have a rough ride with Win-Win Negotiators who don't cower or question their own mental acuity or become rattled by others' sabers.

Win-Win Negotiators wind up with more self-esteem, as well as the esteem of family, friends, and colleagues who will make sacrifices in their behalf because they've done it so often for them. Win-Win Negotiators have the most fruitful life, with less stress, more joy, love and appreciation for and from others, more time to share, the sweet pleasure of being ambitious without being driven, the prospect of a longer life and, conceivably, even more money and power than those tortured, driven stylists who will destroy to get either or both.

Win-Win Negotiators in Brief

ASSETS		LIABILITIES
objective	motivated	ideally, none
non-judgmental	specific	
curious	sensitive	
clear	open	

Your Negotiating Profile

Now that you've met Jungle Fighters, Dictators, Silhouettes, Big Daddies and Mammas, Soothers, and Win-Win Negotiators, it's time to zero in on your own negotiating style—and to alert you to all-important permutations in that style as you meet with different people in different arenas of life. You may be surprised—even shocked—at how you've been digging traps for yourself by using the wrong style in the wrong place with the wrong people.

It's a fairly simple matter to identify the style of another person, once you know what you're looking for. It's something else again when you try to peg yourself. The following exercises are designed to help you do exactly that.

Exercise 1 asks a series of questions to see which of the six different styles seems closest to your own.

Exercise 2 helps you to "hear" yourself in a variety of different situations—at work, at home, with loved ones, with friends, spending money, dealing with service people, dealing with yourself, having sex.

Exercise 3 helps you to "see" yourself in all of these situations.

Try to be as honest with yourself as you can.

Exercise 1

Answer "yes" or "no" to each of the following questions:

Do you usually delegate authority only to people who think the same way you do?

Do you find yourself making all the family, office, and social decisions, from the trivial to the critical?

Do you find yourself disappointed in others because their standards aren't high enough?

Are your conferences with others interrogations rather than dialogues?

Do you find it difficult to express appreciation for good performance by subordinates or members of your family?

Does change make you uncomfortable?

Do you take the same vacation year after year?

Do you generally choose the restaurant your family eats at?

Do you make the final decision about the purchase of major items?

Do you require an accounting of all money spent by other members of your family?

If you have answered "yes" to five of the above ten questions, you have strong dictatorial tendencies. A "yes" answer to six or more questions means that you are probably perceived by your family and colleagues as a Dictator.

Answer "yes" or "no" to each of the following questions:

Do you find it necessary to criticize others in public?

Do you disregard other people's input in joint projects?

Do you use confidential information to attack others?

Do you resort to sarcasm when asking for information?

In dealing with others, do you attack first?

Do you make appointments and invariably keep people waiting?

Do you constantly interrupt to make your point?

When you're uncomfortable in an interaction, do you switch the subject by finding fault with others?

Do you expect others to produce and perform for you regardless of their health or needs?

Do you use threats to get what you want?

If you have answered "yes" to five of the above ten questions, you have strong Jungle Fighter tendencies. A "yes" answer to six or more questions means that you are probably perceived by your family and friends as a Jungle Fighter.

Answer "yes" or "no" to each of the following questions:

Do you prefer to keep your feelings to yourself?
Do you like to work alone?
Do you prefer to ignore or avoid conflicts?
Do social occasions make you uncomfortable?
Are you indifferent to the problems, interests, and needs of the members of your family?
Do you try to avoid discussions of the family's problems?
Do you feel uncomfortable touching or hugging members of your family?
Do brainstorming sessions with family and colleagues make you uncomfortable?
Do you find it hard to give recognition to others?
Do you feel more comfortable in structured work situations than in looser social ones?

If you have answered "yes" to five of the above ten questions, you have the tendencies of a Silhouette. A "yes" answer to six or more questions means that you are probably perceived by your family and friends as a Silhouette.

Answer "yes" or "no" to each of the following questions:

Do you enjoy giving advice to others?
Do you like to take responsibility for other people's problems?
Do you use praise in order to control relationships?
Do you encourage discussion when problems arise, and then solve the problems your way?
Do you offer love, support, and approval to those who agree with you and withhold it from those who disagree?
Do you get angry when others don't follow your advice?
Do you surround yourself only with people who are in need of advice or love or help?
Do you find yourself overwatering your plants, overfeeding your guests, overgiving your advice?

Do you find yourself giving more time and attention to others than to yourself?

Do you find yourself giving partial responsibility but reluctant to give up control?

If you have answered "yes" to five of the above ten questions, you have strong Big Daddy or Big Mamma tendencies. A "yes" answer to six or more questions means that you are probably perceived by your family and friends as a Big Daddy or Big Mamma.

Answer "yes" or "no" to each of the following questions:

Do you dislike making decisions?

Do you ask others to help you select clothing, housing, jobs, lovers?

Do you agree to assume responsibility and then not follow through?

Do you feel victimized by other people?

Are you uncomfortable asking for or refusing?

Does conflict make you so uncomfortable that you'll do anything to avoid it?

Do you blame yourself when things go wrong?

Do you explode at things rather than people?

Do you feel you don't get enough appreciation for what you do for others?

Do you hesitate to state your true feelings about things?

If you have answered "yes" to five of the above ten questions, you have strong Soother tendencies. A "yes" answer to six or more questions means that you are probably perceived as a Soother by your family and colleagues.

Answer "yes" or "no" to each of the following questions:

Do you feel that decision making should be a group activity with input from staff, peers, or family?

Do you feel that other's personal lives are as important as their responsibilities to their jobs?

Do you feel that it is unfair to use attacks in negotiations?

Do you keep personal confidences that others have shared with you rather than use the information against people?

Do you get pleasure from recognizing the achievements of others?

Do you think it is important to get the opinions of others at meetings?

In approaching a new situation, do you listen and observe before jumping in to voice an opinion or take charge?

Do you avoid making decisions in the heat of anger?

In making decisions, do you consider the impact they will have on others?

Do you explore the perceptions of others in order to negotiate more effectively?

If you have answered "yes" to five of the above ten questions, congratulations! You have strong Win/Win Negotiator tendencies. A "yes" answer to six or more questions means that you are probably perceived by your family and colleagues as a Win/Win Negotiator.

Exercise 2

We negotiate in a variety of places with a variety of people. The following exercise will give you some idea of your response patterns in different situations. Check off the one statement in each situation that sounds most like you. A key at the end of the exercise indicates the style your choices most resemble.

FAMILY SPENDING

_____ 1. "Well, just go ahead and get what you think we need. I'm sure whatever you decide will be just fine with me."

_____ 2. "Don will get a bike when, and *only* when, I say so."

_____ 3. "I told you not to bother me with those trivial details."

_____ 4. "Of course this is a family decision. But I'm sure you'll all agree with my conclusion that what we need most is . . . ."

_____ 5. "Let's make a list of what we all think the priorities are, discuss them, and make a decision that benefits us all."

_____ 6. "I've already bought it. Top of the line: Deluxe model. It arrives tomorrow. You'll love it!"

DEALING WITH SERVICE PEOPLE

_____ 7. "Just fix it and leave the bill on the table."

_____ 8. "Gee, it seems to be leaking even more now, but maybe that's just the way it should be and it will fix itself soon. How much do I owe you? Is that all?"

_____ 9. "You call this (cleaned? fixed? installed?) I could do better with my eyes closed!"

_____ 10. "The frame you made is so good. You *almost* did a perfect job. I just had to touch up a few of the scratches on the edge, and now I can recommend you to all of my friends."

_____ 11. "I'm not interested in the way you usually do it. You'll do it my way or I'll find somebody else."

_____ 12. "I'm not satisfied with the way this has been repaired. I'd like to work out an adjustment with you on the price."

DATING

_____ 13. "We're going to the Pierre. I wouldn't be caught dead anywhere else."

_____ 14. "You told me you like jazz, so I've made reservations at the 5-Spot. We'll have dinner afterward, then a drive around the park, then home."

_____ 15. "I don't date, but it's possible you'll see me at the concert. I always sit in the first balcony."

_____ 16. "You said you liked Mexican food, so I called Pancho's and got them to make their specialty. They're all waiting for us. Oh! Sorry, I didn't have time to call you first."

_____ 17. "I don't have any preference. Anything you say. I like everything."

_____ 18. "I've had an unexpectedly long day and don't want to go all the way out to your place. But if you'd be willing to come here, I'll cook dinner for us both."

SEX

_____ 19. "I love it when you touch me here, gently, and I'd love to give you as much pleasure, so tell me what you like."

_____ 20. (after 20 years of nonorgasmic sex) "Dear—I—do you think you could . . . oh, well, it's really my problem. There's something wrong with me."

_____ 21. "Don't be embarrassed. A lot of people have that problem. But I can help you if you give yourself to me completely."

_____ 22. "You're too demanding."

_____ 23. (Male) "If I don't satisfy you enough, that's your problem. I don't do those other things."
(Female) "First do this, then do that, then combine them, then the other side, in that order, and for that long."

_____ 24. (Female) "There's no sense in our getting together again."
(Male) "Not bad, huh? I'll see you soon."

COLLEAGUES

_____ 25. "I hired you to solve problems, not to _discuss_ them with me."

_____ 26. "That report was excellent. I corrected a few minor details, and naturally submitted it under my aegis."

_____ 27. "You call this an idea? This is garbage!"

_____ 28. "Here is a summary of my ideas. I'd appreciate any input you may have within the scope of the study so we can move forward as quickly as possible and get this completed."

_____ 29. "Well, I thought that because you're so much more experienced, you'd want to present the major points in my report at the Board meeting."

_____ 30. "I don't like decision-by-committee. Nothing ever gets done that way."

CHILDREN

_____ 31. (to child learning a new skill) "I could do that twice as well when I was your age. Even younger!"

_____ 32. (to child just beginning to use a fork) "If you drop even one piece on the table, you will go to your room."

_____ 33. "Ask your mother."

_____ 34. "No one will ever love you as much as I do."

_____ 35. "That's okay, dear, that you forgot to do your chores. I'll do them for you tomorrow."

_____ 36. "Yes, you can have the car on Sunday night. I have an appointment on the West Side, but if you drop me off and pick me up, it will work out for both of us."

FRIENDS

_____ 37. _"You_ go to dinner with them. I couldn't care less."

———— 38. "No wonder your friends ignore you. You're a mess!"
———— 39. "I'm sorry to hear about your loss." (Pause.) "What you need to do now is . . ."
———— 40. "Oh, I'm sure she didn't mean those horrible things she said about me. In fact, I've just bought her a present because I didn't want her to get any more upset."
———— 41. "I'm upset about what happened last night. I'd like to know if I provoked it so we can prevent its happening again."
———— 42. "I knew you couldn't tell me, but I could see you were depressed, so I've invited a bunch of people over for a dinner party in your honor."

PARENTS

———— 43. "Mom, we're not going to be able to make it to the city this Christmas. We'd all love to see you. What would be best for you? Thanksgiving? Or a long weekend after the New Year?"
———— 44. "No, you're too old to take that trip alone. I couldn't live with myself if anything should happen to you."
———— 45. "Yes, I'll be busy again this year for the holidays."
———— 46. "Mother, I've planned your day. Be ready by noon."
———— 47. "Oh, no, Mom, don't worry. Of course I'll drive to Washington and pick you up and then drive you back. I'll be over this flu whether I stay in bed or not."
———— 48. "Don't worry, Pop. I'll take care of Mom better than you ever did."

SELF

———— 49. "I will succeed through organization. The others can do the work."
———— 50. "The best approach to problem solving is group interaction with me guiding the group toward the solution I know is best."
———— 51. "I'll do it bigger, better, and faster than anyone else. The others are all losers."
———— 52. "If I know what I want and need and what the other person wants and needs, I can work with the other person to find a solution that benefits us both."
———— 53. "I solve problems most efficiently when I work alone."
———— 54. "The best way to lead your life is to keep people happy. Then everything will run smoothly."

KEY

Jungle Fighters	Dictators	Silhouettes	Big Daddies Big Mammas	Soothers	Win-Win Negotiator
6	2	3	4	1	5
9	11	7	10	8	12
13	14	15	16	17	18
24	23	22	21	20	19
27	30	25	26	29	28
31	32	33	34	35	36
38	39	37	42	40	41
48	46	45	44	47	43
51	49	53	50	54	52

If you have checked five out of nine of the numbers in any column, that's probably indicative of your style in most situations.

Exercise 3

The final exercise will help you to see yourself in your dealings with others—and as others see you.

There are three possible answers: "often," "never," and "sometimes." Be sure to use "sometimes." It may help you to see aspects of yourself that you are unaware of.

The key is at the end of the quiz.

DO YOU FIND YOURSELF . . . .

	Often	Never	Some- times	
1.	____	____	____	not telling someone about a problem if you think it would hurt him or her to hear about it?
2.	____	____	____	in a rage of condemnation directed to family members and/or subordinates?
3.	____	____	____	being available to listen to other people's problems?
4.	____	____	____	insisting that your orders or requests be followed exactly?
5.	____	____	____	saying "Is this okay?" "Tell me what I should do"?
6.	____	____	____	hearing people say "I didn't know you were with the firm"?
7.	____	____	____	feeling that without your help the task just wouldn't get done?
8.	____	____	____	looking at all the options and discussing problems with others?

Often	Never	Some-times	
9. ____	____	____	seeking ways to "get even" with someone who has beaten you in a negotiation or an argument?
10. ____	____	____	untangling problems with the help of family or peers?
11. ____	____	____	promising things and then being unable to keep your promises?
12. ____	____	____	doing the work to get the contract while the rest of the staff takes a dinner break?
13. ____	____	____	supplying sweets, bringing flowers and gifts to members of the staff?
14. ____	____	____	saying "That's a problem we need to talk about" and then not approaching the problem head-on?
15. ____	____	____	feeling anxious when other people are fighting?
16. ____	____	____	using your wits to destroy your competition whether in love or business?
17. ____	____	____	feeling uncomfortable when those around stop working and begin joking and playing?
18. ____	____	____	feeling triumphant when you see your plans carried out by your family or colleagues?
19. ____	____	____	avoiding parties because you feel uncomfortable making small talk?
20. ____	____	____	feeling personally responsible for the development of each staff or family member?
21. ____	____	____	selecting subordinates with a strong emphasis on their personal feeling of warmth and regard for you?
22. ____	____	____	making major financial decisions without consulting with partners or family members?
23. ____	____	____	using your power of persuasion, wealth, or skill to get what you want regardless of the effect on other people?
24. ____	____	____	enjoying the give-and-take of problem solving in family and business relationships?

	Often	Never	Some-times	
25.	___	___	___	thinking out a problem thoroughly before telling others how to handle it?
26.	___	___	___	giving an order, knowing that discussions take too much time?
27.	___	___	___	doing the job instead of asking someone else in the family, firm, or office to help?
28.	___	___	___	becoming impatient with others and taking charge of meetings to get things done more efficiently?
29.	___	___	___	with people who often wonder what you're really thinking?
30.	___	___	___	enjoying the power you have over family and subordinates?
31.	___	___	___	operating on the principle that being liked is essential to getting ahead?
32.	___	___	___	creating fear rather than affection in family and subordinates?
33.	___	___	___	following the same roads, routines, time schedules, and lunch patterns for months at a time?
34.	___	___	___	holding on to people who no longer seem to need your guidance or advice?
35.	___	___	___	choosing gifts or providing opportunities for people because you think they ought to have them?
36.	___	___	___	trying to see things from other people's point of view?
37.	___	___	___	in arguments between close friends, family or associates, being available to diffuse tempers and hear disclosures of both parties privately?
38.	___	___	___	doing nice things for others without receiving appreciation in return?
39.	___	___	___	automatically assuming when things go wrong that it must be your fault?
40.	___	___	___	sending double messages to confuse others so that their confusion gives you an edge?
41.	___	___	___	disliking subordinates and family members who take time discussing issues on which you have made up your mind?
42.	___	___	___	using a letter in preference to a tele-

	Often	Never	Some-times	
				phone and a telephone call in preference to a face-to-face encounter?
43.	____	____	____	possessing confidential information about someone and keeping it confidential?
44.	____	____	____	acting as the individual who approves new experiences for staff or family members?
45.	____	____	____	spending a lot of your time preparing for battles with family, friends, and colleagues?
46.	____	____	____	finishing a negotiation and realizing you forgot to ask for what you wanted?
47.	____	____	____	knowing you had to use guile and shrewdness to get where you are and that you'll have to continue to use them to stay where you are?
48.	____	____	____	asking staff subordinates to write the persuasive letters since your style is clipped and frequently jolting to the recipients?
49.	____	____	____	waiting to be given a promotion instead of going in and asking for what you want?
50.	____	____	____	believing that the rewards of power and wealth go to the ruthless and not to the "humane"?
51.	____	____	____	feeling playful, and feeling free to use humor to deal with situations?
52.	____	____	____	being firm and warm when other staff or family members try to move in unproductive ways?
53.	____	____	____	preferring to finish up a work project on a weekend rather than having friends or family to dinner?
54.	____	____	____	nodding "yes" when you'd like to say "no"?
55.	____	____	____	feeling disappointed and irritated when others do not live up to the high standards and expectations you have set for them?
56.	____	____	____	becoming fearful when people attempt to move to more intimate relationships?

	Often	Never	Some-times	
57.	____	____	____	manipulating everyone around you to adjust to your demands?
58.	____	____	____	being flexible about job pressures when others interfere with your work?
59.	____	____	____	using informal dinners or meetings as a way of displaying your warmth and generosity to others?
60.	____	____	____	exasperated by staff and family members who have obviously not given quality thought to a problem and presume to take your time discussing their ill-formed ideas?

KEY

"Often" answers are grouped below, according to each style. If you answered "Often" to six out of ten questions (1, 5, 11, etc.,) in the first group below, you show definite Soother characteristics. Remember that a "sometimes" answer means that you're closer to an "often" than a "never" in your mind, an indication that you tend strongly toward that behavior pattern.

Soother	Jungle Fighter	Dictator
1.	2.	4.
5.	9.	18.
11.	16.	22.
14.	23.	25.
15.	32.	26.
29.	40.	30.
38.	45.	41.
39.	47.	48.
46.	50.	55.
54.	57.	60.

Silhouette	Big Daddy Big Mamma	Win/Win
6.	7.	3.
12.	13.	8.
17.	20.	10.
19.	21.	24.
27.	28.	35.
33.	31.	36.
42.	34.	43.
49.	37.	51.
53.	44.	52.
56.	59.	58.

Pulling It All Together

These exercises were designed to show the broad strokes you make in your dealings with others—your "central tendencies."

In the first exercise, you'll recall, you were asked to answer "yes" if the behavior described in the questions seemed to be a fair description of you. If you answered "yes" to more than half the questions in any given style, you tended not only to exhibit that style, but to be perceived by others that way.

The second exercise drew attention to the way you speak to others. Talk is something so common and so casual that in most instances you scarcely notice how you speak and what you really say. The fact is that both content and delivery are giveaway clues to style. To prove this point, as well as to help yourself enormously, I urge you to turn on a tape recorder as you begin a discussion with your family, or lover, or friend, or colleagues—assuming, of course, that they're willing. At first you may be self-conscious, knowing that you're being taped. But as you become engrossed in the discussion, you'll assume your normal speaking gait. Later, when you play the tape back, you'll hear an unmistakable negotiating style emerge. Did you encourage others to speak? Did you cut them off? Did you close them out? Were you supportive? Were you threatening? Were you controlling? Were you enjoying yourself? Were you laughing? Were you making others laugh, as well?

The third exercise was designed to probe still deeper into your negotiating style: specifically, how you interact with others, deal with issues, and communicate in verbal and nonverbal ways.

The Complexity of Style

If your response to the three exercises you've just completed has been anything like that of most of the people who have done them, you've undoubtedly discovered that you're a much more complex person than you thought you were. For example, you may have found that you are a Soother at work, a Dictator with your children, and a Big Daddy or Big Mamma with your lover.

Many of us have identified a member of our family as a Soother, for example, only to discover that his peers at the office see him as a Big Daddy. Many wives testify to living with Silhouettes—whose business associates type them as Jungle Fighters. Many Jungle Fighters in the professions are dominated by Dictators at home; that's as quantum a change in style as can possibly be imagined.

When you did the exercises, your responses to the questions most likely varied widely, depending on the particular aspect of your life the questions called to mind—home, work, or social relationships. The differences would have shown up in at least four ways: (1) whether you communicate or don't; (2) whether you cooperate or compete; (3) whether you're rigid or relaxed; and (4) whether you're confrontive or withdrawn. The people you're dealing with, the time of life you're experiencing, the needs you're feeling most strongly—these, too, would affect your responses.

What we're looking for, in all instances, are those broad strokes that enable us to recognize our patterns. *It is the recognition of these patterns that is the indispensable prerequisite to any kind of change.*

Patterns are often unconscious, and unconscious patterns repeat themselves until and unless they are brought to a conscious level. It's those unconscious, rigid patterns that often get people into trouble.

"What do you mean, 'Negotiate with him?'" a client will protest to me. "I've tried for twenty years to negotiate."

"But you've tried the same thing," I'll reply. "Try a different approach, a different style."

One of my clients did just this. Charlotte, a vigorous woman in her thirties, was feeling overwhelmed until, at my urging, she began to monitor her patterns. One day, she said to me, "I finally see it. Part of me is a Big Mamma. A big part of my life is centered around being needed by friends who need me. It's time for me to take down my shingle." That was not all Charlotte saw. She'd been a Dictator at home, issuing nothing but orders to her three children. She'd been a Jungle Fighter in her skirmishes with her Silhouette/Dictator ex-husband. And with her parents, both of them supportive, she'd been playing the role she'd played since childhood, that of an accommodating Soother. If that pattern sounds familiar, it's because it has been adopted, with slight variations, by so many women who have been divorced, are raising children alone, and are simultaneously trying to develop careers. Once she had identified her several other patterns, Charlotte was as resolute in changing them as she had been in ending her Big Mamma role at the office. She scheduled regular family meetings, delegated responsibilities to her children, assumed a more adult stance in her dealings with her parents, and referred her ex-husband to her attorney.

The Chemistry of Style

What a favor you'd be doing yourself if, having charted your own profile, you were now to repeat the exercises with someone else in mind—that spouse or child or parent or colleague or employer with whom you'd like to negotiate. The pattern you'd come up with might be incomplete, or even contain a few distortions, but it would put you in a position to ask some crucial questions:

How does your style mesh, or not mesh, with the style of that other person?

How has your style impeded or facilitated a win in your dealings with that person?

Does the mere mix of the styles presage problems?

Do you continually gravitate toward a certain style?

Certain styles attract one another, forming mergers and partnerships on both a business and a personal level. Styles can be mutually reinforcing, using the chemistry between them as a formula for growth, not surrendering their own structure so much as creating additional forms.

But the chemistry can also be toxic; while the molecules may mix, the product may be deadly. If you've been unfulfilled in love, for example, it may be because you keep getting involved over and over again with the same kind of person— whose style isn't the right match for yours.

Are you permitting another person to provoke you into an alien style? Do you, for example, walk into your office with

STYLES MUTUAL ATTRACTION CHART

HOW THE ELEMENTS OF STYLE MIX WITH ONE ANOTHER

In the lefthand column, find the style that most describes you. Then read across to see how well—or poorly—you're likely to mix with each of the other styles.

RESPOND TO	JUNGLE FIGHTERS	DICTATORS	SILHOUETTES	BIG DADDIES BIG MAMMAS	SOOTHERS	WIN-WIN NEGOTIATORS
JUNGLE FIGHTERS	Red Alert	Challenger vs Champ	The spider and the Fly	Like a penitent to a priest	Lethal	Use everything in the book—even throwing it!
DICTATORS	Champ vs challenger	Tug-of-war	Marching through quicksand	Great debate	Like royalty to commoners	Challenge: to outmaneuver
SILHOUETTES	Brief fascination	Silent standoff	Like ships that pass in the night	"You talk, I'll listen"	With alarm	"At last! Someone who understands me!"
BIG DADDIES BIG MAMMAS	"Now here's someone who really needs me"	Stalemate	"I'll talk; you'll listen"	A classic competition	Diaper-changing time	Looks for chink in armor
SOOTHERS	Masochistically	"I surrender, dear"	Bad news	Parasitic: like babies getting their bottles	A neurotic knot	"Help! Help!"
WIN-WIN NEGOTIATORS	The ultimate challenge	With caution	Appreciates creative silence	Don't want to get caught in the honeypot	Compassionately—for a while	"I like your style."

HOW

your body relaxed and your mind at ease, only to shudder and stiffen up at the sight of one of your colleagues? Do you, by contrast, return home from the office under a black cloud that is suddenly swept away when you see a certain member of your family? Who are these people, and why are they so capable of altering your behavior?

Now let's reverse the process. Are you aware of the impact of your style on the people with whom you work and live? As a Jungle Fighter, you could have others constantly on edge, knowing that they're going to have to compete for whatever they want, no matter how small. As a Dictator, you could have given those around you an acute sense of powerlessness. As a Silhouette, you could have created an atmosphere of total isolation, in which the members of your family, in particular, would live as foreigners to one another's feelings. As a Big Daddy or Mamma, you could have deliberately caused a feeling of perpetual dependency among members of your family. As a Soother, you would have caused others to look upon you with skepticism and distrust, knowing that you are given to mid-stream shifts and that you rarely follow through. Only in the Win-Win Negotiator's intimate circle would there be a feeling of confidence, mutuality, and reciprocity.

The moment you begin to pay attention to style—not just yours, but the other person's—you have begun the process of change.

Choosing the Right Style for You

Perhaps you're dissatisfied with what you've been learning about yourself—that, for example, you're more abrupt than you thought you were, or less flexible, or more demanding. Perhaps you've also picked up some clues as to why you haven't been achieving your objectives in negotiations, that it's been a case of using the wrong style in the wrong place at the wrong time. Perhaps you'd like to make some changes. What kind of changes should they be?

I have a bias: I favor the win-win style. In my years as a therapist and a negotiation trainer, I have seen no persuasive evidence that win-lose, lose-lose, and lose-win styles in interpersonal relationships achieve any lasting victories. Neither in my practice nor in my interviews have I met more than a handful of persons who have achieved their potential with any of these styles.

I'm not suggesting that win-win negotiating is the only choice you have. I'm saying it's an *option*.

I'm not suggesting that your present style must be completely altered. It simply may be out of synchronization with the need of the moment, or with a certain person. One shift in emphasis might maximize your win.

What I am proposing is that you work with what you've got—your history, experience, life choices, and uniqueness—to incorporate more win-win into your style.

If you are a Jungle Fighter, you need to retain your magic or energy or verve, but you will want to learn to listen before you demand, monitor your behavior so that you don't absorb the entire agenda, become aware of your impact on those close to you, ask for others' viewpoints, build on others' ideas, delegate responsibility to subordinates and allow them to perform without issuing put-downs or criticism, be more conscious of others' needs for private time, and above all, acknowledge that you don't need to win it all.

If you are a Dictator, you need not forfeit your extraordinary capacity for leadership and decision, or your propensity to be thorough. But you will want to learn to ask others for their opinions and listen while they are given; to acknowledge that others have leadership qualities, too; to modulate your tone of voice so that it doesn't intimidate subordinates; to listen to the viewpoints of family members rather than issue directives; to let yourself be placed in situations in which, for once, you're not in charge.

If you are a Silhouette, you should continue to cherish your ability to get off into your private world where your creativity is experienced. But you will want to learn to share with colleagues and family your thoughts on issues about which you're well informed, to talk comfortably with your children, to romance your spouse, to develop new contacts and make yourself au courant with the rest of the world. Above all, you will want to learn to be more responsive to the needs of other people.

If you are a Big Daddy or Big Mamma, you will not wish

to diminish your powerful absorption in others, your resonance with them and their concerns, but you will want to learn to ask for and use others' advice, plan trips with members of your family, ask others to do a job without first telling them how, let others lead their own lives without risking the loss of your love and regard.

If you are a Soother, you will not wish to forsake your commendable capacities for loyalty, perseverance, generosity, and appreciation, or to be any less agreeable, but you will want to turn your soothing capacities into quiet grace and determination. You'll want to learn how to risk embarrassment; to talk to the point and not around it; to speak up and out on issues about which you're well informed; to state honestly how you feel; to stick to the issue, become assertive, and stop deprecating yourself.

Everyone has elements of the Win-Win Negotiator. What you need to do is enhance, enrich, share, and use these more often and more effectively. That, as we'll now see, is the path to winning by negotiation.

PART TWO

Tools and Tactics

ATTENDING

At the opening of my seminars on negotiation, I often ask the participants to talk to as many people as they can within a period of ten minutes. In each encounter, the participants exchange answers to two questions. First, "What assets do you bring to a negotiation?" Second, "What liabilities?" This exercise enables the participants to hear over and over again what's helping them and hurting them in their dealings with others. But it's in their second meeting that the real payoff occurs. Once again, I ask the participants to speak to one another. "This time," I say, "tell the person you're talking to one thing you remember about him or her from what he or she told you last night."

Invariably, the request is met with gasps and nervous laughter. To their intense embarrassment, the participants usually remember almost nothing about their encounters with one another. They realize then that they've got to start "attending."

To attend means to pay attention to yourself and others—to see, to hear, to feel, to pick up subtle nuances and shifts in behavior patterns. It is *the* starting point of successful negotiation, and yet it is a point that most people seldom reach. They don't register the environment in which a meeting is taking place. They don't watch the other person for telling behavioral signs. They don't take careful note of idiosyncracies of dress. They don't even listen to what the other person is saying.

SR vs. SRR

Unpracticed negotiators respond to conflict as swiftly as it takes them to flick a wall switch. They want light cast on this dark uncertainty at once. Never mind that the light may be too dim or aimed too poorly to illuminate the problem.

Stimulus response, or SR, may be adequate if you're dealing with someone you've known for years, and with a problem you've resolved before. Otherwise, it puts you at an immediate disadvantage. You've forfeited the opportunity to call up your experience, learn about the other person, and evaluate whether what you're getting is a good exchange for what you're giving up.

The SRR approach (Stop. Reflect. Respond.) enables you to sort through negotiations and to identify the style of the other person. Does that stiff back, averted gaze, cold handshake, and guarded commentary tell you you're dealing with a Silhouette? Is that destructive vituperation coming from a Jungle Fighter? Are those cooing noises and calming words authored by a Big Mamma? What an advantage you're at when you've given yourself time to register and digest the information available to you just by observing and reflecting! "My power comes from observing the other person," one of the most successful negotiators I've dealt with told me once. "I just sit back, lace my hands behind my head, watch, and listen."

Those "Giveaway" Clues

There are dozens of clues available to you as you begin a negotiation if only you will attend the encounter with all your senses alert. Only by attending can you begin to know something about the person with whom you're dealing. By the same token, realize that your own presence is broadcasting clues about you—clues that can be used against you or in your favor, depending on what you're putting out.

We are all signal-and-symbol systems. We are all telling about ourselves in the way we dress, move, speak, glance, handle and attend to others. We all communicate through the same senses, and all these senses are at work bringing in data and communicating responses.

Long before the first word is spoken, communication has begun. Consider all the times on any given day that another person has communicated a need or desire or emotion to you without using a single word.

- The secretary who looked up in anger as you stood before her desk.
- The neighbor in your apartment building who stood at the elevator door studying his shoes.
- The parking lot attendant at your favorite restaurant who left rubber on the pavement as he drove your car away.
- The spouse who went off to work without kissing you good-bye.

A smile, a sigh, a yawn, a giggle, a damp brow or palm— all of these are psychological signals that the acute observer receives and stores for future use. Watch what happens as two persons, one a man, the other a woman, meet. The man's body tenses. The woman's head tilts a fraction; a gush of laughter escapes her. She is the first to extend her hand. He hesitates a fraction of a second before offering his. What are we to make of this brief encounter? Certainly they have met before. But are they old friends? Old foes? Were they once lovers? Did he lose something in his dealings with her, and if so, what? Did she win, and if so, what? Something transpired between them— we know that much—in which she came out better than he did. He is apprehensive; she would like to reassure him.

Suppose these two people had met unexpectedly at a meeting called by you. Had you missed this initial byplay, you would have been completely unprepared for the ensuing difficulties as the tension between them matured. Had you caught the byplay, you would have been able to steer the negotiation away from those difficulties.

Good negotiators are invariably skilled observers. They stock their memories with the symbols and signal patterns of the people with whom they work and live. With such a repertoire of observations, they are able to avoid triggering unproductive responses in others. Nothing in negotiation is more important.

Several years ago, I served on a commission for the evaluation of textbooks used in California's public school system.

I made it a point to be aware of the "body language" of my fellow commission members. I noticed that one particularly conservative member always sat at the head of the table, and that certain members always sat next to like-minded members. I noticed how certain members covered their faces with their hands in order to disguise their reactions. I was so intent on the "body language" of my colleagues, in fact, that in one instance I neglected to tune in on my own. One day as I was about to protest a point under discussion, one of the members said, "Now, Tessa, don't be so argumentative." I was astounded; I hadn't said a word. The same thing happened the next day, not at a commission meeting, but in a private discussion with one of my associates. "Betty, how do all of you know what I'm going to say?" I asked.

Betty laughed. "Because," she said, "each time you're about to raise an objection, you first fiddle with your hair, then you adjust your scarf, then you take your glasses off your nose, point them at the person you're about to take out after, lean forward, and say, 'Madame Chairperson . . . ' "

Your Symbol-and-Signal Inventory

Our bodies give off different clues at different times. The signals we flash vary depending on whether the environment we're in is formal or informal, whether we're at home or in the office, whether we're on public display or in a one-to-one encounter, whether the people we're with are known to us or strangers. To understand the effect we produce on others, we must first be aware of how we appear and react in different settings.

On the next four pages are lists of fifteen different aspects of ourselves through which we broadcast signals. Check the words that best describe your attitudes, manner, or physical response in each of three different settings—home, work, and social gatherings. Think about your answers. Take your time. Be objective.

Gauging Your Responses

Here's how to analyze the results.
First, pay attention to the things you rarely if ever do. Do

BODY

	Home	Work	Social Setting
tense	___	___	___
relaxed	___	___	___
drooping	___	___	___
mobile	___	___	___
athletic	___	___	___
stiff	___	___	___
graceful	___	___	___

OVERALL APPEARANCE

	Home	Work	Social Setting
calm	___	___	___
flamboyant	___	___	___
casual	___	___	___
conservative	___	___	___
femme fatale	___	___	___
macho male	___	___	___
negligent	___	___	___

EYES

	Home	Work	Social Setting
downcast	___	___	___
squinting	___	___	___
roving	___	___	___
darting	___	___	___
expressive	___	___	___
staring	___	___	___
blinking	___	___	___

EYE CONTACT

	Home	Work	Social Setting
direct	___	___	___
indirect	___	___	___
avoiding	___	___	___
confrontive	___	___	___
seductive	___	___	___
scrutinizing	___	___	___
glancing	___	___	___

HAND MOVEMENT

	Home	Work	Social Setting
constant hand movement on body or shaping the air	___	___	___
appropriate gestures	___	___	___
rubbing together	___	___	___
covering mouth	___	___	___
pounding table or backs	___	___	___
finger pointing	___	___	___
no movement	___	___	___

HANDSHAKE

	Home	Work	Social Setting
cordial	___	___	___
firm and responsive	___	___	___
quick and wet	___	___	___
brotherhood/sisterhood grip	___	___	___
overgrip	___	___	___
barely brushing	___	___	___
limp and cold	___	___	___

STANCE

	Home	Work	Social Setting
stooped and burdened	___	___	___
elastic	___	___	___
erect	___	___	___
relaxed and grounded	___	___	___
hands on hip	___	___	___
arms crossed	___	___	___
feet apart	___	___	___

WALK

	Home	Work	Social Setting
fast	___	___	___
slow	___	___	___
youthful	___	___	___
heavy	___	___	___
light	___	___	___
fatigued	___	___	___
shuffling	___	___	___

VOICE—MESSAGE

	Home	Work	Social Setting
hesitant			
understanding			
threatening			
confusing			
confident			
unfeeling			
encouraging			

VOICE—TONE AND QUALITY

	Home	Work	Social Setting
tranquilizing			
piercing			
monotone			
whining			
loud			
modulated			
strained			

HEAD

	Home	Work	Social Setting
shaking			
nodding			
rigid			
responsive			
swaying			
drooped			
tilted			

FACE

	Home	Work	Social Setting
grimacing			
frowning			
smooth-lined			
laugh-lined			
stress-lined			
twitching			
clenched			

SMILE

	Home	Work	Social Setting
intense			
broad			
quick			
constant			
twitch			
frozen			
tight-lipped			

SIT

	Home	Work	Social Setting
slump			
rigid and straight			
legs crossed			
legs apart			
chair straddled			
informal curl			
comfortable			

TOUCHING

	Home	Work	Social Setting
avoids physical contact			
hesitant			
loving			
patronizing			
conciliatory			
pat and peck			
invading			

your responses indicate that you seldom smile, shake hands, move close to others, touch or embrace? If so, the physical part of human contact may be missing from your life.

At home, do you dress casually, curl in a chair, stand relaxed, unclench your teeth, even go without makeup or a shave? If you're not able to do any of these things, it suggests that you're not comfortable. A too laid-back pattern at home, on the other hand, may also suggest some tension; sloppiness carried to the extreme may be uncomfortable to your mate, and a deliberate, if unconscious, signal of dissatisfaction with him or her. At the opposite extreme, excessive formality may be an important signal of strain, too. A certain amount of formality with a Dictator boss may be advisable, but by-the-numbers relationships with colleagues or subordinates or even family and friends require some evaluation on your part.

If you wonder why everyone burdens you with his or her problems, pay attention to your constantly nodding head, your warm, inviting smile, the intensity in your glances, your willingness to pull up a chair and then curl into it.

Conversely, do you wonder why people withdraw from you? It may be because you give off signals of defeat—a stooped body, a shuffling gait, downcast eyes, a low, quiet hesitant voice; or signals of inaccessibility—impatience, turning away, checking your clock or appointment book, a cold, impersonal voice tone; or signals of combativeness—piercing eyes, a loud voice, and too many jabs at the other person's arms.

We flash our signals as we enter a negotiation, expressing our willingness or unwillingness to take part in a dialogue, expressing our emotional state, our degree of intellectual preparedness, our confidence or lack of it. For Win-Win Negotiators, the objective is to flash signals of positive interest: unwavering eye contact, attentive listening, alert response to questions, responsiveness to the issue, the offer of time without pressure.

The key is *congruence:* your verbal and nonverbal message should be saying the same thing. If you feel one thing and say another, you're not going to be convincing. "Yes, I consider that a good trade-off," you say—but your shoulders slump, tears well in your eyes, and a frozen smile poorly masks your anger. Such conflicting messages not only don't convince, they cause suspicions to develop in the people with whom you're negotiating.

Signals and Styles

Signals are like magnets, putting out positive and negative energy that either attracts or repels other people. At the same time, they identify your style.

If *humiliation* is your intent, you will encroach upon another person's space, touch without permission at the wrong time and place, note but not heed others' signs of stress, use distracting tactics, flash signals of impatience. If such signals are in your repertoire, then Jungle Fighting is your style.

If *intimidation* is your mode, you will nod or point your finger to tell others when to speak, control the length of others' presentations by constantly consulting your watch, raise your voice the moment you think you're beginning to lose in order to regain control, raise your eyebrows or throw hard glances to express disapproval, turn your body away if you don't like what's being said, rise, read a memo on your desk or start to make a phone call when you want to end the meeting. Signals like these tell others that you're a Dictator.

If *solitude* is your preference, your most powerful signal is silence. All other signals are muted and economical. Involuntary signals include facial and body twitches, jiggling legs and knees, nervous hands. Combined, these signals portray a Silhouette.

If *barnacling others to you* is your objective, you will stroke, stroke, stroke, nodding your head to encourage the flow of self-disclosure you've turned on in the other person, flashing benevolent glances to reinforce your "approval," disapproving if the person in whom you're cultivating a dependency even faintly hints that he'd like to go independent. Those are all Big Daddy and Mamma signals you're flashing.

If *peace at any price* is what you must have, your repertoire will include myriad signs of compliance—shoulder shrugs, nodding head, a frozen smile, comforting pats; but you'll also flash telltale clues—wet hands, a limp handshake, beads of perspiration, and nervous grimaces—that poorly disguise your inner knowledge. Sound familiar? You may be a Soother.

But if your intent is to *create a dialogue,* your expressions will convey concern and care and genuine interest, and you'll give the other person the time needed to respond. Your body will be relaxed, your gaze steady. You'll punctuate the other person's presentation with agreeable nods and thoughtful questions. Important points will be underscored with emphatic gestures. Those signals you're flashing say, "Win-Win Negotiator."

Monitoring Your Signals

Be conscious of your signals, deliberately flash those signals you'd like others to receive, and minimize or eliminate signals that damage your cause.

Bear in mind that signals are culturally conditioned. They mean different things in different places. The hearty, first-name informality of a Texan may go down very poorly in a New York City boardroom populated by Ivy Leaguers. Signals also mean different things in different eras. What is seen today as a perfectly acceptable greeting from a woman might have been considered a come-on thirty years ago. A warm, responsive handshake may just be a friendly gesture and not a sexual invitation.

How, then, do you know what to do when and where? Your repertoire of observation is developed over time, but the basic rule is to know what message you want to flash, and to inventory the basic means by which to flash it.

PAY ATTENTION TO HOW YOU MOVE: Your movement expresses your confidence or lack of it. An erect (not rigid) posture, a purposeful (not rapid) walk, a sense of where you're going—these are the signals of a Win-Win Negotiator.

If walking into a room full of strangers or superiors, or even peers, is something that disturbs you, here's a suggestion: Before you enter the room, make a decision that once inside the door, you'll move either to the left or to the right. Then, just as you begin to move, pick out a chair, walk purposefully to it, and sit down.

PAY ATTENTION TO NERVOUS MANNERISMS THAT DISTRACT OTHERS FROM YOU AND YOUR MESSAGE:

Hands through hair
Rubbing, touching, smoothing face
Fiddling with jewelry
Fiddling with buttons
Wringing hands
Crossing and uncrossing arms
Adjusting and readjusting glasses
Stringing paper clips
Biting the inside of your cheek
Tapping toes, fingers, and pencils
Capping and uncapping a pen, or clicking a ball-point

PAY ATTENTION TO DRESS AND APPEARANCE. THE KEY WORDS ARE:

Appropriate
Adaptable

PAY ATTENTION TO PSYCHOLOGICAL SIGNALS THAT EXPRESS YOUR INNER TENSIONS:

Giggling at serious times
Sighing as someone enters
Yawning in moments of stress
Expressing signs of anxiety, such as:
  shallow breathing
  rubbing neck
  pulling at collar
  small, uncontrolled twitches
  perspiration

PAY ATTENTION TO THE WAYS YOU EXPRESS AFFECTION:

Touching
Hugging
Kissing

Warm embrace
Handshake
Hand holding
Arm linking
No touching
Smile
Arm around shoulder

PAY ATTENTION TO YOUR SPEECH:

Is your voice firm or hesitant?
Are you speaking at a speed that permits others to
   understand you?
Is your tone friendly and inviting, or hostile and distanc-
   ing?
Are you so intense you're scaring others off?
Are you so loud others wish they could turn you down?
   Or so quiet your words are lost?

PAY ATTENTION TO HOW YOU GAIN ATTENTION:
Screams, tears, complaints of illness, sarcasm, intimidation,
torment, badgering, molesting, heckling, ridiculing, tantalizing,
seducing, or refusing to speak—every one of these is a dis-
credited and outmoded style of gaining attention for your
message.
   What *is* appropriate is to ask for what you want, to use
good-humored humor, to respond to others' goals, to recognize
that others' ability to maintain attention is relative to their interest.

PAY ATTENTION TO YOUR MANNER
OF PRESENTATION:

Arrogant
Compliant
Sarcastic
Cordial
Challenging
Retiring
Embracing

PAY ATTENTION TO HOW YOU'RE FEELING: If your back or shoulder or neck muscles are tight, it may mean you're under stress.

If you can't feel your muscles, it may mean you've worked so hard and neglected yourself so much that you may be a candidate for illness.

If you feel harassed or embittered, or you've lost your sexual appetite or can't remember the last time you had some fun, it may mean your system's overloaded.

If you suddenly realize that you can't remember the last time someone touched you, find someone who will.

If you sense something is amiss, trust your feelings. They may be ahead of your conscious perceptions.

There is no way you can negotiate successfully if you are out of touch with your feelings. When you don't know what you feel, you don't know what you want.

You don't need an advanced degree to know what you feel. Pay attention to the obvious. Remember that whatever you feel affects your ability to negotiate, if only because your feeling is being broadcast to others, no matter how good your acting ability or your attempts at disguise.

Feedback

To discover and evaluate the kinds of signals you're putting out:

Tape your voice.

Rehearse in front of a mirror or before someone you trust.

Ask for comments from friends and family.

Observe others' reactions to your gestures.

Look at photo albums:

How are you standing?

Where are you standing—always in the center or at the edge?

Whom are you standing next to?

Are you:

Touching?

Hugging?

Clowning?

Smiling—genuinely or posed?

Formal or informal?
Never in the family photo album?
Observe media models and how they handle themselves.
Observe those you respect.

Paying Attention to Others

I find in my work that many men who deal sensitively with clues and cues in business relationships proceed in their intimate life as though these same signals were not important. Many women, conversely, traditionally sensitive to others' signals in their personal dealings, ignore the very same signals in their business dealings. How wrong these men and women are.

Timing is the backbone of strategy—whether that strategy be for a major business deal or an everyday family problem. The signals that others flash are the traffic signs of the negotiating process, wherever it takes place. They tell you when to stop and go, when to proceed with caution, when to turn or detour.

Signals can be ploys; you only know that if you have a history with the signaler. Mostly, however, signals have a universal meaning, and tend to mean what they suggest.

SIGNALS THAT TELL YOU TO APPROACH:

An invitation
A welcoming wave
An outstretched arm
An expression of pleasure
Pulling out a chair
Making room for you on the couch
A cessation of activity and a movement toward you when
    you enter
An appropriate smile or nod of the head
Direct eye contact
Head turned toward you

SIGNALS THAT TELL YOU TO HANG IN THERE:
The other person:

Asks questions
Supplements your story
Expresses interest:
   Tilted head
   Body leaning forward
   Still body
   Alert and expressive eyes

SIGNALS THAT TELL YOU TO AVOID:

Signs of anger or hostility:
Shallow breathing
Clenched jaw
Jerky muscle movement
Knotted fist
Inappropriate laughter
Talking through teeth
Jerky hand movements

Signs of disinterest:

Changing issue
Lack of expression
Bland smile
Turning away
Short conversation
Glancing around room

Signs of impatience:

Brusque greeting
Shifting papers
Rattling cups
Disjointed observations
Inappropriate responses

SIGNALS THAT TELL YOU TO WITHDRAW:
The other person:

Doodles
Daydreams
Looks at you with glazed eyes
Looks repeatedly at watch

Taps fingers
Empties coffee cup
Crushes cigarette
Applies makeup
Checks appointment book
Excuses self to make a phone call
Calls in secretary
Asks if it's lunchtime
Makes disjointed observations
Talks through clenched teeth
Shifts voice tone from warm to cold
Speaks with measured words
Shows signs of fatigue

Paying attention consists of more than merely registering physical signals and being alert to habits. It involves an evaluation of what you're experiencing.

An evaluation takes time. Try not to respond in a flash to what you've observed. Sort out the nuances of your observation *before* you respond. When there's no time to be this reflective, trust your intuition. It's generally pretty good, particularly if you've been consciously building your repertoire of observations.

Listening

It's been said that talking is a habit, but listening is an art. It's an art that few people learn. Jungle Fighters, Dictators, Silhouettes, Big Daddies and Mammas, and Soothers are all so self-absorbed that they filter out what they don't want to hear, so worried about how they're going to defend themselves or how smart they're going to sound that they become abysmal spectators. At their worst, they drown out the voices of those with whom they deal.

If you're so preoccupied with your own concerns that you must constantly express them, you miss out on the most vital clues of all to the other person's aspirations—what it is that he *says* he wants. What he says may not be the same as what he really wants, but it's an indispensable starting point.

Careful listening helps you to check out your observations, assumptions, and intuitions. It expresses regard for the other person. It enables you to collect "giveaways," clues unwittingly revealed by the other person.

When you listen, there is much more to be heard than content. The choice of words tells you what kind of person you're dealing with—whether he or she is formal or informal, contemporary or conservative, loose or tight. The speaker's manner gives myriad clues to his or her feeling state—just as your own manner does. Is his or her manner arrogant? retiring? challenging? embracing? compliant? sarcastic? assertive? aggressive? pedantic? emotional? Whatever it is will affect your response.

Listen to more than the other person's words. Note:

- Brittle sounds of statements expressed under stress
- Increase or decrease in liveliness as stress builds
- Misplaced joke or unexpected admission. Is the other person bored, or has a "grave" been walked on?

Watch for:

- The averted eye or face or body. Has tender territory been touched?
- The rapidity of facial expressions, which may denote stress, fatigue, or boredom
- The uncontrolled movement of small muscles, cues to the other's unease
- The rigidity or elasticity with which the body moves in relation to the flow of the encounter—and whether the movements match the flow

The person you're with may be calm on the outside, like a Dictator or a Silhouette, but exhibit subtle signs of inner tension that are often missed unless you attend with all your senses. Some of these signs:

Dilation of the pupils
Perspiration
Blushing

Prolonged, studied ritual when lighting up, especially with
a pipe
Constant application of lipstick
Small muscle movements in the face

You aren't necessarily listening if you're simply being quiet
when another person's talking. Real listening means concen-
trating on what the other person is saying with such intensity
that your own speech-making processes are stilled. It means
being still as well as quiet, assuming an attentive listening
posture, not kicking a leg or running your hand through your
hair or twirling a pen. It means nodding appropriately and
watching intently so that the other person affirms your interest.
It means exclamations of enthusiasm, e.g., "Tell me more!" "Ah
ha." (It doesn't mean forced laughter that is too loud, or long
or vigorous nonstop nodding.) It means asking questions that
show the depth of your understanding of what the other person
is saying. It means not only hearing what the other person says
he or she wants, fears, feels, and needs, but knowing what he
or she *isn't* asking for. When a mate says, "I want you to help
me with the housework," what he or she may really be saying
is, "I want more attention than I'm getting."

Above all, it means not interrupting if you can possibly
help it, so that the other person knows that you are hearing
what he or she is saying, that you are concerned, and that you
are giving him or her your individual attention. Only when
you've created that satisfaction in others will they be willing to
listen attentively to you.

Imagining

There comes a point in experiencing other people when
verbal and nonverbal signals can't tell you everything you might
know, when the subtle nuances of behavior and habit and
attitude remain hidden to even the most penetrating perception.
That is the point at which imagination comes into play.

Novelists frequently base their characters on aspects of
persons they know. They then invent new circumstances for
their "characters." Eventually the novel and its people take on
a life of their own. What the novelist didn't know about the

real people he imagines in behalf of his characters. More often than not the imagined characteristics actually exist in the real person who served as the model.

You don't have to be a novelist to imagine just as accurately. Everyone has a central tendency from which his or her behavior flows.

To ferret out the hidden nuances of another person's behavior, try to put yourself inside that person's skin, to look at a situation through his or her eyes, to think it through in terms of his or her mental processes. You will find that somewhere in your repertoire of observations will be the information you need to put yourself in the other person's shoes.

When I was training to work with blind children some years back, I took a course on mobility training for the blind. For six weeks I was blindfolded for most of the day and night. It wasn't a requirement of the course that I be blindfolded, but I believed that the only way I could begin to understand some of the problems faced by the blind was to deprive myself, temporarily, of sight. One day, learning cane technique, I was required to climb a circular staircase. I'd climbed a number of steps when, suddenly, my cane hit an empty space. I froze. I forgot everything I had learned. I didn't even remember that all I had to do was take off my blindfold in order to see where I was.

My instructor had been observing me silently from the bottom of the stairs. Now he called out quietly, "Tess, I want you to stay where you are. Take some deep breaths. When you've calmed down, think about what you need to do when you get into trouble."

That's what I did—first, because I trusted him; next, because I felt relief that help was nearby; and, finally because I was so involved in what was happening that it *still* didn't occur to me that I could take my blindfold off. For those few moments, I was sightless. I had managed to put my body into another kind of life.

You don't have to walk around with blindfolds in order to imagine what it would be like to confront the other person's obstacles. But if some effort isn't made when needed, you're at a disadvantage in negotiating with that person. You must always be conscious of the balance between "attending" to yourself and "attending" to others. You must be aware of the constant interplay that exists between sender and receiver.

Tools of the Trade

If someone asked you to list the most important tools of business, you probably wouldn't hesitate to name computers, calculators, copiers, and typewriters. But these vital tools would soon be stilled if it weren't for others that are scarcely ever mentioned—agendas, options, trade-offs, cost-benefit analyses, returns-on-investments, contingency plans, and bottom lines. Knowing what these tools are and how to use them is a prerequisite to successful negotiation—whether you're negotiating in the boardroom or the bedroom.

Overt and Hidden Agendas

Most of us bring two agendas to the negotiating table— the first, overt; the second, hidden.

Overt agendas are straightforward. Either they're printed and distributed as a meeting begins, or they're announced by the person who has convened the meeting. There are few problems associated with overt agendas; all parties to the negotiation can agree on the words being used, if not on the meanings each of them gives those words.

Hidden agendas are another matter. They represent the real, but unannounced, purpose of each participant. There may be as many hidden agendas as there are people present. Overt and hidden agendas are as constant a fixture of family negotiations as they are of business meetings. The family's overt agenda as it gathers to discuss vacation is to plan a trip that everyone will enjoy. But Father's hidden agenda may be to guarantee himself some skiing. Mother's hidden agenda may be to keep down the cost, so that they can stay longer. The children's hidden agenda may be to push for the kind of vacation in which they're away from their parents' supervision throughout the day.

Overt agendas usually deal with a common concern. Hidden agendas usually express self-interest. The two agendas may or may not be at cross-purposes, but they almost surely produce some conflict.

The best way to defuse the possibly explosive impact of a hidden agenda is to give others sufficient indication of its existence. That was the strategy of a career woman, married and with two teenaged sons, who was also a Win-Win Negotiator. One day, she summoned her sons to a family meeting. "I'm concerned that neither of you knows how to cook," she began. "It means that you're essentially helpless when I'm not here. Cooking is one of life's most basic necessities. I'll teach you everything I know about cooking. In exchange, all I'd like you to do is prepare your own lunches—and mine, too, while you're at it."

The boys eagerly agreed. Not only were they voracious eaters, they liked the idea of being independent. So keenly did they approach the project that, in addition to preparing their lunches, they were soon cooking dinner one or two days a week. Both of the boys were aware that their mother's hidden agenda was to free herself from the preparation of as many meals as possible so that she could devote more time to her business. But because she really didn't try to disguise that objective, they didn't resent it at all.

Those Mighty Tools Called "Options"

Options are negotiation's heavy-duty tools—potential alternatives for dealing with situations. Every alternative is not necessarily an option. It only becomes an option when it becomes a real possibility for action.

Without options, you're helpless. With them, you're agile and strong. The person with the most and best options is the one who most often gets what he or she is after in a negotiation.

We all have options, but not all of us recognize that we do. I once knew a woman, the wife of a commercial artist who worked at home, who, in addition to raising three children and caring for their house, had cooked three hot meals a day for her husband every day of their married life. When she came to me, she was worn out, bored, and resentful. "Why didn't you ask your husband to eat his lunch in a restaurant?" I asked her. "You had the option to do that."

The woman sighed. "I didn't know I had options," she said. "I thought I only had endurance."

Most people really know what they want. They just lack the courage or the enterprise or the stimulation to bring their distress to the surface.

In every circumstance, excepting only those in which you're facing dangerous physical abuse, there are three basic options. You can stay. You can leave. You can modify.

The business equivalent for staying is "holding to the contract." Leaving is known as "buying out." Modifying is known, in business parlance, as "optimizing" the situation. To the nonprofessional, business decisions may often seem arcane or exotic, but fundamentally they consist of choosing one of these three options.

Once the decision has been taken, it's your responsibility to execute.

If you've made the decision to stay, you've declared that the status quo is tolerable enough for you to accept it, and that you can cope with the situation as is. So long as this remains your choice, *stop putting energy into other options.*

If your choice is to leave, it's because you know yourself and the other person or the environment in which you've been functioning, you've evaluated your needs and wants as well as the consequences of your departure, and you've decided that what exists simply doesn't work. Once you've come to that awareness, why hang in there? Leave before there's a crisis. Whether it's a job, a relationship, or a marriage, face your fears and move on.

One couple I know tried everything they could think of

with one another to make their marriage a good one. They talked their problems through, kept the problems to themselves, placated one another, fought with one another, experimented with almost every known form of therapy. One day, at last, the husband said to his wife, "Look, we're two terrific people—we're just not terrific together. Let's each of us live our lives." And they did.

If it's a job you're leaving, and you have money in the bank and another job waiting, you can leave at any time. Otherwise, you have to leave with care. Never quit a job in a fit of emotion, to prove a point or make a gesture, or in the midst of an argument. Let that argument be your catalyst. Then set a time schedule, get your résumé in order, put out some feelers, and go on a budget.

Option three: modify. You know the situation has to change—and that the change must begin with you. Do what business does; "optimize" the situation. Find out how to do that by asking, and answering, these questions:

What's the major problem?

I'm not getting attention from my husband. I'm bored. I suspect he's bored too.

What part of the problem can I change?

All of it eventually, I hope, but I could do something now about my boredom.

How can I change it?

I can begin to do the things I used to do from which I derived great pleasure—go to concerts, and ballets, give small dinner parties. I can look for a job, or plan a small business.

What am I willing to do?

I'm willing to do things alone, if necessary.

What are the ground rules?

To tell my husband what I'm planning, so that he can join me if he wishes. To expect him not to join me, and be pleasantly surprised if he does. To be available, if I'm free, when he makes plans that include me.

How much time do I have?

Three months. If I'm still bored, I'll try something else.

What is my contingency plan?

My original plan is to stay and modify. If that does not work, my plan is to leave.

The Art of Making Trade-Offs

Trade-offs, in their most classic sense, are exchanges that people make. It's the old barter system: I'll give you this if you give me that. A secretary in my building wanted to take my negotiating seminar but didn't have the money. We made the obvious trade-off: she took the course for nothing, and worked for me on weekends.

Options and trade-offs are like chickens and eggs. You can't have one without the other. There is, however, no argument as to which comes first. Without options, there are no possibilities for trade-offs.

A trade-off is not a thing. It's a process—of weighing and sorting and judging and deciding, finally, which option will work most effectively for you and the other person. Trade-offs don't necessarily occur between two people; many, if not most, occur within the self. When you're making a trade-off, you're asking yourself, in effect, "What am I getting in exchange for what I'm giving up?" The answer to that question is determined by your *values*.

Options develop from your values. Many alternatives don't become options precisely because they're inconsistent with your values. The more diverse your background, the more diverse your values. The more rigid you are about your values, the more likely you are to experience conflict—both within yourself and with another person when the matter of trade-offs arises.

In the past, many women have traded off ambition, adventure, and even their identity and sexuality in exchange for economic security. I shall never forget the despair of a mother of three: "Tess, when you have children, a mortgage, and no skills, you will sell anything to make do, even if it's your self-esteem. I stayed in a relationship I hated for ten years, until I could learn a skill and take care of my children. And I would do it again."

For men, the basic trade-off has usually been time with their families for achievement at the office. Having made such a sacrifice, they are bewildered these days to discover that they're not getting what they signed up for. They had thought they were marrying women who, whatever else they represented, would function as custodians. Now, they find, they are living with wives for whom such trade-offs are no longer acceptable. These women want lives of their own outside the household, and have the skills to negotiate for them. The increased assertiveness of wives comes at a particularly difficult time for many men who are themselves in transition, having decided that they are no longer willing to endanger their home lives in behalf of their careers.

Trading the Present for the Future

Often it's not enough to ask yourself, "What am I getting for what I'm giving?" The more pertinent question may be, "What am I giving up *now* for what I'll gain *later on?*"

Consider Ted and Margie, a couple in their late thirties with a high regard for one another but a listlessness to their marriage. Their sex life, especially, was tepid. Both acknowledged the need to confront this problem. Margie admitted that she was restless. She didn't want to be a caretaker all her life. She wanted to return to school to earn an advanced degree. Ted knew that if she did, it would be at considerable cost, not just in money but in comforts and attention. Nonetheless, they agreed to finance her return to school. Three years later, Margie radiated a sense of self-possession and vitality that made her an exciting person and a good companion.

Trade-offs can never be accomplished unless you're willing to give something up.

We all have different styles of giving and taking. There are those of us who give something first to get something back; those who give everything too early and too fast and have nothing to trade off down the line; those who give everything without thinking they deserve anything back; those who give a little and take a lot; and, finally, those who give nothing and take everything. When people walk away from a negotiation feeling that they haven't received enough of a trade-off in terms of what they've given, nothing is permanently settled. The trade-off won't work or endure. The most difficult aspect of making a trade-off is being able to let go of what you're trading off. Stylists raised in an economy-of-scarcity framework really choke up here, because they fear that what they're letting go of may never be replaced. With your trade-off ought to go a *resolve* not to look back. You're getting something you want. Instead of mourning the loss, celebrate the gain.

Making Your Cost-Benefit Analysis

Before a business makes a commitment, its executives examine all possible ramifications of the move. They project the costs, and compare them to potential benefits. What business does can and ought to be done in the personal realm.

But can costs and benefits be quantified when they're measured in terms of subjective values rather than dollars and cents? Yes, they can—not as precisely as dollars and cents, perhaps, but accurately enough to help you make your choice. Here's how to do that:

Step One: Make two columns. At the top of the left-hand column, write the word "Costs." At the top of the right-hand column, write the word "Benefits."

Step Two: Make a list of every cost, or loss, you can think of, no matter how small it is, if you make the trade-off in question. Then list every benefit, or gain, you can think of, again, no matter how small.

It may be that just this simple exercise will create such a vivid comparison you won't have to go any further to establish whether the trade-off is one you want to make. But if the comparison doesn't make your decision obvious, the next step should do the trick.

Step Three: To each item in both columns, add the number 1, 2, or 3.

1. Negotiable. Not too important. Could live without it.
2. Might be negotiable.
3. Not negotiable. Essential. Must have it.

When you've finished, add up the numbers in each column. The higher total gives you a strong indication which category— costs or benefits—outweighs the other.

I say "strong indication" for a reason. It may be that one or more of those threes, those nonnegotiable considerations, are so important to your life that the grand total doesn't matter.

But since there will be threes on both sides of the ledger, you're well advised to count them up and see which side has more. At this point, you ought to take a very hard look at those threes to see whether they can't be reduced to twos. If, at the end, you still have more threes on the one side than the other, you may have to decide in terms of the can't-do-withouts, on the ground that you can take only so much deprivation of vital needs.

A journalist I know was recruited by *The New York Times* to be the newspaper's chief Latin American correspondent. He was enormously tempted by the offer: the position was prestigious, and he and his wife loved Rio de Janeiro, where they once had lived, and where his new bureau would be located. However, he already had an excellent job, he and his wife had just bought an apartment in Manhattan, and their children were enjoying life in the United States after several disruptive years. The two opportunities seemed impossible to compare until he did a cost-benefit analysis, assessing not only the material aspects, but the emotional and psychological ramifications for his family as well as himself.

His calculation slightly favored the career with *The New York Times*. But there was one three on the "costs" side of his ledger that made all the benefits immaterial. He knew that foreign correspondents of the *Times* were away far more often than they were home. His present job kept him away from home as much as he could bear. So he stayed where he was.

In the end, this major career decision came down to a matter of feeling. The following diagram indicates how important feelings are in considering options.

OPTION	COSTS	BENEFITS	FEELING	ACTION
To stay, leave, or modify	Leave present position	Prestige	Disquiet at the possibility of not maintaining family unit	Stayed
	Leave newly purchased apartment	Adventure		
		Comfortable life in dramatic country		
	Disrupt children		Possible loneliness	
	Frequent separation from family		Possible guilt	

You can waste a lot of time asking others' opinions about

what you ought to do when you know the answer in your heart. Certainly, an informed opinion can be helpful, but much of the time when you seek such opinions what you're really doing is avoiding making your own choice. Making a cost-benefit analysis of your options, taking care to include your feelings, can take a lot of the pain and indecision out of the decision-making process.

Contingency Plans: How and When to Use Them

A contingency plan is not another option. It is a whole new strategy, with a beginning, middle, and end. It must be prepared in advance of your negotiation, whenever you have reason to believe that your initial plan won't succeed. You invoke your contingency plan when you've tried all your original options and they've proved unacceptable.

Suppose you've taken the initial program through discussion and dissection and encountered no enthusiasm for it. The first "no" you receive is a strong and clear signal that your first option isn't going to work. Don't abandon your objectives, but do try hard to come up with other options. Wait a few days, watching for positive cues, and then make another attempt, using the other options. If, at this point, you meet solid silence, outright aggression, or uncomprehending vacuity, don't persist. Change to your contingency plan.

There are people who don't switch to a contingency plan because they don't have one. But there are many others who, even though they have contingency plans, never use them because they're so convinced that their initial options should be persuasive and work. That makes as much sense as practicing a physical movement over and over again that you weren't doing right in the first place.

Whenever I make a plan with a client, I ask, "If this plan doesn't work, what else can you do?" The most frequent answer is, "Nothing." But when we explore a little, we find several possible contingency plans, any one of which, if successful, will satisfy.

In the worst of circumstances, contingency plans also function as your escape hatch. When a relationship becomes abusive or life threatening, that's the time to get out. Because you generally need a plan to do that well, it's wise to have one ready.

Be sure you have money in the bank, gas in the tank, and a place to stay for yourself and your children, if you have them. Let your relatives and friends know where you intend to be. Bone up on your rights before the fact.

The Bottom Line

You've reached that point when you say, "Enough!" You've given and given, made trade-offs and concessions until you've been picked clean. One more concession on your part would make the cost too great. At this point, that's just what you must make clear.

It's not easy to say "no." Agreeing to a request is a guarantee of continuity, whereas saying "no" invites rupture in the relationship.

There are inevitable consequences to saying "no," some of which may be uncomfortable. But the consequences of not saying "no" can be just as bad, and usually are. One young couple went on a vacation to Spain in a very hostile mood. She had wanted the trip; he hadn't. His response was silence—until they reached their destination at the end of the day, usually a romantic *parador.* Then he wanted sex. Halfway through the trip she invoked the bottom line.

"It's very hard for me to be receptive and responsive at night when you've been mean as hell all day," she told him. "I'm really not willing to do that."

"Have I been that bad?" her husband asked. At which point she told him what it was like to endure his silences.

Had the young woman remained silent herself, she would have accumulated a mountain of bitterness. By announcing her bottom line, she managed to put their relationship back into balance.

Many people tend to come to their bottom line too quickly, almost before they understand the problem. Worse yet, they'll announce their ultimatum, and then not execute. Their bottom line will keep stretching and stretching until it's lost its snap. Parents often threaten their children, then don't carry through. The children, as a consequence, often don't develop a sense of limits or responsibilities.

Once you've reached your bottom line, you must have the courage to act. But before you act, you must be certain that you've exhausted all your options, that your decision is rational rather than emotional—bottom lines are usually reached at a high emotional pitch—that you're not being precipitous. Any or all of these last-minute checks may prompt you to back away.

Age, money, health, needs, increased information, increased awareness, a change in position from middle to top management, from liberal to conservative, from single to partnered—any of these variables can relocate your bottom line. What you were willing to tolerate a year ago may be intolerable today. A competent and mature woman executive went to work in a division of a corporation whose Jungle Fighter supervisor immediately began to take credit for her outstanding work. Because she was new to the firm, she remained silent. A year later, she asked him for a raise and received such an insulting response that she went to the company president and announced her resignation. Somehow the president had become aware of the circumstances under which she'd been working, and had also recognized her talent. "What will make you happy?" he asked. "What will it take to make you stay?" She requested a raise twice as large as the one she'd originally had in mind—and got it.

Anger may be your dominant emotion as you reach your bottom line, but it may be underlined with relief. When you've thought, studied, learned, developed realistic options, optimized the other's benefits, and still gotten nowhere, you have really come to a moment of intense self-awareness. There is no person more formidable than one who knows what he or she wants—and what he or she will pay to get it.

Stylists at the Line

The likelihood that a person will invoke his or her bottom line, and then use it, varies widely, depending on his or her style.

JUNGLE FIGHTERS: Quick to threaten, but rarely carry out their worst threats because they need you to push around. When they do act, however, they are unmerciful.

DICTATORS: They usually control the situation so completely that their bottom line is seldom reached. Once there, action is swift and final.

SILHOUETTES: Little or no advance warning; they'll simply disappear into their cloister.

BIG DADDIES AND BIG MAMMAS: No savagery involved, just subtle, gentle threats that they won't love you anymore.

SOOTHERS: Their bottom line keeps stretching and stretching, if they have one at all. They'll do anything to avoid confrontation: their biggest fear is rejection.

WIN-WIN NEGOTIATORS: They'll go to their bottom line only in an emergency, and even then with great reluctance. They'll execute without ambivalence, but only after preparing a way back to the negotiating table if they feel there's the slightest reason to do so. Win-Win Negotiators seldom find themselves without enough options and alternative strategies to continue a negotiation. Rather than reach the bottom line, they'll try a lateral move.

R.O.I. (Return on Investment)

The wise investor plays for the long term. He doesn't become disheartened if the value of his investment diminishes initially, so long as his long-range objectives remain intact. He will take less now for more later.

The same standards apply to any investment you make in a career, an education, or another person. It's the final payoff that matters.

When you make your initial investment—be it time, effort, or love—it's in the anticipation that your eventual return will be at least equal to or greater than the amount you're putting in. But that doesn't mean that there won't be costs and risks along the line, and that you won't be the one making a larger investment. If you're the person who wants to turn a nonnegotiator into a negotiator, then you're the one who has to do the work. If you're the person who wants the change, you have to explore the option, make the plan, and put it into effect.

The most impressive and valuable tools in existence aren't worth a nickel if they're not in operation. If you have paused, reflected, evaluated, designed options and trade-offs, you must risk and act if you want your life to change.

Tactics

Tactics are a series of steps in pursuit of an objective. No single tactic is expected to carry the day. Rather, each tactic is designed to make a specific contribution toward the ultimate goal.

Opening Ceremonies

You're about to negotiate with someone—spouse, lover, parent, child, boss, assistant—about something—time, attention, money, a new roof, a hike in the rent—somewhere—in your living room or kitchen or bedroom, your office or boardroom, a bank, an attorney's or doctor's office, on a golf course or tennis court. Every one of these variables could call for a different approach.

Preparation for the opening ceremonies begins long before they take place. You prepare physically by eating and drinking with moderation the night before, and getting a good night's sleep—this against the background of a consistent fitness program. You prepare intellectually by analyzing your position and your strategies, with particular reference to the style of the person with whom you'll be negotiating. If the person is someone with whom you've dealt before, you draw from your repertoire of observations. If he or she is a stranger, you try to gather impressions from other sources, and you make assumptions based on the person's record that you'll check against reality the moment you meet. If past dealings with this person have left you with unresolved problems, you may be carrying around an emotional hangover. You've got to attend to whatever you're feeling before the negotiation begins.

The most successful negotiators I've known will go so far as to cancel a negotiation if they haven't had time to do their emotional housekeeping. If that's not possible, they'll listen during the negotiation, but steadfastly refuse to make decisions.

Among the stylists, Dictators, Silhouettes, and Win-Win Negotiators are less vulnerable to emotions than the others. Jungle Fighters and Soothers are extremely vulnerable. Big Daddies and Mammas are vulnerable, too, but they're also adept at converting their emotionalism into a tactic to use against you.

Opening ceremonies may be formal or informal, depending on the degree of familiarity of the participants. When you're dealing with intimates, the opening ceremonies can be fairly perfunctory, but I, personally, am saddened by the laid-back casualness with which many families carry on negotiations today. In part, this offhand style is a healthy reaction to the formality of bygone days, but it is often carried to a point where we treat business associates and friends with greater warmth than those we supposedly love. Cavalier treatment is resented, no matter who receives it. If you're planning an important negotiation with members of your family or other intimates, you should prepare your opening ceremonies with at least as much care as you would the opening ceremonies of a business meeting.

There are time-honored rituals between hosts and guests. The host:

- Sets the time and place of the meeting
- Creates the environment of trust—or competition or intimidation, as some prefer
- Prepares a greeting that establishes the climate of discussions
- Determines when the agenda will begin
- Does not attack the guest

The guest:

- Gives the host time to play his role—but not too much time
- Modifies the emotional climate if it's going against his best interests
- Participates in establishing the agenda
- Makes certain that his priorities are represented on the agenda if he sees that the host is blocking them
- Does not attack the host

Both host and guest are responsible for seeing that the ground rules reflect each of their interests, that the issues have been stated with clarity, and that the time to deal with the issues has been fairly apportioned.

These protocols are observed as though they are accompaniments to a theme. That theme is *awareness* of what you're seeing and hearing and feeling because from the moment you meet the person with whom you're to negotiate, your world has been transformed by his or her presence, and his or hers by yours.

Small Talk, and How to Speak It

Certain negotiators, most notably Dictators and Silhouettes, have low tolerance, or sometimes none at all, for "small talk," the language of opening ceremonies. They may ask a perfunctory question—"How are the kids?"—but your answer scarcely registers. The next question, or statement, pertains to the agenda. But for most of us, small talk is the social lubricant that gets us working smoothly with one another. It's not simply a form of mutual courtesy by which we help one another relax. It's a means to gain important knowledge.

By listening to small talk, we begin to learn about the other person's communication style—whether it's fast, slow, articulate, inarticulate, interesting, boring, focused, or unfocused. Some people can talk only about their children or money or tennis or World War II. Others can give a generous glimpse of their lives in the span of fifteen minutes. The difference between them is the difference between one dimension and many; you can be reasonably certain that the first person will see problems from a fixed viewpoint, whereas the second will be more willing to entertain options.

Small talk can help you relax, provided you know how to speak it. It can produce the opposite effect if you don't. Then, every new encounter seems as uncomfortable as those first moments at a cocktail party completely filled with strangers when you rush for a drink and retreat to a corner or inspect the books and paintings.

One of the most frequent questions I get from members of my men's seminar on negotiating is, "How do I communicate at a party? I don't know how to begin a conversation." The one surefire way is to ask an open-ended question—the kind that requires more than a one-word response. Closed-ended questions are those that can be answered with a word, usually "yes" or "no."

YOU: Enjoying the party?
STRANGER: Yes.

And you're back to square one.

But when you ask an open-ended question, you're bound to get a response.

YOU: What brings you to the party?
STRANGER: Fred's my oldest friend.

What the stranger's just given you is an entrée to his life story—and Fred's, to boot.

The basic idea is the same in any small-talk situation: get the other person talking. But you should expect to do some talking, too. You want the other person to know something about you, so that he or she will also be at ease. Self-disclosure in those opening moments of small talk helps to create rapport.

If, on the other hand, the other person has talked for twenty minutes and shown no interest in you, you're onto a good clue. There are stylists who give endless accounts of their own accomplishments, feelings, and needs. Dictators want adulation. Jungle Fighters and Big Daddies and Mammas want an audience. Soothers want couch time. You're not going to achieve with these people what small talk is meant to do—create a bond between you.

When you're using small talk, be alert to the other person's mood and circumstances. You wouldn't use small talk with someone who's about to leave for the airport, or when you're ushered in for a ten-minute appointment with the president of your company.

The Warm-Up

It's exactly what the name implies, a preparation for the introduction of an idea or the start of a negotiation.

Suppose you've been in a relationship for several months, and have decided that a long-term commitment isn't what you want. Yet you care about the other person and would like to prepare him or her without a cut-and-run approach. "I'd like to spend more time alone," you say. "I don't feel our relationship is moving us closer together. I've been thinking about living alone. Think about it and give me your thoughts." You haven't said you're going to move out, you've simply indicated which direction your thinking is taking, and asked for some feedback.

The Probe

The probe is analogous to dipping your toe in the lake before you dive in. You've learned what to expect, but haven't committed.

Probes are efforts to reach a deeper level of information and insight. They can tell you how much work you still need to do, whether your position is viable, whether the issue is negotiable. Probes can be used at any time in a negotiation except at the close. Once your probes have helped you select an option and the negotiation has focused on that option, further probes are not only no longer needed, they can be distracting.

Probes must be used with care. Most people protect not only their physical space but their psychological privacy. Probes that are too deep or made too abruptly can rupture a dialogue.

Jungle Fighters are savage probers. They rarely respect others' privacy, and feel a proprietary right with a subordinate or child. Big Mammas and Daddies are at the other extreme, so smooth and slick with their probes that they've learned about your negotiating strategy and its emotional components before you realize what they're doing. Soothers often get into trouble by making irrelevant probes after they've gotten what they were after. Silhouettes don't do much probing themselves; when you're the one making the probe, proceed with caution; too strong a probe might send them into hiding.

Here are some sample introductory remarks you can use when you're making a probe:

"What are your feelings . . ."

"Have you given any thought . . ."

"I've been wrestling with a problem, and was wondering if you could give me some input."

"How do you think this idea would work . . ."

The Full Thrust

The full thrust is the quick, direct, often blunt, presentation of your need, request, or feeling. It's a dangerous but sometimes necessary and even fruitful technique—provided you use it with skill.

The key is to be as informative as possible in the least amount of time. "Frank, I have just fifteen minutes to resolve a problem. I need a decision because . . ." And then tell Frank as briefly as possible why the matter is so urgent.

The full thrust is a particularly effective business approach with the Dictator, who cares about decision making and solutions. But it's too forceful a tactic for most personal situations. If you have to use it, try to mitigate its impact.

It's the nature of the relationship that tells you whether to use a warm-up or a full thrust. Only you can gauge the other person's tolerance. If you're dealing with a Jungle Fighter, don't worry about his sensibilities; he'll surely parry your thrust. You can also use full thrusts with confidence when dealing with Silhouettes. Small talk makes them nervous; they'd just as soon be rid of the interruption your inquiry represents. Sample: "I've decided I want a full-time career. It will change our household in many ways. I'm going to need your help. I feel this will work for the good of us all, and here's what I propose . . ." No hedging, but no hostility or sarcasm, either. Be specific, clear, and committed.

What if you're on the receiving end of a full thrust and you're not prepared to deal with it? If you have the self-esteem to do so, throw back your head and laugh. "I'm not up to that right now."

Other tactics:

Postpone: "Let's take that up tomorrow."

Be "out front": "I don't agree. Here's why . . ."

Defuse: "We may not agree, but I know you have the family's interest at heart."

Establish priorities: "It sounds like you have a lot to say. Let's take the most important issue first."

Mid-Course Correction

You've been pursuing a discussion of an option and its ramifications. Suddenly, you begin to note changes in the other negotiator's speech and manner. These changes tell you that the option you've been discussing isn't being well received. You make a mid-course correction by shifting to an alternative option.

Mid-course corrections are often initiated when you become aware that you've miscued. You thought you'd identified the other person's negotiating style and planned your tactics accordingly. Now that the negotiation's under way, you discover that he's hidden his real style behind a facade. You realize that the option under discussion will never work. Switch to another option.

Time Out

Calling time is a potent tactic. You can use it to monitor your conduct, control your anger, order your thoughts, or secure additional data. But use it sparingly, because repeated use can make you seem vulnerable, particularly if you're dealing with a manipulative negotiator.

With intimates be up front. Say, "I'm not able to talk right now. Let's break for thirty minutes." Use the time to think through another approach to the problem, and to regain control of your emotions. If you need more than half an hour, tell the others: "What you've said puts a new perspective on things. I need to think about it overnight."

If the problem is more substance than emotion, a time-out is essential. Request it at once: "We've discussed this issue for two hours and haven't gotten anywhere. Let's come back tomorrow and make another try."

A time-out can also be called in the midst of a positive negotiation when you know you're making progress, but aren't quite at the point where you want to make your bargain. "I think we've done very well. Let's meet again tomorrow and see if we can't nail this down."

In a troubled personal interrelationship, the implied goal of calling time can be a reconciliation, which is worth all the time it needs. The length can be anything—overnight, a week, three months. "I need to be away from you for a while," you explain. "I need time to think about us." If energy is intense and emotions are at high pitch and no reconciliation is in sight, give reason a chance to fight its way back through the psychological barricades. According to Dr. John Stratton, when people go into crisis emotions run very high and reason very low. It's like a seesaw. The conflict cannot be resolved until balance is restored.

Breaking a Deadlock

A deadlock exists when communication has ceased. But *why* has it ceased? Do you really have nothing further to say to one another? Or are you both using the deadlock as a tactic to wear one another down? The only way you're going to know whether the deadlock is genuine is to know the history and style of the other person and, of course, your own.

Before you announce your bottom line, ask yourself these questions:

Have I been clear enough? decisive enough? persuasive enough? warm enough?

Have I used all my research? my materials? my arguments?

Are there options I haven't used—changing the setting? calling for time?

Are there outside resources I haven't used—friends? colleagues? co-workers? persons with special qualifications?

Have I considered the consequences with all the care they deserve?

It's when others cry "Deadlock!" that the best negotiators shine. They consistently ask themselves, "What else can I do?" They try to break the rhythm that's gotten them to the deadlock by buying time and doing something different—gardening, exercising, making love, building a shelf, watching a funny movie. A change of pace helps the most creative negotiators to come up with that one extra alternative within their negotiable options.

Whammies

Most of us enjoy a surprise—party, present, visit, treat. Some people enjoy giving surprises for their shock value. They are indeed surprises, but they also put you off guard and divert your attention. You are not left with a sense of joy and celebration. You know you've been had and you don't like it. You like it even less when you're put at a tactical disadvantage.

You arrange a meeting to discuss a personal issue, but the other party brings an attorney.

You thought the meeting was for further discussion, but the other party insists on making a deal.

The agenda was for adding to inventory, but the president announces a budget cut.

Your spouse deals with an impasse at home by announcing a sudden trip—alone.

These are examples of "whammies." Whammies can be devastating. They are almost never used by Win-Win Negotiators or other shrewd people except possibly when they are deadlocked hopelessly with a Dictator or Jungle Fighter or anyone else who has negotiated so aggressively that he or she has failed totally to listen to the other side.

The recipients of whammies rarely forget them—particularly if they've lost face in public. I see such examples of public humiliation all the time. One spouse to another, in the midst of friends at a party: "Don't you think you've had enough to drink?" In offices where I'm called to consult, an employer will tell a subordinate, in my presence, "Can't you use your head?"

That's equivalent to parents who criticize their children in public—"Can't you do anything right?" The cruelest whammies of all, perhaps, are those directed at elderly parents by their grown children. "That's the fifth time you've told me the same story. Why do you always repeat yourself?"

If you've noticed lately that others have been withdrawing from you, maybe you're the one giving the whammies. Even if others say "no" when you ask if you've offended them, watch their nonverbal signals to see if they're congruent with that answer. If the other person won't look you in the eye when he speaks, or kicks his foot or rubs his neck, he's probably not telling the truth.

Whether you're giving or getting whammies, pay attention to the circumstances in which they're delivered. Take steps to diminish them if you're a sender, and to learn how to cope with them if you're a recipient. If you've been hit with a whammy, address the issue. If you let it slide, you'll be hit again.

Closing Ceremonies

You've finally reached a point where you believe you've made a deal. In a business negotiation, you want a memorandum of understanding or a signed agreement. In a personal relationship a formal agreement would be an indication of mistrust, but nonetheless you want just as clear and firm an understanding of what it is you've agreed to.

Close with style and grace—but close. Many a deal, in business and love, has been lost because the negotiator tried a new probe or continued talking long after he had achieved his objective.

Closing ceremonies should be as gracious and attentive as opening ceremonies. They're designed to put the other person at ease, to make him glad he came, to make him want to come again.

Bridging

No matter how acerbic or uncomfortable a negotiation has been, there is every likelihood you'll have to negotiate with the same people again. Only when you've bought a house or an automobile does the person with whom you've made the deal pass from your life—and sometimes not even then. The maintenance or restoration of good relationships—cooling down from the heat of argument to the warmth of friendship and love—is the objective of "bridging."

Bridging develops a sense of continuity. It builds a way back. Without bridging, you almost have to start over again the next time, forfeiting all the understandings that have developed between you, dealing, in effect, with a stranger instead of a friend.

Bridging is not difficult, but you do have to work at it. It won't just happen. You may be able to build your bridge simply by inviting the other person for a drink to celebrate your agreement. A difficult family meeting on the household budget can be followed by a jog around the block. Even a promise of a future meeting can do the job: "I'll see you in town next week . . . I'll call you as soon as the papers arrive."

If it's the other person who's attempting to bridge, you want to be alert to your responses, lest you destroy his effort. A don't-call-me-I'll-call-you attitude will blow the bridge. Silence in the face of his invitation to meet next week will do the same. A put-off rarely fools anyone. If you really want to bridge, don't say, "Yeah, sure," when the other person says, "Let's have lunch." Say, "When?"

Be particularly specific when you're dealing with children. "I'll see you in a couple of weeks" seems forever to a child. Tell the child: "I'll be here two weeks from today at two o'clock. If I'm going to be late, I'll call you."

A responsibility goes with bridging; it's your job to follow it up.

The Follow Through

Make a phone call. Write a note. Send flowers and a card. Do something to express your pleasure or satisfaction to the person with whom you've dealt. "Just wanted you to know how much I enjoyed dealing with you." "Thanks for a lovely evening." "Looking forward to our next meeting." "Really excited about getting together." Any of these will do. What *won't* do is forgetting to follow through.

Matching Tactics to the Stylists

Bearing in mind that every individual responds in his own way to different situations, here's a summary of the tactics to use in dealing with each of the stylists:

JUNGLE FIGHTERS: They can be as gracious as any Win-Win Negotiator at the outset, but they will move quickly to take over the agenda—at which point they will pour on the derogation, particularly if you're in a less powerful position.

Tactics: Watch out for the *magic,* the *muscle,* and the *misinformation.* Otherwise your opening ceremonies may be your closing ceremonies as well. Make certain that you both came to discuss the same agenda. Remember that the Jungle Fighter has the ability either to bully or to charm you away from the issue at hand. Stay with the agenda, and make certain that it doesn't become absorbed by less important issues. If derogation and abuse persist, reset the agenda.

DICTATORS: They can be charming hosts when on their own turf. That's what they prefer. They say, "Let them come to me." They'll be cordial at the outset if you're important to them and time permits, but even that period will be perfunctory. Dictators are usually all business. They'll make it known that the burden of proof rests with you.

Tactics: Recognize that Dictators' opening ceremonies are short, particularly if they don't consider you important. Be well groomed; if you're a guest, be on time. If it's business, be early. If you're making a presentation, restrain your razzle-dazzle. Dictators don't want to be challenged; open at their pace. Know your data; be prepared to answer penetrating questions. And be careful; Dictators tend to hear only what they already know.

SILHOUETTES: Their brusque manner and pained expression will broadcast their feeling that your presence is an intrusion.

Tactics: Ignore their silent language, because it always says "Do not disturb." Keep your opening ceremonies brief and cordial. Address the agenda. Be crisp and to the point throughout. Ask specifically for any decision you need. Wait for it. If you don't get it, ask for it again; and again, wait for the answer. Close when you've said what you came to say. Then leave.

BIG DADDIES AND MAMMAS: They will make you feel, at first, that you are the agenda. In reality, they'll be busily determining how they can juggle the agenda so that their concerns are paramount and your success depends on them. As you reel with delight from their love, care, and concern, the negotiation is suddenly over.

Tactics: Work on yourself, not on them. Be aware of your susceptibility to flattery and your need for approval. Be alert to their efforts to ease you away from your purpose. Don't be afraid to move away from their "concern" about you and back to the issue at hand. Watch your time carefully; they'll try to preempt it in order to keep you from working through your agenda.

SOOTHERS: They'll offer you coffee, ask repeatedly if you're comfortable, and inquire about your interests—anything to avoid confronting the real purpose of the meeting.

Tactics: You take charge, because they never will. Know when it's time to shift to the agenda. Be specific. Tell them how much time you need to state your case. Ask them how much time they require. Be certain that they use it. Call for answers and decisions.

WIN-WIN NEGOTIATORS: They use opening ceremonies to build trust, as well as to monitor signals of concern, nervousness, or agreement. They listen attentively to the language and pattern and rhythm of your speech, in particular for those little signs of anxiety. The clues they pick up help them to orchestrate the timing and thrust of the meeting. Once they know something about you and have established a constructive environment for negotiation, they'll focus quickly on the agenda, announce their own, and ask for input.

Tactics: These are task-oriented negotiators. Stay with them. Follow their timing. Be prepared, because they'll expect you to talk.

12

Four Steps to a Win-Win

If confronting a new problem gives you a helpless feeling, welcome to the club. Nothing is more normal. So many of my students, in fact, complained about this paralysis that I designed a simple four-step system to take the fear out of the problem-solving process. Many students tell me that it's the most valuable tool they learn.

Here's the four-step process:

1. Define the problem.
2. Decide what you want.
3. Design a strategy.
4. Do it.

Let's take them one at a time.

Step One: Defining the Problem

Successful business people never let a problem fester if they can possibly help it. They acknowledge the existence of the problem the moment it appears, and ask the following questions:

What is the source of the problem?
Who and what are involved?
Is the problem external or internal?

132

What aspects of the problem are controllable?
What aspects are soluble?
What aspects require outside help?

The overriding concern of management is to resolve the problem before it gains size and force and a life of its own. That is exactly the objective people should have in their personal lives, and yet often they choose to ignore a problem in the hope that, if they don't acknowledge it, it will go away. Before they know it, the problem has preempted most of their time and energy, and destroyed their relationships.

You don't need experts to certify that you're unhappy or restless or dissatisfied. You know when you've got a problem. You may even know what seems to be provoking you—a dull job, a poor relationship, a troublesome child, heavy debts, lack of recognition or appreciation, or all of these and still others.

But defining your problem in terms of its impact on you alone won't reveal all of its dimensions.

Remember the kaleidoscope you used to play with as a child, that rotating tube with bits of glass and beads held loosely at one end? One slight turn of the tube and the entire picture changed. That's the way it is with problems. Shift just the smallest bit and you get a different view.

When you look at a problem, you tend to see it from your perspective, which is natural but not comprehensive. Until you've managed to see the problem from the other person's perspective as well, you haven't really defined it. Watch how different a problem becomes each time it's modified:

You don't love your spouse any longer.

You don't love your spouse any longer, but your spouse continues to love you.

You don't love your spouse any longer, nor does your spouse love you.

Examining the other person's side is not something most people readily do. Yet until you understand the problem as he or she sees it, you can't deal effectively with the problem itself.

At some point, you *have* to address the issue with the other person. When you do that, try to disengage from your view of the problem, from your own sense of rightness. As you hear the replies, try to visualize the other person's concerns, to feel what the other person is feeling, to recognize his or her fears. Use what you know about the other person's history to put the problem into perspective.

Suppose you have a standing date every Wednesday evening for dinner with a friend. In the last month, however, your friend has been consistently, and flagrantly, late. You're angry and hurt.

Questions:

Does your friend have a history of tardiness?

Has his or her behavior changed in any other respect?

Has his or her life changed in a manner that could explain the behavior?

What you construe as an intent to hurt may be a problem with schedules, late meetings at work, or traffic. Set dinner an hour later, and see if the behavior continues. If it does, you know that the problem is not a matter of logistics, but has something to do with the emotional part of your relationship.

Whenever you define a problem, it's imperative that you deal with its stripped-down reality, rather than with your analysis of the problem's causes or consequences.

PROBLEM	INFERENCE
Lover gets home late.	Lover no longer loves me.
Child hits me.	Child hates me.
Mother doesn't call for weeks.	Mother doesn't care about me.
Boss says, "Get on the ball."	Boss intends to fire me.

Some of those fantasies may come true, particularly if you continue to believe them. You won't be at your best in negotiating the problem if you're burdened with worry. The best approach to negotiation is to address the issue, not the inference.

"I hate having you get home late."

"It hurts me when you hit me."

"I've missed hearing from you."

"I'd like you to tell me what you meant when you said, 'Get on the ball.' "

Acknowledge the problem, above all. Pay attention to your feelings. Pay particular attention to the style of the person with whom you're negotiating—and to your own style, as well.

Jungle Fighters, Dictators, and Big Daddies and Mammas have no trouble, as a rule, in acknowledging that a problem exists. But they rarely, if ever, see the problem from the other person's point of view. Silhouettes, too, readily recognize problems, but just as readily walk away from them. "You take care of it," they say. If you recognize Silhouette tendencies in yourself, beware. When you defer to another person, you may not like his or her solution to the problem.

If you have Soother tendencies, you're most likely not only turning your back on the problem, you're trying to deny its existence. But unconsciously, you know that it's there. In the meanwhile, it may be eating a hole in your stomach lining.

There are very few Win-Win Negotiators with holes in their stomach lining. They deal with problems as each problem appears. They attempt to come to a resolution by getting an immediate idea of how the other person perceives the problem. That's the best ulcer preventive I know.

Step Two: Decide What You Want

"I don't *know* what I want. That's my problem."

I hear that statement at least once and often twice or three times a day.

When people tell me that they don't know what they want, my first advice to them is to determine what they *don't* want. That's often a good deal easier; the "don'ts" usually gush forth:

"I don't want to be unhappy."

"I don't want to take verbal abuse from my child."

"I don't want to feel battered."

"I don't want to be poor."

"I don't want to be stuck at home any longer."

If it's so easy to acknowledge what you don't want, why is it so difficult to discover what you *do* want?

Fear is part of the answer. Many people are afraid of the consequences of their desires. Once they knew what they wanted, they would presumably want to go after it. That means they'd suddenly be at risk. Far safer to pretend they don't know.

Whatever the cause, the fact is that most people don't have the *habit* of looking for what they want. They tend to want what they think they can get, just as many children do. Their deeper desires go unfulfilled.

Many of my clients seem almost completely unaware of the resources life has given them. One of my first tasks is to help them draw on these resources by remembering and projecting. They need to recall experiences that gave them satisfaction in the past, and to test them as possibilities for the future. They need to call up an old friend for a lunch date, to join a volunteer group, to skate or jog or swim again, to teach something, to learn something.

The remedy for fear is knowledge. You need to become specific about what the consequences of a different course of action might be at a time when the risk is lowest. One question gets right to the heart of the issue: *"What's the worst thing that could happen to me?"* Even forgetting that the worst is only one of several possible outcomes, you often discover that it isn't as bad as the present reality.

What a joyous task unearthing your deep desires can be! You are completely free of risk, able to sift through all the myriad fantasies that, if brought to reality, could enhance your life. Long before you ever come to your three basic options— to stay, to leave, or to modify—you are expanding your knowledge of what it would take to make you happier than you are. You are sifting through your past to determine what worked for you before, evaluating the lives of your friends to determine what has worked for them. Don't wait until you're miserable to begin to explore your options; do so when you're on vacation, or taking a long weekend, or relaxing for an hour or so when the children are off at school.

Clarity about your wants, needs, thoughts, and purposes comes from making choices. You do this by first exploring, then narrowing, and finally choosing options.

EXPLORING: In the exploratory stage, you expand your relationships, activities, and thoughts to test for your wants and desires, via three basic techniques:

1. Finding your "deep wish." Here is a simple, tested method we use in therapy to center people's thoughts in such a manner that they are able to visualize their optimum wants.

- Close your eyes. Put yourself into a state of relaxation, using deep breathing or meditation.

Breathing: Focus your mind on the very act of breathing. Feel the air going into your nostrils. Be aware of the second's pause as you complete the inhalation. Then feel the air being expelled from your nostrils. Then be aware of the second's pause before the cycle repeats.

Meditation: Breathing deeply, repeat a single word at the end of each cycle. Try "flow" or "open" or any word that soothes you. Focus on the word. Empty your mind of thoughts.

- Visualize a setting, a stage on which you are the leading performer. It may be your home, your office, a club, a playing field.
- Identify the people. Watch the action. What's on the stage with you? What's missing? Who's with you? What are they doing? Who's missing? What are you doing? What are you feeling?

2. Interstices: Have you ever stood and admired the delicate tracery of a spider web and thought how beautiful the filaments were? Did you also consider that without the spaces between the strands there would be no perceptible design?

Life, too, is a web of connections and open spaces. Many aspects of our life are clearly organized patterns of roles and expectations. But no matter how organized life is, there are corners, crevices, and spaces—interstices—that exist within the webbing. They are unutilized, unoccupied aspects of our lives. It's in them that we can find many options.

Think of interstices as moments you capture and put to creative use. You speak with someone you've never spoken to before and learn something you've never known. You do a small job that others haven't time to do, and you gain your boss's eye.

Think of interstices as empty physical spaces that, imaginatively utilized, transform the environment—even if just a little. That dead space at the end of the corridor becomes an attractive rest area with the addition of two seldom-used chairs, a small table, and a plant. A bunch of pillows turns a sofa you've all been ignoring into the family meeting place. The empty walls of your office become a gallery for employee art.

Think of interstices as opportunities unrealized until someone does something about them.

3. Brainstorming: Business uses this technique all the time. It's a process of letting your thoughts fly. No idea is too ridiculous. None is judged at this point. Brainstorming is done best by groups of people—friends, family, colleagues. Each person thinks of you, the problem, and possible solutions to it. The purpose is to get many possibilities into the open. A young woman in one of my seminar groups was losing her son to her estranged husband. She thought she had no possibilities. Fellow students in her seminar thought up twenty alternatives with her. It was her task then to change these alternatives to options.

Brainstorming can be used anywhere, at any time—in a general meeting called to stimulate a flow of ideas, in negotiations, during a coffee break, or even in the privacy or your own mind. Wherever and whenever, heed the following rules:

1. Be spontaneous; say whatever comes to mind that's relevant and constructive.
2. Don't discuss, evaluate, or criticize any statements.
3. Repeat ideas if you wish.
4. Piggyback on others' ideas if you wish, adding to or slightly changing their suggestions.
5. Keep going, even when you have to wait out a prolonged silence.

NARROWING YOUR OPTIONS: Now that you've developed options using the above techniques, the time has come to review them. You begin to organize your behavior, considering such questions as when you'll negotiate and where. And you take a very close look at the forces that motivate your choice.

You want to make sure that the answer you've come up with is yours, and not someone else's idea of the person you ought to be. Here are some sample questions with which you can test your results:

"Do I want it because my partner wants it?"
"Do I want it because others expect it of me?"
"Do I want it because it's the fashion?"
"Do I want it because of the equal rights movement?"
"Do I want it because it's comfortable?"

Choose an option based on a realistic *self-assessment*. Motivation based on an unrealistic self-appraisal is highly destructive. Such assessment may be inspired by others to the point where it creates self-delusion. I see many people who got into serious trouble by trying to prove something to a parent. "My mother was a lawyer, my father was a lawyer, and so I became a lawyer," a young woman in one of my seminars told her group. She got a lot of approval and acceptance for following in her parents' footsteps, but she was also miserable—and not a very good lawyer.

Watch out for options based on "unconscious contracts." Such contracts involve both an overt and covert choice. The overt choice reflects what you truly want; the covert choice is motivated by desires of which you may not be consciously aware.

Suppose you have an affair with a Jungle Fighter. You tell yourself that the power you share vicariously as a consequence of her success is more than an adequate trade-off for the abuse she gives you. That's your overt choice. But what you may have signed on for—unbeknownst to you—is the manner in which she validates your worthlessness. Your covert choice, your "unconscious contract," may bring you much win-lose negotiation.

Relationships with Dictators may be motivated by an unconscious need to be dominated; relationships with a Big Daddy or Big Mamma may stem from a need to be protected; relationships with Soothers may come from a need to ignore reality just as they do.

Your choice of options should suit your style. Are you someone who needs support and guidance and consistent demonstrations of affection? Don't become involved with a Silhouette. Are you a creative person who needs quiet and lack of pressure? Don't choose involvement with Jungle Fighters or Dictators—unless you select a benevolent Dictator who will assume responsibility for the routine tasks of life.

And what of the styles of the other people in your life? Will your choice accord with their habits and ideas? You may decide you want an open marriage, but if your partner is monogamous by nature you've got trouble ahead. If your life partner wants to live on a houseboat in the Florida Keys but you need the stimulus of a city, neither one of you may be capable of making a major investment in the relationship.

Your "I want" not only must accord with the people in your life, it must accord with your institutional involvements. If you've decided to organize a protest against rising fuel prices, you'd probably be well-advised to quit your job with a major oil company. You may think you're more competent than your boss and that the company would be better off if you replaced him, but if you go over his head and try to impress the president of the company directly, you may wind up getting fired.

Perhaps the most important question to ask yourself is whether the answer to "What do I want?" corresponds to the relations of your life and its physical and psychological under-pinnings. If you are a single parent with two children and you're responsible for their financial welfare, a career as a free-lance writer or artist may not be feasible, however appealing the thought of such an independent life might be. If turmoil and shouting and deadline pressures drain your energies, a competitive advertising agency is not the place for you.

CHOOSING YOUR OPTIONS: It's time to select the option that you want to take to the negotiating table, to analyze your potential trade-offs, and to consider which of your values will surface and be served. It's time, in short, for your cost-benefit analysis. (See page 112.)

First, list all the costs and benefits you can think of. Then rate each of them. When you've finished, add up the totals. The higher total will give you an indication as to which category—costs or benefits—outweighs the other.

Consider Sarah, a young, highly intelligent junior executive, restless with her life, not really knowing why. Sarah, a Big Mamma, lives with David, a Silhouette. Their relationship is tentative; they've been together only a short while. David is wary of Sarah's restlessness; he suspects it might somehow impinge on his own solitary style. One day, at last, Sarah recognizes what it is that's been troubling her. She sees that life as she's living it has serious limitations.

But Sarah also knows that to take two steps forward, she must first take one step back; she will have to quit her job and return to school for the college degree she's always coveted. Sarah's scared: she doesn't know what it will be like to let go of a stable job; she doesn't know if David will help her financially, or even emotionally. But she's also persistent; she does her homework, investigating all her possible options—getting a part-time job, applying for a scholarship, assessing the costs and benefits of her contemplated decision. Here is how they finally stack up:

COSTS

I'll lose financial security	3
My relationship with David will change	2
I won't be doing something comfortable and familiar	1
I'll be giving up many social experiences	1
I'll be giving up leisure time with friends	1
TOTAL	8

BENEFITS

I'll grow intellectually	3
I'll develop skills for a new career	3
Eventually, I'll earn more money	3
I'll expand my professional options	3
I'll be independent	3
I'll expand my contacts	3
I'll fulfill my fantasy	3
TOTAL	21

For Sarah, the choice is now fairly clear. But not entirely clear, because it's not easy to quantify a feeling, and not comprehensive either. Rating costs and benefits with numbers is just a beginning way of objectifying personal/subjective issues. Once you have your totals you need to review them against your values and other feelings, asking yourself whether the results seem honest and real in terms of your objectives. This is what Sarah now does.

Sarah values her relationship with David and recognizes

that his need for privacy will fit in with her need for further education. She will need time to study and carry a part-time job, David will have time alone, and there will still be time for them to be together. Sarah's overall strategy is to elicit David's financial and emotional cooperation without threatening their relationship. She must now design a specific strategy. Here's how it's done.

Step Three: Design a Strategy

Strategy is a plan of action designed to achieve your objective. How people arrive at strategies differs tremendously.

There are instinctual strategists, those who simply know what to do without really studying the matter. There are studied strategists, who design their every move. There are antistrategists, whose "strategy" is to ignore everything. And, finally, there are the serendipitous strategists, who just happen to fall into the proper grooves.

Regardless of what approach is taken, no strategy succeeds unless it springs from self-esteem—that positive sense of self-worth that energizes us to act and to persist in goal-directed behavior. Self-esteem derives, in no small part, from the ability to control situations. All of the stylists—even Soothers—are capable of doing this; in the process, all but the Win-Win Negotiators may be destructive to peers, family, and lovers. Only the Win-Win Negotiator embeds a concern for others into his overall strategy.

Timing is the key to strategy. If you want something, you're far more likely to get it if you ask for it at the right time. That advice may sound almost simplistic, but you would be astounded by the numbers of negotiations that are lost because the timing is inappropriate.

- Don't negotiate for more time together when your lover has to fly to Alaska.
- Don't ask the kids to help you prepare packages for Aunt Maude on the night of the big game.
- Don't ask your boss for a raise when you just lost a client.
- Don't ask you girl friend for attention when she's studying for her bar exam.

- Don't set important negotiations when:

  You or others are tired.
  You or others have had a negative encounter.
  You or others have another important commitment on your minds.
  You or others don't have sufficient time.

Manipulative stylists will seek to deal with the other person when he or she is not at his best; Win-Winners seek a time when both they and those with whom they're to negotiate are hassle-free and task oriented.

Win-Winners also pay careful attention to the *setting* in which they negotiate. They try to choose an auspicious one. Manipulative stylists choose territory that places them in command and the other person in subservience. They insist that meetings take place in their office, where they can keep you waiting by taking phone calls and can rally their forces, if necessary. They'll usually sit behind their desk in a chair higher than yours, and have you facing the light. Win-Winners set meetings where they know everyone will be at ease. One, recently named the president of a major communications company, has furnished her office like a living room. It doesn't even contain a desk. She even goes so far as to hold conferences in the office library, so that none of her associates will feel at a disadvantage.

The early stages of a negotiation can be held in one or the other side's offices. But if a conflict develops, it's wise to move to neutral territory. The same for personal conflicts. Don't discuss them in your bedroom, or even in the house. Go to a restaurant or a park.

Step Four: Do It!

You've come a long way to get to this point. Your decision to act has been carefully considered. You've chosen your options, determined your bottom line, thought through your strategy. You've taken your own style and the other person's into consideration. The time has come to act.

TRUST YOURSELF: The precondition of action is self-trust. You can't take risks without it. Each time you take a risk, you increase your self-esteem. Increased self-esteem leads to multiple options, experiences, and risks.

You alone know if you're ready. Does your inner voice say, "Move ahead?" If it doesn't, don't proceed. Sleep on your decision. Reflect on it. Continue your preparations. Whatever you do, trust your feelings, and don't act when you know you're not ready.

JOIN THE RISKERS: My interviews with successful negotiators show "riskers" to be people with a strong reality focus. They prepare. They try. They know there is another day. They enjoy the game of life and they don't want to settle for second best—unless they have to.

It takes courage to do something different, to make a change. Your first attempts to negotiate may be awkward. But you can improve. Treat yourself with compassion. Remember the simple cues for risk reduction:

- Be clear in stating your problem.
- Know your contingency plan.
- Know your trade-offs and bottom line.
- Keep focused on the problem.
- Seek help from those you trust.

LEARN HOW TO DEAL WITH YOUR DISASTER FANTASIES: These fantasies occur when you're facing a problem so critical to your own survival that deep anxieties are aroused within you. If you go to work, your teenager will take drugs. If you ask for a raise, you'll be fired. If you ask your lover for more time alone together, your lover will reject you. Often these anxieties stem from past experiences. More often, they stem from fear of the unknown.

To deal with these fantasies:

- Objectify. Examine the reality of your options, trade-offs, bottom line, so that you have something concrete to pit against the scary scenarios produced by your imagination.
- Check out the reality of your fantasy against what you

know—what happened in the past when similar requests were made, how you or others resolved the problem before. Playing out the consequences in your head or in a discussion can diffuse much of your anxiety.

- Analyze your feelings. Is it terror you're feeling, or is it simply anxiety? Be specific about your fear. If you're truly frightened, afraid to walk out of the house, then no negotiation technique can help you. But if you can see that the degree of anxiety you're experiencing is appropriate to the risk, then you're not only reacting normally, you've gone on "alert" in anticipation of the task.

TAKE THE FIRST STEP: For most people, this is the toughest part of all. They know that there's a consequence for every act. But not all negotiations are terrifying. To the contrary, most of them can be as engrossing as a well-played game.

Now you're ready to make your move. Pick up that phone, knock on that door, ask that first question! Remember your tools and tactics; you've got them all. Opening ceremonies, small talk, just enough to warm the atmosphere, a little probe now, good, good, you're watching intently and listening carefully for what is and isn't being said. Above all, you're *staying focused* on the needs, problems, options, trade-offs, and bottom line you've brought to the negotiating table, and you won't be diverted from them. It's time now for that trade-off you've prepared, based on an acceptable option. Keep watching the other person! Check to see if your strategy is in gear with his behavior; if it isn't, get ready for your mid-course correction. Bring out your contingency plan. Don't let that first "no" from a Dictator or Jungle Fighter dismay you; they're just using some tactics of their own. Have they countered with a proposal? Remember the high cost disclosed by your cost-benefit analysis. If you need more time, tell them you want more. Keep watching more than ever now. Watch for the quiet nod of the head, or the look that passes between the members of the other side. A frown or a curled lip means resistance. How about a whammy? Or maybe that's too drastic. Maybe you should pull back a moment and give them time to calculate their own risks. An offer's made—close, but not quite right. What's that? They want *what?* Repeat your position. That's out of the question. Rephrase your request—pull out another trade-off. They're pushing me to my bottom line, you think. I'd like to avoid it. I'll try a mid-course correction. There, that's better. It was only a trial balloon.

You've got what you want now. Time to check if they're feeling okay, too. They seem satisfied. Good. Come to closure. No more talk about the issue. Be cordial. Build your bridge. Make small talk about getting together soon. And be sure to follow up.

13

Negotiating Cripplers—
And How to Deal with
Them

There are many negotiating cripplers: for example, lack of self-esteem, lack of preparation, and self-deception. But anxiety and anger are cripplers in a category all their own, if only because, involving principally your emotions, they can overpower you in a flash.

Some of the most successful negotiators I've interviewed, persons who have read all the literature and memorized the tools and tactics and had years of practice, confessed that when they lost it was because they hadn't confronted, diffused, or controlled a powerful emotion.

There are special tools for doing exactly that with the two emotions most damaging to a successful negotiation.

Anxiety

Anxiety accompanies most significant changes, regardless of the degree. When it's in full bloom, it can color, distort, and reshape to such an extent that good looks bad and bad looks good. You become immobilized, confused, disoriented, and disorganized, and tend to make inappropriate and negative conclusions. But a normal increment of anxiety is absolutely essential to good performance. Like other emotions, it produces energy, wakes up your brain, puts your body on alert, makes your muscles stronger, and increases your endurance. If you can regulate your body's response to anxiety, you can turn it to good use.

The first step in dealing with anxiety is to understand that it takes three forms, and to identify which form you're experiencing.

The first level is the heightened sense of awareness that alerts your body and senses. You not only have nothing to worry about in this state, you should be grateful for its presence.

The second level is anxiousness. Your loved one's an hour overdue. Has he or she been in an accident? Why no phone call? Or perhaps you've had to do two days' work in five hours, or you've just delivered a new ad campaign to the firm's biggest client, or you're meeting your new boss. If you're not anxious in these moments, you wouldn't be responding normally: in any case, the anxiousness dissipates once the issue is resolved.

The third level is the heightened anxiety that produces fear and the kind of immobilizing symptoms we've described.

The body's response is a clue to what's going on. If you have excessive perspiration, shallow breathing, and palpitations your body is giving you a signal that you may be entering an anxiety state. It's your job now to figure out why. Pay attention to the circumstances. When did it happen? With whom did it happen? What was at issue when it happened?

Riding Herd on Your Tremors

First, be conscious of your body. Listen to what it's telling you.

Second, be aware that what you're feeling isn't permanent. Unless you're a person with chronic anxiety, the feeling will go away.

I had a client who became exceedingly fearful before every examination she took. She would invariably overprepare. The day before an examination, her mind would go blank. She could not remember a single fact she had studied. Her anxiety would feed on itself, to the point where she could hardly order her legs to take her into the examination room. But once inside that room, and once the test had begun, she would be fine. She never flunked a test.

Then, a few days before her most recent test, the young woman's eyesight became so blurred she couldn't read. Instead of panicking and running to the eye doctor as she usually did, she recognized the symptom for what it was—an expression of her anxiety. By the time she took her examination, she had calmed considerably, because she knew that, in spite of her anxiety, she was well prepared, and sure enough, her sight cleared.

The third short-range measure is to be active. Walk. Jog. Run. Play tennis. I know a man who immediately begins to polish his car as soon as he feels unduly anxious. Those big muscle movements calm his body considerably.

A fourth remedy is to try to imagine what will happen as a consequence of the problem you're confronting. Often, just facing the possibilities will make them seem less ominous.

Fifth, fantasize. You can do this best if you've put yourself into a state of relaxation by breathing deeply through your nostrils, preferably with your eyes shut. Once you feel your body relaxing, try to imagine yourself lying in a field of tall grass, looking up at the sky, watching the clouds pass overhead. Then climb or jump or leap up onto one of the clouds, and float along, watching the earth below. At last you come to a familiar setting. There you are down below, surrounded by your problem. Perhaps you're in your office. Perhaps you're with your lover, confronting the issue that's been bothering you. Fantasize the best possible outcome and how you'd achieve it. Now, slowly come down from the cloud, examine the prospect, and determine how you might react if it became a reality. If you find the prospect agreeable, look for the new options that make it a reality.

The sixth anxiety-diminisher is word repetition. Use a familiar word or phrase. I encourage my students to write out a very short phrase that applies to their own circumstances. "I can do it"; "I've done it before"; "I'm well-prepared." As one of my clients put it, "It's my negotiation mantra."

During the negotiation itself, there are a number of anxiety reducers to employ:

- Press your thumb against your index finger. This allows your brain to concentrate on your muscle movement instead of on your fear.

- Put your papers in order.
- Move your body around until you feel that it's in a relaxed position.
- Use your hands and body and eyes in responding to the other participants.
- Breathe deeply, preferably through your nose.
- Expand and contract your big muscles, particularly in your arms and legs and back.
- Listen acutely to what others are saying.
- Ask for a break, and take a walk.

Win-Win Negotiators usually deal with their emotions before a negotiation. They analyze the potential severity of the encounter and make all necessary preparations. At a minimum, they would spend a quiet period before the negotiation doing relaxation exercises. If they felt extremely anxious—even Win-Winners get the tremors—they would take a brisk walk around the block or do something else physical. In the negotiation itself, they're at a tremendous advantage; because they don't feel the necessity of talking at every moment, they can use their silences to compose themselves and listen attentively to others' presentations. Jungle Fighters and Dictators rarely have such opportunities because their style requires them to take over all the spaces.

In the heat of negotiations, Win-Winners, like everyone else, move their bodies forward as they emphasize their points. But then, to calm down, they lean back so that they are physically disengaged.

The best of all remedies for anxiety is preparation. If you are aware of the negotiation process, if you know what you want and have a good idea what others want, if you have developed options and prepared and rehearsed your script, your fears will probably subside, and with them, your anxiety.

Anger

Anger is as inevitable as anxiety. Like anxiety, it can render you useless in a negotiation. Sometimes you may think you are anxious when you are indeed angry. And, just like anxiety, anger can be turned to good use.

Most people are able to control their anger at the office,

where it is considered inappropriate. That doesn't mean it doesn't appear; it means that most people tend to restrain themselves in an office setting. Home is another matter. That's where the anger not discharged at the office tends to vent itself. Men, in particular, seem to know that they need to keep cool at the office, above all, whereas anger is an emotion they're allowed to release at home. So they release the anger at home precisely because it's supposed to be inappropriate at the office. For women, anger is another matter altogether: They have been conditioned to express their anger in a disguised rather than a pure form, such as depression, physical ailments, anxiety and over-eating. It's long been accepted in our society that women will be emotional and temperamental; many women use tears and body aches as negotiating devices. In some professions, emotionality is seen as a form of creative expression, but it is a deadly way to negotiate in the long run; it simply doesn't work.

It's usually the emotional issues hidden underneath your anger that get in the way of dialogue—revenge, disappointment, expectation, jealousy. Whatever offer you bring to a negotiation, you also bring an attitude. The attitude, formed by your history, very often gets between you and your offer, thereby creating problems in your negotiation that otherwise wouldn't exist.

"Open Links"

The anger that spoils a negotiation is not usually the anger of the moment. It's something from the past that never got resolved. I have an expression for such unresolved conflicts. I call them "open links."

When a couple discusses a conflict, brings feelings openly into it, plays with various options, and comes to a resolution, the circle is then closed. In most relationships, however, problems are rarely resolved because they are insufficiently discussed. Each person sees the problem from his viewpoint only because options are not discussed and talk is limited, dishonest, or nonexistent. Each person fears the possible consequences of failure if he were to initiate a discussion, perhaps a breakdown or rupture in the relationship. And so life is experienced as a series of open links, circles that are never closed. When a new problem arises, it is perceived in the context of many previous unresolved conflicts out of the couple's own experience. The chances of resolution in this new instance are poor to nil.

There are several responses to such misery. The most common is to run away. The action may be more figurative than literal; rather than divorce, the couple may have affairs, overwork, or lose themselves in drugs. Television is another form of escape—living life through vicarious imagery. Whatever the expedient, it serves the same purpose; for a while, it obliterates the pain.

Old Business

People go into negotiations more often than not with their emotions not tidied up. Now there are certain emotions they may not be able to tidy up by themselves; to do so may require the help of competent professionals. But eighty percent of such emotional freight is the residue of previous battles, wounds suffered in a previous negotiation that can be confronted and put in perspective if they're simply addressed.

Suppose you're about to deal with someone with whom you've had a previous encounter. Perhaps you felt in your last encounter that you were ignored or rejected or persecuted or even betrayed. If you don't take care of these feelings prior to your new attempts, they will exacerbate, expand, explode, because anger that isn't dealt with when it occurs will fester just like an illness. Pretty soon, all you're dealing with in your new negotiation is the illness and not the issues.

This "old business" needs to be dealt with before you enter into a new negotiation. You'd say to that person, "I'd like to take care of some old business." Over lunch or a drink, you'd do that. Conceivably, the old emotions could become so aroused once more that you might not be able to get to the new business. Well and good; if there's that much unresolved anger there, you ought to know about it out front, before you're surprised and before the old emotion sabotages your new efforts.

There's a further complication. Frequently, old business may have nothing to do with the person with whom you're now dealing. Often people let the feelings they experienced in one arena cripple them in another arena where the feelings don't—

CLOSED LINKS

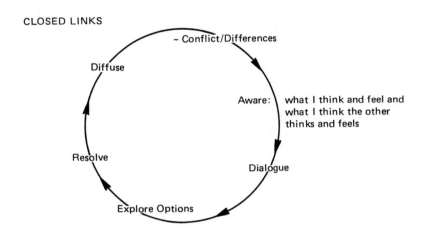

- Conflict/Differences

Diffuse

Aware: what I think and feel and
what I think the other
thinks and feels

Resolve

Dialogue

Explore Options

OPEN LINKS

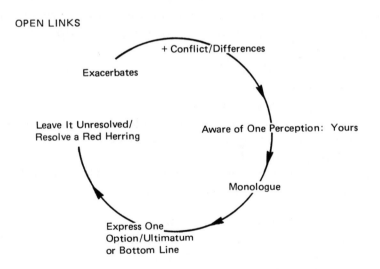

+ Conflict/Differences

Exacerbates

Leave It Unresolved/
Resolve a Red Herring

Aware of One Perception: Yours

Monologue

Express One
Option/Ultimatum
or Bottom Line

or shouldn't—apply. There's no isolation of the experience. An argument at breakfast with your mate turns into a diatribe a few hours later against your secretary. The only connection between the issues is the carrier of the anger.

Positive Ways to Vent Anger

I have never experienced a negotiation in which sending an amount of anger equivalent to what you're receiving has done anything positive for that negotiation. The louder the other person becomes, the quieter I usually become—particularly if the other person is a Jungle Fighter.

But anger needs to be vented. Even the Win-Win Negotiator expresses his anger. It's healthy to do that. It's essential. But you have to pick your spots. Venting your anger in the midst of a negotiation, even if it's controlled, isn't always the best strategy. It's certainly not wise to make a critical decision when you're angered or enraged.

Anger should be expressed appropriately, and to the right person, and briefly. Be sure to explain yourself. Describe the cause of your anger as directly as you can, and then drop it, write it off. It may take you a few minutes to calm down. As much as you want to lay it on, try to resist the temptation.

CLOSE THE TIME GAP. Don't wait three months, three weeks, or even three hours to deal with the issue. Step away just long enough to gain control, to identify the cause, to make sure that what you think you're angry about is the real issue, that the source isn't some hidden issue. Determine what you want and *then* go out and discuss it.

Take care of business when the business arises. The longer you wait, the more complicated it becomes.

STICK TO TODAY'S ISSUE. Don't start reminding your friend that he didn't come to the hospital ten years ago when you had your appendix out. Tell him you're upset because you couldn't be together today.

CALL TIME OUT. When football and basketball teams get into trouble, they call time out. The same technique works for relationships. If you're having an argument and not getting anywhere, say to your partner, "Let's take ten minutes. You go to the kitchen. I'll go to the study. We'll both think about it. Because all we're doing now is screaming, and we're not getting anywhere."

During that ten-minute interlude, you can deep breathe, you can meditate, you can ask yourself whether you've really told the other person what it is that you're angry about, or what it is that you want, or whether you've really learned what he or she wants. You can come back with three different ways to solve the problem. If you haven't come up with new solutions, you can say, "This is really much more complicated than I thought. What I'd like to do is discuss only one part of it now, and then come back later after we've both had a chance to think about it."

There are moments in a negotiation when anger can be very useful. You have to pick your spot. Jungle Fighters are incapable of doing this; they spray their anger indiscriminately. But a Win-Win Negotiator uses his anger as a barometer; it tells him the storm has arrived and he's got to take cover. So he says, "I want to call a halt to what's going on here." Just like that. He hasn't called anyone a name. He's simply alerted the others to the fact that the meeting has gotten out of hand. Then he brings the argument back to the issues.

If an argument of any kind goes more than three minutes with battering and personal abuse and no good discussion, you've got to call a halt because you're not going to get anywhere. Say: "I want the abuse to stop. Tell me what the issue is. Tell me what the problem is. Tell me what you want. I'm willing to talk to you, but I'm not willing to take the abuse."

"Who's abusing you?" the other person may say, at which point you can respond, "I'm feeling abused, even though you may not be meaning it and may not even think it's happening."

Using Your "Anger Diary"

In Chapter 9, we focused on the importance of paying attention to others' and your own responses, mannerisms, and behavior patterns. But there are certain elements of behavior that can't be fully understood and utilized to your advantage simply by attending with your senses. You have to pay attention to your own patterns in a more thorough manner, by recording your behavior. Only when you become consciously aware of your unconscious behavior patterns does change become possible.

Unconscious behavior is repetitive. If you're not aware of the way you're living your life or how you're behaving, you're going to keep repeating that behavior.

Learning what makes you angry is a marvelous place to begin a systematic appraisal of your overall behavior. It's for this purpose that I've developed the Anger Diary.

When you're angry but don't know why you're angry, with whom you're angry, about what you're angry, or even what the feelings are that have taken command of your mind and body, you've been rendered effectively powerless. There is no way that you can negotiate to restore the balance or redress the grievance or get rid of the issue at hand. Something—and you can't identify it—keeps stoking your fire.

But if you register the components of your anger each time it occurs, you will see definite patterns emerge. Perhaps you become inflamed primarily at work. Perhaps one person, in particular, gets to you with the same techniques over and over again. Surely, your body is giving signals every time you're angered.

In the Anger Diary, every episode of anger is inventoried in six different categories:

First, the date and the time.
Second, a description of the negotiation situation.
Third, how your body reacted.
Fourth, your emotional feelings.
Fifth, your response, including the tools and tactics you employed.
Sixth, the outcome. Did both of you win? Did only one win? Did both lose?

On page 158 is the Anger Diary of one of my clients, a professional woman in her early forties. Take a look at it.

Now, what does the anger diary show? The last entries record her analysis of her patterns. The foremost indication is a central tendency to be a Soother, with the exception of certain instances at her office in which a streak of Jungle Fighter emerges. From the body cues recorded, this woman can see that she is courting serious body disabilities—an ulcer, high blood pressure, colitis, etc. Her unverbalized feelings of worthlessness express themselves in a lack of self-esteem. Her expectations that she will be treated without respect only increase her disappointment. Her actions are indirect and self-destructive; she reacts to her co-workers' slights in an aggressive manner. Instead of tools, she uses weapons against herself, such as drinking and silence. The natural consequence of this behavior pattern is a consistent "lose."

By keeping a similar inventory of your angry moments and doing a similar analysis, you can bring your repetitive unconscious patterns to a conscious level.

Suppose you become angry with yourself because you apologized to another person when the unpleasantness was really his or her fault. If you were to enter the components of the experience in your Anger Diary, you would probably soon discover, to your amazement, that you apologize to others far more than you ever dreamed you did, and usually for the same reason.

Suppose you become angry with another person for refusing to give you time and attention and consideration. By entering your reactions and the circumstances each time it happened, you might soon discover that you were dealing with an "empty bucket," someone who has nothing to give you.

Keeping your Anger Diary will quickly enable you to identify the people who make you angry and the circumstances that accompany your bouts of anger. The patterns will simply leap out at you. *Then* you'll have the information you need to change the patterns and eliminate the anger.

Why not try it? You have nothing to lose and everything to gain. A chart for your use is on pages 160–161.

Diffusing Your Anger

When I talk about emotional housekeeping, I'm not suggesting that you become a robot and walk into a room without feeling. Men, in particular, have done that for too long, to a point where they have even learned to monitor the muscles on their faces. What I am suggesting is that you do something

ANGER DIARY

Date and Time	Negotiation Situation (Indicate Before, During, After)	Body Cues	Feeling Cues	Response (Indicate Tools and Tactics Used)	Outcome Win/Win Win/Lose Lose/Win Lose/Lose
11/11 4:30 P.M.	Father issued ultimatum: "You *will* be here for the holidays"	Light-headed, mouth dry, sweaty palms, stammering	Resentment, regression, "childish"	Sulked, verbally agreed, said, "I'm catching a cold. Hope it's okay by then"	L/W
11/11 5:30 P.M.	Intimate complained in public about my drinking	Hands shaking, stomach tight, dizzy, perspiring	Humiliated, embarrassed, worthless	Had another drink and pretended I didn't hear	L/W
11/12 10:00 A.M.	Secretary ignored request to redo last-minute report	Head aching and heart racing	Disappointment and rage	Verbal tirade	L/L
11/12 3:00 P.M.	Overheard coworkers discussing me as a "whining bitch"	Tight stomach, pounding headache	Misunderstood, unappreciated	Didn't speak to coworkers for balance of the week, set late meeting	L/L

11/12 4:30 P.M.	Passed over for promotion	Tight band in head, trembling, tight stomach	Unappreciated, ignored, worthless, despairing	Remained silent, seething inside	L/W
11/15 9:30 A.M.	Friend demanded more of my time	Inside suffocation	Rage, guilt	Gave him additional time and was late for the next meeting	L/W
11/16 6:30 P.M.	Lost negotiation with my son over household chores. Did it myself	Heart beating, stomach tense, mind went blank	Humiliated, impotent, disappointed	Complained to spouse and had three drinks for dinner	L/W
	Pattern: Soother pattern with friends and family, Jungle Fighter with secretary	Pattern: Headache, "eating a hole in the stomach"	Pattern: Humiliation and lack of self-worth	Pattern: Indirect aggression	Pattern: L/W

© 1977 by Tessa Albert-Warschaw, Ph.D.
Note: No reprint without permission of the author.

ANGER DIARY

Date and Time	Negotiation Situation (Indicate Before, During, After)	Body Cues	Feeling Cues	Response (Indicate Tools and Tactics Used)	Outcome Win/Win Win/Lose Lose/Win Lose/Lose

Pattern:					
Pattern:					
Pattern:					
Pattern:					
Pattern:					

© 1977 by Tessa Albert-Warschaw, Ph.D.
Note: No reprint without permission of the author.

about those feelings before you enter a new arena, so that you can make the necessary transition. A period when you're raging is no time to attempt to reach a solution. At that point, you're not thinking. You're just dealing with emotion. Take a break. Have a cup of coffee. Read a newspaper. Tell a joke. Take deep breaths. Sing yourself a song. Take a walk.

Don't let anger debilitate you. Take care of it as soon as you are aware of its presence, source or effect. "If you address your anger at once," according to Dr. Connell Cowan, "it's clearly related to the issue at hand. If it is allowed to fester the temptation is to bring in old business and diffuse the importance of the present issue." Express your anger in some nondestructive way.

- Go off alone somewhere and scream.
- Punch a pillow.
- Tell the other person exactly what you're feeling. "I feel _____ when you _____ because_____."
- Make a date with yourself to analyze your anger, and create strategies for dealing with it.

Whatever you do, confront your anger. Reduce the time gap between the initial hurt and the expression of that hurt. Intercede before the emotion boils over.

Finally, remember that in negotiating for any kind of change, you've had a long time to think about it. Those who will be affected by your decision need to think about it too. You can reduce the prospects of anxiety and anger all around by understanding that change is going to take time.

14

Sending Your Message

All negotiation involves communication. Finding out what you want by examining and choosing your options won't help you much if you can't advertise your knowledge. No tools or tactics, no powers of observation, no awareness of your own and others' wants is going to be of help, in the final sense, if you are unable to send your message.

Many people can't—not assertively, at least. One of the more common reasons for negotiation breakdowns is the failure of people to communicate their desires. As severe as the problem may be in the workaday world, it is infinitely more serious at home. Hundreds of couples with whom I've worked are capable of sending positive messages on the outside, both singly and together, and yet, when they return home in the evening, are incapable of talking to one another. "To the world, we're the golden twosome—vivacious, interesting, articulate, well informed. But the moment we get home, the TV turns on and the talking turns off," one dispirited wife laments.

Silence is not the only problem. Effective communication requires dialogue. But for many stylists, monologue, not dialogue, is the norm. Jungle Fighters and Dictators constantly render others speechless through verbal and physical domination. Silhouettes issue cryptic bulletins, when they talk at all, and then scurry out of earshot. Big Daddies and Big Mammas and Soothers smother your assertions in goodness and kindness; it's hard to ask for a raise when you're surrounded by so much love. "Who talks?" the husband of a Big Mamma asked rhetorically in my office one day. "She talks for me." He might have been speaking for myriad people who let such problem stylists silence them.

Static

Why is it that so many of us have so much trouble sending our message in a manner that will be absorbed and understood? The reasons have to do with a multiple of fears:

- We're afraid we don't have the skills.
- We're afraid of saying something that won't be approved.
- We're afraid of not living up to expectations.
- We're afraid of hurting the other person.
- We're afraid that we'll be refused—or, conversely, that we won't be, in which case we're accountable in ways we weren't before.
- We're afraid we're not worthy.

The ability to send your message—which gives you a great deal of power—begins with self-esteem. You have it when you believe in yourself and in your capacity to accomplish what you want. You lose it, or never develop it, when you fail to recognize that you have something—talent, knowledge, love, whatever— the other person wants.

That failure may not be entirely attributable to you. Most aggressive stylists attempt to diminish your self-esteem or destroy it altogether. They intimidate, distract, and demean, attacking aspects of you they know to be especially vulnerable. They make you wait. They show you in unspoken ways— twirling a pen, lifting an eyebrow—that your words are un- important. If none of the above is sufficient, they may take overt action.

One evening, eight business associates and friends, myself among them, met for dinner to discuss a project of mutual benefit. After the dishes had been cleared and we were sipping coffee, a woman with strong Soother tendencies began to make a presentation. To her right sat a Jungle Fighter whose negative energy I'd been feeling ever since the dinner began. Now, as the Soother spoke, the Jungle Fighter began to flick her bright red nails and bite on her ruby lips. As the others in our group responded more and more warmly to the Soother's presentation, the Jungle Fighter slowly moved a water glass closer and closer to the edge of the table. Suddenly with a movement so fast that I wouldn't have seen it if I hadn't been watching, the Jungle Fighter gave one final flick of her fingernails and sent the water glass tumbling into the Soother's lap. Immediately, the Soother burst into tears and her presentation ended; she had no resources to deal with this humiliation.

Putting Out Your Sound

The tremendous interest in assertiveness training attests to a twofold desire, first, to learn how to deal with the attacks of authority figures—Dictators and Jungle Fighters and Silhouettes and even Big Daddies and Mammas—and, second, to learn how to send one's message.

Assertiveness training gives you the tools to ask for what you want, to say, "I feel, I need." It diminishes your fears about the consequences of your request. You learn that asking for a raise may create some tension between you and your boss for a few days, but that it won't, in all likelihood, get you fired. You learn how to get what you've earned.

Dr. Adele Scheele, who has taught hundreds of people how to make themselves more visible, points out that achievers live totally different lives from the people she calls "sustainers"— those who maintain their jobs but don't move ahead. The difference between them, she notes, is largely their sense of purpose. Whereas the sustainers perform their jobs and then wait like good students for recognition, promotion, or permission, achievers not only perform their jobs but also "put their sounds out." Doing their jobs is only fifty percent of their effort. The other fifty percent—usually hidden from others' eyes—is the exercise of skills in self-presentation, positioning, and connecting. Dr. Scheele gives the example of achievers making a report. They don't just put pieces of paper on the president's desk. They highlight the report for the president, and tell him why, specifically, it's a breakthrough, different from all previous work they've done. Or suppose they've prepared a special dinner. They'll describe the recipe just enough to tantalize their guests—informing them, without saying so directly, that a special effort has been made.

This isn't boastfulness. It's the expression of enlightened

self-interest. Winning negotiators have no trouble broadcasting their own strengths in a manner acceptable to others. Losing negotiators find themselves incapable of doing that—if not because of a deficiency of self-esteem, then because they are paralyzed by society's taboo on self-promotion, which is usually interpreted as self-centeredness.

The fact is that self-confidence and self-centeredness aren't the same thing at all. Self-centeredness usually excludes others' welfare from consideration. Self-confidence is an outgrowth of self-acceptance, without which no one can function. Promoting yourself in as positive way as you can, taking care of yourself without hurting others, are expressions of enlightened self-interest.

And who, more logically than you, should be artfully calling attention to your attributes? You know them better than anyone else, and you're the one most interested in your own success. How will others know what you have to offer unless you advertise? Advertising needn't be boastful. It can be a reflection of your quiet belief in your own strength and talent, backed by proven success.

Now, how can you determine whether you're putting out a confident sound?

LISTEN TO YOURSELF. If you're someone who has a problem communicating, you may discover that yours is the sound of silence. If you're a nontalker, you'll know it the moment you begin to pay attention to what you're saying—or not saying.

Most people, however, talk to someone, somewhere, about something. You need only to make an inventory to find out what circumstances make you talk. With whom do you talk? Where do you talk? What do you talk about? Do you talk your head off at the office and then say nothing at home? One week of personal observation will tell you, and you'll have gained vital knowledge.

RECOGNIZE YOUR STYLE. Your style of sending may open or close communication. Positive senders are flexible, responsive, active, participating, as well as silent at the proper times, all of which lead to openness. Negative senders are indirect, defensive, indulgent, threatening, psychoanalytic, any or all of which closes off dialogue.

ADDRESS THE ISSUE. If you've taken inventory and discovered that your dialogues are closed, or abortive or empty, it's time to "confront the obvious," as Dr. Don Dossey puts it. Instead of pretending that something is happening, express the truth: "We never talk." *Then talk about the fact that you never talk.*

The Icebreaker

There are numbers of ways to start talking. "Small talk," which we discussed in Chapter 11, is a technique widely used by successful negotiators in business to warm up the proceedings and establish a friendly climate. The technique is perfectly adaptable to personal relationships. The key, as we saw, is to ask open-ended rather than closed-ended questions.

There *are* times for closed-ended questions: Is the bathroom this way? Do we have enough wine for the party? They ask for, and get, information swiftly and efficiently. But if it's a dialogue you're after, make your questions open-ended.

Other methods for breaking the ice:

- Monologues: Select a subject that concerns a joint goal. First, one person speaks without interruption for five minutes. Then the other person speaks.
- Taping: Agree that you will let a tape recorder run during meals or other times together. Put the tape away for a week. Then play it, and discuss it.
- Pretending: Practice a negotiation trade-off in behalf of someone else. Talking to others about the way you negotiate may be uncomfortable when you're out of practice. But if you set up a situation in which you pretend you're someone else, you're not as vulnerable. You're able to "play the fool," as Dr. Eleanor Haspel-Portner counsels. If what you propose to say seems awkward or unfamiliar, you can say it anyway. You can be candid, frank, and honest.

Don't respond immediately—think about what the other person has said and dialogue later.

The best way I know to break the ice is to play a game I call—naturally—the Icebreaker.

For the game, each participant will need a writing pad and a pen or pencil.

Step One: Write down two things that you like about the other person. Be specific, e.g., "I like the way you appreciate the sunset." Not "I like you." Then exchange papers and discuss your answers.

Step Two: Write down one thing that you don't like about the other person. Once again, exchange papers and discuss.

Step Three: Describe the last positive experience the two of you had together. Exchange papers and discuss.

Step Four: Describe the last negative experience the two of you had together. Exchange papers and discuss.

Step Five: Describe one thing about the other person that you would like him or her to change. Be specific. Exchange papers and discuss.

The Icebreaker is meant to get you talking. But don't discontinue the game just because you've started. Mere talk isn't necessarily negotiation; to get a true dialogue going, all questions should be answered. If there's any reason why they might not be because of lack of time, limit your responses to a specific period.

If you give yourselves enough time and both of you answer the questions in good faith, you can reach levels of understanding you never knew existed. In the process you may well be giving your partner the very thing he or she most wants.

The Missing Ingredient: Recognition

One of America's major corporations did a survey among its employees to find out what single aspect of their work made them the most unhappy. The result was overwhelming—not lack of money or fringe benefits or time off or better working conditions but lack of *recognition.*

Recognition is a critical ingredient in any human interaction. If you ignore or demean another person, he or she will get back at you somewhere down the line, regardless of whether your neglect or slight was deliberate or accidental.

Often you can recognize people simply by showing your appreciation. Spending time together, sending flowers, cooking a dinner, buying his or her favorite record, taking a picture, paying a compliment—such expressions of regard tell the other person that he or she is important to you. Even a smile and a simple greeting can do wonders for a relationship.

But it's got to be genuine. You know it when you get a phony greeting. So does the other person.

A few words can often do the trick:

"I care about you."
"I like your work."
"I appreciate your help."
"Thanks for the call."

Your nonverbal response can make that connection, too:

Attentiveness when the other person is speaking
Walking together
Touching an arm or a shoulder
Hugging
Smiling

Very often, the persons to whom we show the least recognition are those with whom we work and live—not because we don't love them but because we take them for granted. If you expect to be heard by your loved ones, it's imperative that you spend time with them, that you support them at critical moments, that you be as excited about their triumphs as you are about your own.

Getting Attention

Before you can send your message in the confidence that it will be received, you not only have to create a receptive audience, you have to get its attention. How you do that depends on the style of the people listening.

There are, admittedly, some moments when communicating with the other stylists can tax the patience of the most positive Win-Win Negotiator. In those moments, it seems that if you want to send a message to a Jungle Fighter, you should send Tarzan; to a Dictator, a telegram; to Big Daddies or Mammas, flowers; to Silhouettes, three little words; to a Soother, Kleenex.

If you work with Jungle Fighters or Dictators, the only way you'll get your message to them is if it somehow gratifies their ego or facilitates their objectives. Shouting, screaming, crying, getting sick, getting drunk, overcharging at department stores—none of these attention getters of yore will do you a bit of good. Dictators, in particular, don't respond to emotion. The only thing that attracts their attention is something that's pertinent to their goals, presented in a well-prepared manner, with obvious profit potential for them. As to Jungle Fighters, a crisis or an intrigue that compliments their strategy will catch their eye, but only because they might turn one or the other to their advantage.

There is one splendid, if paradoxical, method with which to communicate with the intimidating stylists—Jungle Fighters, Dictators, and Silhouettes—and that is to use silence (along with some concentrated eye contact).

"Dad," the young man said to his Dictator father, "I've got something important to discuss with you."

"I'm reading, son," the Dictator said. "This is the time I read."

"That's okay. I'll just stay here until you finish. But don't worry. I'll be quiet." The son got his audience with his father.

Verbal aggressors like the Dictator and Jungle Fighter are usually surprised by a quiet, calm approach. Their own noise level diminishes. Flustered, they'll ask that sudden question or give you that little opening that enables you to slip your agenda in: "I know you've only got a few minutes. My contract's up for renewal. Here's a summary of my work during the last eleven months. I particularly want to point out my work on the Bramley job."

Silhouettes are accustomed to fending off or fleeing from noise. Silence will surprise them. Use that unguarded moment to introduce your agenda, preceded by a brief but gracious opening if you know the Silhouette well.

Ego gratification is the key to gaining the attention of Big Daddies and Mammas. Give them credit for the amount of help they've given you and you'll have an attentive audience for your request.

Your Message Sending Checklist

BE SURE YOU'RE TALKING TO THE RIGHT PERSON. The right person, for these purposes, is someone who has the power to give you what you want. It's useless to deal with "empty buckets," people whose lives are so out of synchronization with your own that you're incapable of satisfying one another. They may not recognize it, but you should. There's no point in asking for a loan from a lover you've rejected, or in continuing to seek attention from an ex-lover who's left you for someone else. In business, if you're dealing with an intermediary, your request may trigger a set of alarms connected to that person's own circuit breaker. He or she may not want to champion or even forward your request for reasons of his or her own. Jungle Fighters and Dictators tend to perceive others' ideas or competence or ambition as a threat to their own position. Silhouettes may not want to be bothered. Big Daddies and Mammas may not like your independence or may decide that they're not getting enough credit. Soothers will find a dozen things to worry about, all of them connected to their fear of making waves. Only Win-Win Negotiators have the self-confidence and mutuality of interest to consider your request exclusively on its merits.

USE "I" STATEMENTS. Say, "I'd like you to think about . . ." Or, "I want . . ." Don't start with what the other person might want, because the other person might shut you out before your own request has been made.

USE CLARITY AND SPECIFICITY. Express what you want without disguise. Don't ask for one thing when you want another.

BE STRAIGHTFORWARD. Negotiation is often thought of as a crafty, Machiavellian business. Not in my counseling. Too much energy is lost in being devious, too much confusion created, too many bad feelings aroused, too much credibility sacrificed—not to mention your own potential loss of self-esteem. There is literally nothing you could gain by being devious that wouldn't cost you as much or more.

AVOID APOLOGY. Don't be ashamed that you're making a request. Don't start off by saying, "I'm sorry to bother you," or, "I know that this has been a bad week for you, but . . ." The other person will only agree with you and wonder why you're intruding.

DON'T WEAKEN YOUR REQUEST WITH MEANINGLESS PHRASES: "I was kind of counting on . . . " "I sort of thought

. . . " or "I kind of wanted . . . " are phrases that go along for the ride. They waste everybody's time.

EXPRESS A BELIEVABLE "NO." If your spouse's or live-in partner's proposal strikes you as out of the question, say so: "That's nonnegotiable."

If only part of what he or she is asking for is nonnegotiable, say so: "I wouldn't be willing to negotiate X, but I would consider Y."

If the problem's a matter of time, say so: "I can't even consider it now. Let's talk about it next week."

If the other person won't take no for an answer, ask yourself whether your body language was in harmony with your verbal message. A big smile and an up-and-down motion of the head can vitiate even the most emphatic "no." If that's not the problem, and you're still being pressed, try the "broken record" technique: keep repeating your refusal. Finally, hold your ground, and don't let the other person make you feel guilty.

But if you're the one who's pressing, it's another matter altogether.

GO FOR IT! When you want something, there's no such thing as waiting for the other person to meet you halfway. You go one hundred percent of the way if you have to. Don't expect the other person to call. If it's something you want, make the call yourself.

But be sure you've prepared your script.

Scripting

A script is a tool. Its purpose is to reduce anxiety. It allows you to think through a problem with the other person in mind. It fosters specificity: you see at a glance if you are talking too much or too defensively. It enables you to diffuse inappropriate emotions that could spill onto the negotiating table and stop the dialogue. It provides a means to stay focused on the problem. It causes you to do your homework.

Every negotiation is a performance. Performances are almost always based on scripts. Your performance as a negotiator will profit greatly if you'll write yourself a script. It needn't be elaborate; a page, two paragraphs, even a line will sometimes do.

Every script has three ingredients—a description of the setting, a description of the characters, and dialogue. If you were writing a film script, you'd begin first by visualizing the setting. That's a good place to start in preparing your negotiating script.

SETTING: Imagine what the room looks like in which your negotiation will take place. Ask yourself whether this room is the best possible setting for the negotiation, or whether you'd do better elsewhere—at lunch in a restaurant, perhaps. Once you've settled on a locale, pick a place to sit where you'll feel most at ease.

CHARACTERS: Analyze the style or styles of the people you're meeting with and how they relate to your own. What sort of treatment would you normally expect from a Dictator or Big Daddy or whomever else you're meeting? How do their styles mix with your pronounced Soother tendencies—or whatever tendencies you have?

Are the people you're meeting well known to you, or are they strangers? If they're well known, you have a history to add to the mix. With strangers, you can only make assumptions based on what little contact you've had over the phone or in correspondence, or what you've heard of them. During the negotiation, you'll need to test your assumptions against the reality.

If you're a man and you'll be dealing with a woman, be careful about making assumptions as to her weakness or lack of competence. You may find she's both strong and competent. In preparing your script, assume that she is. Conversely, if you're a woman and you'll be dealing with a man, don't assume that he's your enemy. He could very well be an ally.

DIALOGUE: To keep yourself focused on your agenda, write out several lines, in this order:

1. Your request
2. The rationale in support of your request
3. The action you desire

Build the scene with lines that alternate between you and

the other person. Ask yourself what response will most likely come from the other person, given his or her style. Then prepare your response. Again, just a line or two.

Almost everyone who has tried it reports that scripting reduces the anxiety in a negotiation. And why shouldn't it? Scripting focuses you on your agenda. It tells you what you're to say. All you're lacking now is adeptness at delivery.

Practice in Safe Places

Learning how to send your message doesn't immediately equip you to do it. You've got to get in some practice, and that practice ought to be unpressured. In effect, that means a dry run.

If you want to transform yourself from a C to a B tennis player, you have to carve out a period of time for yourself in which you try to remake your game. You take lessons from a competent teacher, and then you practice what your teacher's taught you in a setting absolutely devoid of pressure. Laurence E. Morehouse, an expert on human performance, recommends you abstain from competition until your old habit has been replaced by a new and better one. If you return to competition too soon, the chances are that the pressure will cause you to revert to your old habit simply because it feels more reliable. You may win the point, but you'll break the new habit in the process.

The theory applies no less to negotiation. If you've been a Soother all your life and you want to become a Win-Win Negotiator, you've got to practice in a safe place. That can be in front of a mirror, or with a loved one or good friend.

One test you can easily make is to determine whether you are persuaded by your own argument. The way to find out is to tape your rehearsal, and then play it back. Would you give a raise to the person speaking? Would you marry him or her? Even though it's your own voice coming back at you, even though the arguments are yours, try to imagine that you're listening to someone else.

Don't feel ashamed or inadequate if you fail to persuade yourself. If you're not used to talking, you don't have the skills. As the physiologists say, "Use makes the organ." Just practice using your voice with a positive flow and the competence will come.

The Magic Ingredient: Trust

Trust is the oil of the negotiating process. Without it, nothing moves smoothly. You question credibility, withhold feelings, thoughts, opinions, and information, concentrate on your position to the exclusion of the other person's. Above all, you don't take risks. Without risks you are stuck in a standoff or deadlock or losing position.

Trust doesn't develop overnight. It is a product of history, of relationships in which people have given satisfaction to one another. The standards of satisfaction differ; what might be a satisfying marriage for one couple might not work for another.

Trust also implies an absence of surprises—emotional outbursts, double messages, whammies, bullying.

There are occasions when you're going to negotiate without trust, either because you have no history with the other person, or a poor history. That doesn't mean you can't negotiate. You simply do it differently. Rather than relying on your past intimacy, stick tenaciously to the issues. Avoid at all cost who-did-what-to-whom arguments about the past.

You don't have to love or even like another person in order to be able to accomplish a task together. Nor do you have to trust in all areas people you otherwise care for. Example: A husband and wife have a tendency to overspend. Rather than arguing about which one of them is to blame, they agree to meet once a week to review the past week's expenses, and to contribute a fixed sum toward the payment of their outstanding debts. They stay focused on the problem, and explore together their options for outside help, such as hiring a money manager or consolidating their debts through a bank loan that is repaid via mandatory monthly deductions from their checking account. If that's not enough to solve the problem, they can cut up their credit cards and pay cash for everything.

Building Trust with the Stylists

Whether in business or personal life, you create an environment of trust principally *by trusting yourself.* There are variables, however, depending on the styles of the people involved.

JUNGLE FIGHTERS: Creating an environment of trust with them is probably more difficult than with any other stylists because they're always baiting you, trying to make you lose your cool so that you'll tell them more than you really should. In business life, never, under any circumstances, trust them with personal information. Be specific, even cryptic, in your responses. If you have a confrontation with a Jungle Fighter business colleague, write a memorandum to yourself of everything that's been said. If you're personally involved with a Jungle Fighter, the problem's somewhat different. It's almost impossible to avoid revealing your thoughts and feelings. Inevitably, the Jungle Fighter will learn about you, whether you express yourself or not. To the extent that you can, monitor your self-disclosures, and always try to deal with him or her when he or she is in a calm, relaxed state. When you have something to discuss, take your Jungle Fighter partner somewhere quiet where there aren't a lot of people and he or she can't be diverted. Always remember that the Jungle Fighter has no respect for privacy and will use your secrets to hurt you.

If you're a Jungle Fighter yourself and you want to create an environment of trust, watch those verbal thrusts that demean and wound others.

DICTATORS: Whether you're living with them or working for them, the same dynamic is operating: they're frightened of losing control. For this reason, they must know—or think they know—everything. To create an environment of trust, try not to challenge their knowledge. Build on their ideas. If you're married to a Dictator, any project you want to advance, such as remodeling your home, should be presented in a manner that points up how it will serve his or her interests. Even then, the Dictator will trust your judgment only if your argument is well prepared, clear, and concise. Never promise more than you can deliver, and emphasize your seriousness. The best way—and perhaps the only way—to get the Dictator to ease up on the reins is to persuade him or her that letting others share in decisions would make life less burdensome.

If you're a Dictator yourself and want to create an environment of trust, try to listen to the other person's point of view.

SILHOUETTES: You can trust them with your most personal secrets because they don't talk. That doesn't mean that you'll receive confidences in return. A Silhouette spouse is not going to give you long dissertations about his or her feelings; if you want to build a relationship of trust, keep your encounters short. One Big Mamma client of mine was having no success in gaining access to her Silhouette boyfriend's feelings until she realized that the prospect of an hour of intimate discussion terrified him. The moment she reduced their encounters to fifteen minutes, he opened up—not much, but enough.

Encourage self-disclosures by monitoring your own behavior. Keep your meetings short and your statements precise and clear. Emotions should not intrude; any issue with the hint of an emotional charge should be withheld from the agenda. Don't expect, or seek, compliments or recognition. If you want to build a personal relationship with a Silhouette colleague, do it after working hours, because the Silhouette is mostly problem oriented and will stick to the problem in a business setting.

If you're a Silhouette yourself and you want to create an environment of trust, try to express a feeling.

BIG DADDIES AND MAMMAS: Tone down your own trust of the trusting environment created and controlled by these parent figures, or you'll find yourself trusting them for your every decision. You want to encourage their help but not their continued takeover. To perpetuate a relationship, show your appreciation but hang on to your identity. Remember that Big Daddies and Mammas need to be needed. They need to hear that they've guided and helped you and still maintain an important influence over your life. The environment of trust will be enhanced when you begin to share their thoughts, ideas, and problems and come up with creative solutions for them.

If you're a Big Daddy or Mamma interested in creating trust, try to restrain your stroking and touching, and encourage others' independent actions.

SOOTHERS: They bring so much anxiety to the encounter, so much desire to avoid conflict, so much need for approval that they're bound to be vague or seemingly indifferent about the issues you're supposed to discuss. To build trust, be conscious of their anxiety, and encourage them to express their opinions. But it's your responsibility to set the agenda and even to take it over, if necessary, being very clear and even repetitive. You've got to be careful that you're not being ambiguous; this can happen easily when you deal with a Soother, because his or her concerns are so unfocused. Tell the Soother what you expect. Always set a deadline; unless you say "Tuesday" the Soother will put it off until Friday.

If you're a Soother yourself and want to encourage trust, try to be specific, and to reach your own opinion—one you trust yourself and on which you're willing to follow through.

WIN-WIN NEGOTIATORS: It's easy to develop trust with them. They'll help you do it. Trust develops because your relationship is noncombative; you have freedom of expression without fear of retaliation.

It's also easy to communicate with Win-Winners. They know what they want, and they know you. They've practiced and role-played. They've seen all the tactics—solid silence, wild accusations, numbing indifference—and dealt with them all. Their own emotions are in check. Their agenda is clear. They ask for what they want. They don't expect instant success from every first effort. But they're willing to modify their request and try again, if necessary. They almost always succeed.

So will you, if you keep their example in mind. The most singular characteristic of Win-Win Negotiators, perhaps, is that they *trust themselves.* With self-trust, you can deal with any of the other stylists. Your lack of fear opens you up, lets you hear clearly, even if you're being attacked, and enables you to present your own case with confidence. Self-trust is what deflects the thrusts of the Jungle Fighter, who, filled with fear himself, tries to find out how fearful you are. Self-trust cuts through the defenses of all the stylists, introducing trust itself into the negotiating process. Without it, little can be accomplished.

Sending your message begins and ends with self-trust— trusting your judgment, planning, and ability to execute.

You're a negotiator now, in theory. You know what the best of them do. You're equipped with their tools and tactics. It's time now to put them to work—and to trust that you can.

PART THREE

Negotiations

15

Negotiating for Power

Ah, power! What a sensation! You can see it, feel it, smell it, sense it. It's the most sought after of all commodities. People work, sacrifice, fight, and trade for it—and then abuse it, waste it, and throw it away.

To most people, power means control over other people, whether that control is exercised in negotiating a treaty or in deciding where to eat a hamburger. Not surprisingly, the mere thought of power frightens a good many people. When I ask my clients to tell me what words they associate with power, they offer, "Tyranny . . . dominance . . . limitation . . . hurting others . . . depriving others . . . coercion . . . dirty."

But power is not a dirty word. Its primary meaning is none of the above. It's "To be able . . . the ability to do or act . . . capability of doing or accomplishing something."

"Power is potential," as one of my very perceptive clients said. "It's not even how you wield it or what you actually do. It is what people perceive you could do. That's power."

True negotiating power comes from inside out. If you come to a negotiation with a prior conviction that you're capable of doing what you're there to do, you're bringing power to bear. It's not power against another person, it's power in behalf of the task.

Knowledge plus skills plus self-esteem equals competence, according to R. W. White. You can gain knowledge and learn skills, but it's self-esteem that activates you to use the other two.

Just as competence flows from self-esteem, so power flows from competence.

You know when power is yours. Others listen when you speak. Your phone calls are returned. At dinner parties, you're seated to the right of the host or hostess. Your luncheon calendar is full. Before an important meeting others consult with you. When you're introduced to people, they say, "Oh, yes, I've heard about you." You're asked to sit in on meetings. Your children seek your guidance. And when your friends get into trouble, you're the one they come to.

Power: How You Get It

The key element in negotiation, as we've seen, is knowing what you want. That knowledge alone gives you an enormous amount of power—or, at the very least, access to it.

You and a friend go to an employment agency together. Your friend is "fishing"; she doesn't really know what she wants. You know that you want to work with older people. "I have an opening at a seniors' center," the interviewer says. "How does that strike you?"

Your friend hesitates.

"That's exactly what I want," you say. Suddenly, the power is yours.

Power is sometimes achieved in the simplest of ways. Suppose you're the newest member of a team, or the most junior member of a firm, painfully conscious that you haven't been accepted by the others or even included in their vital meetings. Two immediate steps on your part can do much to change the power equation.

The first is to inventory your verbal and nonverbal signals. Are you stiff, withdrawn, defensive? The chances are that you may be, partly because you're new, partly because you're apprehensive. Monitor your speech and manner. Walk briskly into a room. Sit or stand in an erect, alert posture. Ask and answer questions briefly and vigorously. Acknowledge your own competence. You wouldn't be there if you weren't good enough to have been wanted in the first place. That sense of self-esteem will begin to send out automatic signals that the others can't miss, signals that say you're neither intimidated nor aloof.

Your second step is to assert your most minimal rights. Tell whoever is in charge you would appreciate being advised promptly as to the time, place, and agenda whenever a meeting is convened.

Or consider the kind of situation all of us have found ourselves in at one time or another—being in a room deathly quiet except for a single voice, that of a Jungle Fighter/Dictator secreting venom that has paralyzed everyone there.

This style can be handled. Your tactic is *attentive disengagement.* Instead of cringing in your chair, as your colleagues are doing, lean forward and engage the speaker with your eyes; it's consistent eye contact that mutes high volatile responses. Attempt to control expressions that might reveal signs of anger or anxiety. Avoid emotion; it only enables him or her to keep going. Avoid talk as much as you can; use your silence as a tool to blunt the Jungle Fighter/Dictator's thrusts. If you're pressed for a response, be cryptic, sharp, and clear. At the same time, acknowledge the speaker's problem. "I can tell this has been a rough one." Or, "I know this is troubling you. I'll be glad to talk to you further. What are your major concerns?" As you speak, watch your voice tone; you want it to be controlled, even, never angry. Disengagement *can* mean lack of attention; your intent, however, is to intensify your concentration in this cool, collected way.

You gain and sustain power by knowing your own limits, knowing the right time to make certain moves, building a track record, and knowing the strengths, vulnerabilities, and needs of others—in short, knowing their styles.

The Power Game—and How to Play It with Each Stylist

With the exception of Win-Win Negotiators, all the stylists, even Soothers, play the power game. Here's how to play it with them:

JUNGLE FIGHTERS: They love power. To them, it's the name of the game, the reason for the combat—much more of a reason, often, than what power acquires.

We know that they can be savage and merciless in the pursuit of their objectives. But they can be handled, whether you're living with them or working for them.

The first step is to figure out why you're putting up with the ceaseless battering they inflict on you in order to render you powerless. What's your hidden agenda? What type of trade-off have you made? Are you accepting the abuse in exchange for money, prestige, status? Or is it the intrigue you respond to?

Once you've identified your hidden agenda, set a time line for its achievement. Tell yourself, "I have a deadline for leaving. Right now, I need the experience, the money, and the time." At the same time, begin to develop other options, so that you can leave if and when you want to. Develop a contingency plan that instructs you in exactly how to depart. Develop a support network—a "web"—of family, friends, and colleagues to call on if and when you need help.

Don't be intimidated! Don't let the Jungle Fighter think for a moment that you're afraid of him or her.

DICTATORS: As long as you live or work with them, you can expect to be in a power struggle—unless you simply acquiesce. Dictators must have control, and they will have it so long as you follow their lead. In order to gain parity with your Dictator spouse or boss:

Decrease your feelings of intimidation by identifying your specific fear and having options to reduce it. Intimidation decreases as your recognition of the assets you bring to the negotiation increases. The *best* way to reduce your intimidation is to learn the strategies involved in dealing with Dictators; such as planting a seed, knowing their agendas and priorities and keeping a lid on your oversell.

Identify the trade-offs you're getting by remaining with the Dictator and recognize your hidden agenda. Make time your ally by planting a series of seeds over a gradual period when your viewpoints are in conflict. Don't look knowledgeable when you're not—on the other hand, don't look vacant, keep composed. If you use words to cover up your confusion you'll only dig yourself in deeper. Ask short questions to clarify your confusion. And above all, keep cool! Dictators see emotions as weakness and they will attack.

Make yourself valuable to those in the Dictator's inner circle. They'll boost your stock if and when they can.

If a task strikes you as impossible, point out specifically

why it can't be done and that, if you are pressed to stick to the deadline the quality will suffer. If the Dictator insists that it can be done, don't then drive yourself into the ground—only to prove that he's right.

If you've never before said "no" to your Dictator spouse, don't start out by taking him on over a big issue. Start with a "simple" no. If he wants chicken rice soup, hold out for chicken noodle.

Insist on becoming a joint decision maker—again, by sticking, at first, to issues on which you know you can win.

SILHOUETTES: You feel powerless with them because of their silence. They may give you an opinion, but they won't give you any information about themselves to go on. The key to power parity with Silhouettes is to refuse to fill in the silent spaces with your own voice. Eventually, they'll have to speak for themselves.

Let them be silent. Maintain your own contacts, so that their silence doesn't get to you and you don't find yourself cut off.

Gather as much information from outside sources as you can, knowing that you won't be getting any information from Silhouettes.

When you do talk to them, don't use small talk or warm-ups. If you do, you'll lose them. And pick the right time; if they're on one of their solo flights, they literally won't hear you.

BIG MAMMAS AND DADDIES: Remember that they wield power as none of the others, because where the others deal in fear and threats, they control with love and approval.

Don't ask them for approval. Instead of saying, "How do I look?" say, "I like the way I look today."

Don't come to them with problems to solve. As long as you do, they'll continue to treat you like a child.

Go slowly. Break away step by step. Remember that not being betrayed by you is paramount to them.

Use silence as a tool.

Establish outside contacts. Big Mammas and Daddies manipulate you by putting you into contact with their network, which is simply an extension of their control. Only when you have your own network are you free of dependency on theirs.

Keep your bridge to them intact. You want to leave, but you always want to be able to go back.

SOOTHERS: They control you with their powerlessness. Their message is that they always need your help. The way to achieve power parity with them is to make them take responsibility for themselves.

Deprive them of excuses. Don't say, "I know you've had a hard day," or "I know you weren't feeling well."

Don't cancel your plans on their account. Soothers will get a headache when you're about to do something they don't want you to do.

Address the issue. Say, "We're getting off the track. Let's discuss our problem."

Insist on a commitment. Say, "I'm taking more responsibility than I want to. What are you willing to do?"

Don't give them five things to do. Give them one thing to do. Say, "I'd like this taken care of by Monday at four o'clock."

Keep an agenda. Be certain to follow through on raises, requests, favors, reports, or any agenda item.

Don't get seduced by the "guilts." Soothers will try to make you feel guilty by saying, "I can't do it alone." Say to them, "I'm sure you can manage" or "I know you can do it." Curb your desire to feel sorry for them.

And be aware of your own hidden agenda. You may be dealing with a Soother because you need to be taking care of someone.

The Gentle Approach to Parity

How do you change the balance in a relationship you want to maintain without destroying the relationship? This problem expresses itself in almost every power struggle. Its most common expression these days is among women who, after years of nurturing their families, now want to develop themselves in new ways.

Suppose you are such a woman. Here is how to proceed:

ATTEND AND OBSERVE: Are you saying "yes" to everything your husband asks? Do you act exclusively on the options he provides, and offer none of your own? The only way you'll gain independence is to stop letting him make all your decisions and to provide options of your own.

DO A SERIES OF WARM-UPS: Warm-up One: "I'm finding I have a lot of time on my hands these days." (Be prepared for your husband to come back with some new household projects.) Warm-up Two: "What I want to do is see what I might be interested in pursuing in the future." Make it clear that you're not thinking of leaving him; you just want to add to your life.

EXPLORE: Test your options in terms of your present reality. If your husband likes to have dinner at 6:00 P.M. and your class breaks at 6:30 P.M., suggest he relax and have dinner at 7:30 or meet you at a restaurant or start fixing dinner himself.

SET THE AGENDA: "I'm going to take a class." Note that it's not a full thrust, e.g., "I'm going to educate myself for a career." Then reassure your husband that your class won't affect your life together. If he resists, say, "This is important to me—" and say it as many times as necessary to get your point across. Often, it's repetition that best achieves communication.

If your husband really digs in his heels, tell him, "I need to be planning what I'm going to be doing five years from now. You have enthusiasm for your work, and I've supported you all this time. Now I need your support. Five years from now I want to be as excited about my work as you are about yours."

At this point, you want to show your husband a cost-benefit analysis that demonstrates how *he* will benefit, and to show it in the context of your appreciation for his efforts.

Remember that your power originates with options of your own. It's you who must develop them.

Gaining Parity with Parent Figures

Whether parents are natural ones or adoptive Big Daddies and Mammas, there comes a time when their children must break the symbiotic bond. The art is to be able to do so without destroying the relationship. The guiding principle is to move slowly. Any swift, overt severance could be destructive to both sides.

All parents consider children their protégés and extensions of themselves. But you may be reinforcing the problem.

Attend and observe. Do you play child a lot? Do you come to your parents with problems? If you want to grow up and move out on your own, don't come with problems, come with solutions.

Be specific about what you want. Don't make your desire for independence your hidden agenda. Make it your priority.

Write a line that gives focus to your desires. Make that line a probe. "I'm feeling that I'd like to have some new experiences. Do you have any ideas?" You may know very well what you have in mind, but if you present it right away, the response could be, "You're not experienced enough for that."

Remember, early on, to acknowledge your parent's contribution to your welfare. Say, "I've had a terrific learning year. You've given me the confidence to try something on my own." Then talk about that specific "something."

Dealing with Ph. Deities

Professors sometimes act as though they are guardians of a special castle of knowledge. Once they themselves have gained entry, they raise the bridge and lock the gates. Does their heart warm to gifted students? Or do they see them as potential rivals whose ascendancy might threaten their own position? Students often compound the problem by treating professors with the deference accorded heroes, a syndrome particularly noticeable in mature women returning to school after many years away, not at all certain that they can literally make the grade.

The strategy for negotiating with professors applies to any situation in which you're a subordinate dealing with someone in an exalted role.

Make a decision that you have a right to be there. You wouldn't be there in the first place if you didn't have the qualifications. You're also there to learn; you're not supposed to know as much as the authority figure, even though you sometimes do.

Attend and observe. What characteristics does he have that will make it easy or difficult to negotiate with him? Is this professor really knowledgeable? Sometimes professors will attempt to overwhelm you with words. But what about those words? How good are they?

Pay attention to your own patterns of intimidation. Do you want to be put in a dependent position? Are you letting it happen? Are you not speaking up when the professor moves too quickly, or doesn't make himself understood? One of my clients enrolled in a middle-level Spanish conversation class, only to find the professor, an academic aristocrat, teaching the course as though it were populated by graduate students. Nor did the professor pick up on the ample clues that he wasn't connecting—the silence of the class, a complete lack of questions, whispered conferences among the students during breaks. My client asked to see the professor privately. He deliberately spoke in a mixture of Spanish and English, a hidden agenda stratagem designed to convey that he wasn't an expert. He gave the professor recognition by complimenting his brilliance. Then he confronted the issue by informing the professor, without hostility, that this was not the course he'd signed up for. And because he was something of a Big Daddy, my client proposed that his view was shared by the rest of the class. The professor made a mid-course correction.

Pay attention to the professor's patterns of intimidation. He may be trying to bait and goad you. Medical students and law students are frequently subjected to almost unbearable forms of cruelty because their professors feel they have to be toughened up for the competition and trauma they'll experience as professionals. Don't respond with hostility. Keep focused on your goal. If the professor's not going to be your friend, at least don't make him your enemy.

Protecting Your Power

When it comes to preserving your power, allies can protect you only to a point. Beyond that, you're on your own.

No one ever gets used to office politics. It's always an upsetting and often a frightening business. The only way to diminish your fear is to learn how to play the game the Win-Win way.

What follows is the story of Susie, a twenty-three-year-old Soother, a complex person with a brisk outward manner but little inner confidence. Susie began work at seventeen with a leading movie producer; at twenty-two, she accepted an offer from another firm at lower pay so that she could work with a man she felt would push her career faster. A year after joining the new firm, Susie was recognized by everyone as a winner, warm to those with whom she worked, proceeding exclusively on the basis of competence rather than sexual messages.

And then Susie learned that the company was about to hire a man who would have exactly the same responsibilities she did, but at a considerably higher salary. As galling as the inequity was, what bothered her far more was its implication— that despite her seniority, Steve, the new man, would have the inside track on future advancement.

Susie was so furious that she was all set to take her boss on. "I'm going in there and I'm going to demand the money," she told me.

"Susie, you're going to lose if you do that," I told her. Together we worked out a strategy.

The next day, Susie went in to her boss and asked if he would be willing to give her a job evaluation, as well as to compare her job with Steve's. Susie's boss was a classic Soother, very bright and intelligent, but a poor administrator. He didn't know how to delegate responsibility, mostly because he was afraid to use his own authority. He would promise to take care of something and then never follow through. Now her boss told Susie that he would be happy to give her an evaluation— in a few days. When a few days passed and nothing happened, Susie repeated her request. "Why do you keep pestering me with this?" the Soother shouted. "Have I ever let you down? You're the youngest person in this office. Look at all I've done for you."

"That's not the issue," Susie said. "The issue is that I'm interested in having a job evaluation." When it was obvious that she wasn't going to get it, she came to the next line in her script. "I'm sensing this is the wrong time to go forward with this matter. Let's talk about it tomorrow." (Never try to negotiate with someone who's enraged.)

When it became apparent that the Soother wouldn't evaluate her job for her, Susie wrote out a job description herself and asked him to review it. He said he would but he didn't. He promised to speak to the personnel director in Susie's behalf, but he didn't. Susie pressed on. Each time she asked for her evaluation, she said it was to "assess" her future, an adroit way of letting him know that she would not ultimately stand for what had happened. Four weeks passed without action. Finally, Susie set her deadline. She told her boss, "I'm going to the personnel director today to get information about a leave of absence. I'm planning to take a leave of absence until this matter's resolved."

The Soother boss said nothing.

Susie did go to the personnel director, who, like any good personnel director, smelled trouble and investigated. Susie not only made the point that her duties were exactly equal to those being performed by Steve, she reminded the personnel director of the Equal Opportunity Act and its provision that persons performing the same work must be paid the same salary, irrespective of sex.

Not only did Susie receive her raise, it was made retroactive to Steve's first day on the job. Like the Win-Win Negotiator she was becoming, Susie did not flaunt her victory in her Soother boss's face. You gain nothing but enmity if you gloat or otherwise embarrass another person.

How to Avoid Giving Power Away

Power can do strange things to you if you are one of those who fear it or are even mildly apprehensive about it. You may seek to avoid it, or ignore it, or try to give it away, often without consciously realizing what you're doing. You'll arrive late for an important meeting—too late to be in on the decision. Or you'll be too tired to function, or operate on the notion that if you lose on one issue, you've lost the entire negotiation. Early surrender, that's called.

You may give away power because you want to be liked. It's so much more agreeable, after all, if you don't make waves, if you're pleasant and cooperative, if you don't stand up strongly for yourself or your ideas, if you don't resist the arguments of others unduly or aggressively.

Sometimes we behave as though we expect others to remind us that we have power, to support us when we relinquish it, to award us by not taking advantage of our vulnerability. It doesn't work that way. You have to take care of yourself. It's your responsibility to hold on to your power.

Every time you hesitate or needlessly apologize or disparage your own statements, you weaken your power. You also risk losing power if you talk too much or listen too little. Any or all of these mannerisms appear when you're feeling intimidated.

You give power away whenever you let yourself be intimidated. You give others permission to intimidate you when you:

- defer uncritically to authority
- trade off attention and affection for lack of firm decisions
- continue to stretch your bottom line
- communicate weakness with your body—slumped shoulders, sagging head, slow gait, frown, etc.
- don't speak up, or use tentative language

If you're readily intimidated, you ought, first of all, to acknowledge the fact. That's not complex; it requires no expert certification to establish when you're uneasy. Just pay attention to your body. Whenever you're in an uncomfortable situation, your body's going to tell you. You perspire; your mouth and throat feel dry; your stomach constricts; your breathing becomes more rapid.

Next, pay attention to *when* you're feeling intimidated, and who's intimidating you, and what the circumstances are when it happens—keeping an "intimidation diary," in effect, exactly like your Anger Diary.

Take the problem step by step. Ask yourself what is the least frightening first step you can take to make a transition.

When you're dealing with people who intimidate you or disrespect you, you can, and usually should, go very quickly to your bottom line. Watch how swiftly a situation can change.

A divorced Jungle Fighter father often arrived very late to pick up his son for the weekend, and sometimes didn't show up at all. When the mother asked me how to handle the problem, I suggested that she establish rigid ground rules. The next time her former husband arrived late, she said, "I expect you to call me if you're not going to be here on time. If you haven't called, I will wait thirty minutes, then leave and take John with me." The Jungle Fighter thought she was joking, particularly since he could withhold child support. But when he arrived forty-five minutes late the next time, he found no one home. He hasn't been late since.

When you state your intentions, you have to carry them through. One deviation from your word and you'll never be taken seriously again.

Recent studies have focused on what researchers call "women's speech," although many men use it as well. Such speech can be hesitant, reticent, unspecific, imprecise, indirect, uninformed, and uncontrolled. This "question mark" in the voice may be due to inexperience or lack of confidence, or both. But sometimes it's not the voice that's the problem; it's the minds of the listeners. Many people tend to discount statements from women that would be accepted if made by men. One of my clients, a very stylish woman, was on board a yacht one day when it was suddenly closed in by fog. "We're on a collision course," she announced some minutes later. Even though her voice carried a sense of emergency, she was not believed. In desperation she said, "My husband is a ship's captain. I know boats and sailing well. We are on a collision course." Only then did those on deck move to safety and the skipper of the yacht change course.

Take that question mark out of your voice if you want to retain your power. Believe in what you have to give, and say what you believe.

Be certain, as well, that when you're talking, it's to the right people. Power is dispensed by people who have it to give. Power, therefore, is transitory; it shifts from hand to hand, and year to year. This year's champion may be next year's chump. The question uppermost in your mind ought to be whether the person from whom you're seeking the power to accomplish something has it to give to you.

Negotiating for Money

The most successful negotiators I know have a positive attitude toward money. They think big. They want to win. They're not afraid of money, not afraid to say they want it, not afraid to use it, not afraid to spend it or invest it or share it or trade it off in behalf of common goals. There is a persistence and drive to their search for money that losing negotiators rarely have.

Losing negotiators, by contrast, tend to ask not only for less than they're worth, but for less than the other person is willing to give them. As one of my clients put it, "On my side, it's a squeamish request for more, in which I anticipate the answer 'no.' Afterward, I have the feeling that it wasn't a negotiation at all, but a settling for whatever the other party thought he could get away with. I can see clearly that I could have gotten more."

You're going to learn how to "get more"—to negotiate a raise, earn what you're worth, make that sale, pay a fair price. And because emotions are such a tremendous factor in the acquisition and disposition of money, you're going to learn, as well, how to deal with each of the stylists in money matters, particularly in the home.

Hari-Kiri in the Marketplace

Most of us harbor the suspicion that money might put something between us and the people with whom we negotiate, that it might somehow distort the feelings and the relationships. It's this fear that keeps us from asking for what's owed us, whether that be in the form of a bill past due or a merit raise. When we ask for more money, what's uppermost in our minds is the meaning and consequence of a "no." The refusal, we fear, will validate that we're not liked, not appreciated, not perceived as worthy. The consequence we fear most is a possible rupture in the relationship, either an unstated acknowledgment of low esteem or some form of walking papers. Women, in this regard, have historically had a far graver problem than men, because they have tended to be more spectators than participants in the money economy, completely dependent on their mates.

Studies cited by Caroline Bird in *The Two Paycheck Marriage* show that only three women in five have joint checking accounts with their husbands and that, of the women who do, only one in five has a say about how the money will be spent. Women, by tradition, were expected to make the purchases but men allocated the money. Women were expected to go to the department store but not the accountant.

That tradition has led to an attitude about money, even today, that is a real negotiation crippler. It is a defensive attitude that places more value on approval than on money. Psychologists have tested men and women to determine their sense of self-worth. In one test, the participants were asked to say how much compensation they should receive if they lost an arm or a leg or an eye or an organ, or the use of some other part of their body in an accident. On average, the men valued the parts of their bodies higher by thousands of dollars than the women. They also knew their value in the marketplace. Many women don't. The traditional woman has had no way of putting a dollar figure on her value.

There are many different forms of self-sabotage, be it undervaluing your worth, or not asking for a raise at the peak of your success, or telling a dirty joke as you're ready to close the sale—somehow, some way mucking it up for yourself.

Suppose you find yourself in your dream job: excitement, glamour, money, and purpose. The one hitch is your boss, a Silhouette/Dictator, who's used to doing everything alone. He doesn't have the time to introduce you to contacts or give you feedback about your performance. You begin to brood. Meetings in which you do participate are carried on as if you're not present. The quieter you become, the more depressed and less productive you are. You begin to hate yourself and your job. You hear yourself telling others about the S.O.B. who's "doing it" to you. Three weeks later, the word is out that you can't work with others, and a week after that you're fired.

What went wrong?

You didn't acknowledge the problem of your own Soother-like tendencies not to address the issue.

You didn't identify your Silhouette/Dictator boss's style of wanting clear and precise solutions.

You crippled yourself by not speaking to him directly and by speaking behind his back.

You didn't observe how others worked effectively with him.

You didn't develop allies within his inner circle.

How to Make Others Value Your Presence

People used to think that if they worked hard and stuck to business, their efforts would be perceived and rewarded. You've already seen in Chapter 14, "Sending Your Message," that that's not the case. It was Dr. Adele Scheele's finding that the achievers, the ones who get what's coming to them, are those who spend fifty percent of their time performing their work and the other fifty percent calling attention to it in assertive but nonboastful ways. Self-promotion means, as well, taking on extra responsibilities, getting active, joining organizations. It means coming up with creative ideas. It means inviting your colleagues to lunch, to your home or your weekend retreat. Help your colleagues with a problem, and you'll be identified overnight as a problem solver. If you've discovered a way to cut through administrivia, don't keep it a secret. Put the word out, either by pitching it during a conference or, even better, by writing and distributing a memorandum. Use memos. They not only make you visible, they memorialize an idea as yours. Send them to all the appropriate people. Wide distribution is particularly important if you're working for a Soother, because the Soother won't follow through. He'll tell you it's a fine idea, and then bury it on his desk. But before distributing your memo, be certain that the practice is consistent with the policies, as well as the realities, of your organization. Learn how change takes place before you attempt to effect it. If you're working for a Dictator or Jungle Fighter or Big Daddy/Big Mamma to whom control is imperative, then your memo could backfire, unless you check beforehand, thus:

"I've got an idea I'm extremely excited about. I'll be sending [Not, "May I send . . . ?"] a memo to you and copies to the other departments." That was a probe you just made. You've given your boss a chance to raise any objections.

If you like to write, write an article for a professional magazine—after clearing the project with your boss. You probably won't get money for this but your R.O.I. will be the enhancement of your reputation. Or try some of the approaches a client of mine did when she moved to a small community to establish a therapy practice. She gave free lectures to local organizations and church groups. She wrote articles for the local newspaper. She approached the owner of the local radio station with a proposal for a talk show. Six months after arriving as a stranger, she was a celebrity.

How to Ask For—and Get—a Raise

If you're convinced you deserve a raise, pin one word on your wall, chant it like a mantra, write it out a hundred times.

The word is "timing."

Timing pertains to you. Are you "hot"? Have you just closed a deal, won a case, set a sales record? Go for it.

Timing pertains to your organization. What's its wage or salary policy? Is your request in line with that policy, or it is out of order?

Let's walk through the Four Step Process now with that word in mind:

1. DEFINE THE PROBLEM: You've landed three major accounts in the last year, but your salary's lower than others' whose work isn't as good. You're feeling unappreciated and ignored. You're overdue for a raise.

2. DECIDE WHAT YOU WANT: Immediate or long-term satisfaction? A big job downstream, or a big raise right now? What trade-offs are you willing to make if you don't get your raise? Title? Better office? Company car? What's your bottom line? What are you prepared to do if the answer's "no" to everything?

3. DESIGN A STRATEGY: Write your script. Be certain it reflects an awareness of the current condition of the company. Is business good? Has the stock just been split? Right on. A budget cut? A bad time to ask for money, but *not* a bad time to remind management of your situation, to tell them you'll be asking for a raise three months hence and that, in the meanwhile, you'd like time off for additional training at company expense. This is also a good time to negotiate for stock options, which require no cash outlay.

Before you can get more money, you have to find out what you're worth in management's eyes. If there are aspects of your work that need improvement, you want to know about them before you ask for your raise. Asking for a job evaluation is good strategy at any time.

4. DO IT: Make an appointment. Read the mood of the person to whom you're making your request. Is his smile for real? Does he seem impatient? Tell him you'd like to see him tomorrow, or the next day, but pin him down. If he says he's just too busy, tell him you'll write him a memo with an alternative salary suggestion. Be absolutely certain you know what that figure is. Many losing negotiators are caught flat-footed when they're asked, "How much do you want?" Have a "wide band" in mind—one figure that would call for champagne, and another you could live with.

Never, never ask for a raise when you're in trouble, or when you're broke and behind on your payments. A raise won't solve your immediate problem; what you need is a bank loan. Asking for a raise at an anxious moment will give the game away; your anxiety will seep through.

By the same token, don't look for another job when you're feeling anxious or desperate. Your prospective employers will divine your mood, and file you away under "Loser."

Don't quit one job until you have another one, because the

worst time to find a job is when you're unemployed. The more desperate you are, the less persuasive you'll be.

If you simply have to quit your job because you can't stand it, be sure you have enough money in the bank to cover five or six months' expenses.

Know Your Boss—and Keep His Style in Mind

Your tactics in negotiating for a raise must be keyed to the style of your boss.

JUNGLE FIGHTERS: They'll try to distract you with criticism of your past deficiencies, real or imagined. Stick with your agenda. They'll fence with you for the sheer love of combat, so be ready with parries and thrusts. Duel with them just after you've contributed to their success.

DICTATORS: Use nothing but logic and fact. Have your homework well done, your script practiced so that your speech is clear and your argument specific. Have your emotional housekeeping well done. Negotiate for important issues, not for trivia, and always when you're on the crest of a wave. Don't be slick, but do be classy. Cite authorities, if that is relevant. Be as brief as possible, but be comprehensive as well. Listen carefully for his or her ending cues. And remember, Dictators go according to the book. If government policy is for no more than say, 7 percent wage increases and you feel you deserve more, you'd better present a terrific case.

SILHOUETTES: As with the Dictator, bring facts, bring data, make your presentation clear and crisp. "I've been here seven months. We agreed that this would be the month we would discuss my raise. Here's what I believe I've done for the company." Tick off your accomplishments. Then wait silently for a reply.

If you receive a "yes," the conversation's over. Go call your mate, or take a friend to lunch. If you receive a "no," you have to have prepared a rebuttal.

BOSS: I know we talked about that, and you're quite right. Your assessment of your work seems accurate. However, you've heard that we're trying to hold costs down in anticipation of the recession.

YOU: I understand the problem. However, three other people in my division have just received raises. The amount of revenue I've brought in during the last seven months is greater than what any of them has brought in.

BIG DADDIES OR BIG MAMMAS: Be prepared to spend some time. Have ready one or more illustrations of how their advice and support have helped you progress during the past year. Tell them how much you enjoyed working with them. As long as you're dealing with a Big Daddy or Mamma, you have to deal with demands for your loyalty and dependence.

With Big D and Big M, as well as Jungle Fighters and Dictators, always ask for more: "I'd like a two-thousand-dollar raise this year." They'll cut your request down, simply to express their control. "Let's give you fifteen hundred, so you'll have something to shoot for."

SOOTHERS: Press—gently but firmly and persistently until you get an answer. Whatever you request, the Soother will say, "I'll have to check with top management." You say: "Okay, but I'd like an answer by Friday." On Friday, ask for the answer. And don't waffle. If the answer isn't forthcoming, have something ready that will put pressure on the Soother—your own resolve to go to top management yourself.

If You're Turned Down

It's foolish to quit a good situation just because you've been turned down on your most recent request for a raise. It's even more foolish to jeopardize your position by indulging your anger. An outburst could get you fired—or, if you've been negotiating for more money from your mate, cost you your relationship. So before you express your anger, be sure that you have chips in the pot, many options, and a support system to call on. Even then be careful to discharge your anger in a safe way:

Talk the situation out with a friend.
Call on your web.

Write a nasty letter that you don't mail.
Punch a pillow.

Once you've dissipated your anger, you may realize you're getting a valuable trade-off—experience, visibility, prestige. The next time you go in for a raise or promotion, you'll know better than to go empty-handed. You'll have consulted with your web, you'll have put out some feelers, you'll have options.

No one is ever the "complete strategist" on all occasions. Even the most competent Win-Win Negotiator will lose an argument, a contract, a job, or a lover. But the Win-Winner will review the steps that led to the loss and make positive preparations for the next encounter with his or her strategy revised. The Win-Winner is generally gracious in defeat, making sure to "bridge" for the next encounter. The important point is to discharge your rancor and be able to recover.

When Agreements Aren't Kept

You went to work for a firm with the understanding that, between salary and commissions, you would earn $30,000 a year. At the end of the first year, your income from both totals $20,000. What do you do?

1. Diffuse your anger safely, in the ways we've just discussed.
2. Prepare a contingency plan that will enable you to survive if you quit your job.
3. Write and rehearse a script in which you praise the company, its product and management, but add, "In spite of all this, I can't afford you."
4. If the original promises are renewed, negotiate an agreement that requires a review of your earnings in three to six months. If you're still not being paid what's been promised, go to your bottom line. (Women have a tendency to wait too long.) There may be problems you don't know about, and this is a sure way to smoke them out.

One of my clients went to her bottom line when her commissions hadn't been paid; she filed a claim with the Department of Labor.

Suppose you've fulfilled your end of a contract, sent a bill, and haven't been paid. After a reasonable amount of time, you've called and been greeted with Soother calm and praise. "I had no idea this had happened. I put the payment order through weeks ago. Let me check into it, and get back to you." At this point you say, "If I haven't heard from you by [set an appropriate deadline] I'll call you." Make that call, and as many others as are necessary until you're paid.

The important thing is to take the position that you'll be paid eventually. The moment you take the reverse position the process becomes self-fulfilling, if only because your very attitude is an acknowledgment that you're not going to be paid.

How to Succeed Without Putting Out

Everyone wishes to choose where, when, and with whom he or she will experience sex. The statistics, however, tell another story. Sexual harassment in the work arena has reached epidemic proportions. Most of it is initiated by men asking or demanding favors of women in exchange for raises, promotions, or sales contracts.

If you find yourself in such a predicament, it is unrealistic to expect that the practice will stop. Your only power is in learning how to discourage such advances.

BE CLEAR ABOUT YOUR AGENDA. Make certain that your enthusiasm is invested in the product or idea you're selling, and not in the person to whom you're selling it. Stay focused on your objective. Don't even hint at a hidden agenda. Ultimately, your enthusiasm will transmit itself to the buyer because your product or idea, not you, is his primary interest, too.

AVOID A CASUAL APPROACH. Be gracious and cordial, but thoroughly professional. An informal approach may be misinterpreted as a desire to use the business meeting as a bridge to a personal relationship.

ATTEND AND OBSERVE. If you've had previous dealings, you know the style of the other person. If not, try to get information about him or her from others who have. Listen for verbal innuendo, e.g., "It's about time they sent me someone who knows how to sell." Be alert to nonverbal messages, e.g., a lingering handshake, bumping shoulders, prolonged stare, etc.

MONITOR YOUR OWN STYLE. If you're a Big Mamma (or Big Daddy) and touching is a natural part of your style, you may be sending ambiguous signals. If you're a Jungle Fighter *and* a woman, harsh language, particularly four-letter words, can send a signal you don't intend. If you're being propositioned everywhere you go, the chances are that you're flashing some sort of come-on. If, having monitored your style, you find that it is not you but the other person, change your job or territory.

ADDRESS—AND STAY WITH—THE ISSUE. If you're feeling harassed, say so! "Thanks for your time, and this order. I'd like to continue to do business with you, but I'm not comfortable with your innuendo. How can we work comfortably together?" If the other person is a Jungle Fighter, he may respond, "We could take off our clothes." At this point, go directly to your bottom line, even if it means losing the sale.

If you're confronted with a direct invitation, say "no," and continue with the business discussion.

JUNGLE FIGHTER: I'd like to discuss sales over dinner, honey. I'm interested in your product.
YOU: Dinner's not negotiable, but the price for bulk buying is.

KNOW THE LAW. The Equal Opportunity Act, Title IX, protects you against sexual harassment. There is no need to be silent. If your boss is a Dictator or a Silhouette, write a script with a minimum of emotionalism before you lodge your complaint. If your boss is a Jungle Fighter, he'll probably accuse you of enticing the client with whom you're having trouble. If other colleagues are having the same problem, you may want to consult an attorney.

Selling, in most situations, produces an atmosphere charged with sexuality. There will be cases where you must be willing to lose the sale. Better that than your self-esteem.

Money and the Stylists

Thus far we've been talking about money and the marketplace. Let's enlarge the focus now, and deal with the inner attitudes that we find among the styles.

JUNGLE FIGHTERS: To them money is a tool to be used. Getting it and keeping it is part of the process of power. They persuade themselves that they can buy anything with it— love, happiness, others. They are inveterate risk-takers and heavy plungers. They love the trappings that money buys. Their appetites are enormous and usually insatiable, because they are always trying to replace what money can't buy— continuity and deep, sustaining relationships.

DICTATORS: They control money as they control people. Ideal corporate leaders and family providers, they investigate meticulously before they invest or spend their money, and they must be absolutely certain that the R.O.I. is a big one. In business relationships, they hold staff members responsible for producing high R.O.I.s. Those who don't, are replaced. Dictators are often zealous savers and quiet spenders. They make decisions, as does the Jungle Fighter, without consulting family members or business subordinates. But those who profit from the Dictator's financial success pay the price in loss of independence.

SILHOUETTES: They are hoarders of money—for what, only they know for sure. If another word can also be used to describe their money attitude, it is "penurious." It's not that they love poverty, it's that they don't want to spend money on the trappings of success that mean so much to Jungle Fighters and Dictators. Wives, children, and business associates know these individuals as "tightwads." Silhouettes derive pleasure from the *pursuit* of money, not from spending it.

BIG DADDIES AND BIG MAMMAS: They're generous to a fault; but be careful to look closely for the strings. Their largesse is almost always a trade-off for loyalty and devotion.

You know you're in for a good dinner when they're picking up the check. Not only are they generous, they live life with zest. They give lots of gifts, principally because they like the "giving" image. They also buy what they think you should have. Big Daddies and Mammas will frequently lend money, with no thought of ever being repaid. Having you in their debt gives them control, although their expectations are so subtle, you may never realize it.

SOOTHERS: Money is a real problem for them. They *can't* ask for it because they're constitutionally incapable. And, besides, they know they won't get it. Yet Soothers have a great need for money because they are helpless consumers. They have zero resistance to a sales pitch, principally because they're afraid to say no. They're always picking up the tab in the hope that they'll be liked, and they're almost always in debt because of their unresisting consumerism. Ironically, Soothers have tremendous power without being aware of it because they're the ones the sellers delight in going after.

WIN-WIN NEGOTIATORS: They enjoy earning money, whether for themselves or others. They enjoy using it as well, to further their careers, enhance their families' lives or purchase pleasures. They're never reluctant to spend if the trade-off is a good one. They usually invest well, and rarely get into debt.

When You've Been Kept in the Dark

In a majority of households, one of the partners is usually kept in ignorance about money. In a small number of cases, that partner is a man; overwhelmingly, it's the woman. Such women try to make light of the matter. "Why is it important for me to become aware of our finances?" they'll ask "I've been well taken care of for thirty years."

Here are four reasons why: your spouse's possible illness, his eventual death, your decision to leave him, or his to leave you.

On a deeper level, ignorance about money matters has to have diminished your self-esteem. When a "caretaker" husband makes all financial decisions, he's sending a hidden message that he doesn't value you or your decision-making ability. This message has to communicate itself somehow. Lack of information also creates fear; admit it or not, you know you're not in charge of your life.

Any man who is still excluding his wife from the family's financial proceedings is only building trouble for himself. Even if his wife is not working outside the home and not contributing dollars to the family pot, she is aware, first, that her work in the home and in behalf of the family has value and, second, that other women are successfully negotiating for participation.

Any woman who has, in effect, defaulted from participation by failing to inform herself on financial matters is also building trouble for herself. Admittedly there are profound cultural reasons why women do default. From their earliest years, they have been conditioned—at least until present times—to be dependent on the men in their lives. They grow up believing that there is a man out there somewhere who is going to take care of them. They even pass such messages on to their daughters. In effect, the message is, "You don't have to trouble yourself with money problems. You don't need to know how to solve them." Women, as a consequence, are not only ill prepared but *ill disposed* to deal with problems when they must inevitably confront them. If a well-meaning husband attempts to discuss what resources his wife will have in the event of his death, she will often say, "I don't want to talk about it." But how else will the woman inform herself about life insurance, investments, and debts if she doesn't talk about "it"?

The inability or unwillingness of adults to talk about money is exceeded only by their unwillingness to discuss sex or death. When a woman recently widowed comes to me for help, feeling overwhelmed by her new responsibilities, I say, "Did you ever ask? Did you assume your partnership role?" The response is almost always the same: "I meant to, but something always came up." Women can't keep putting the blame on men for not letting them know. They have a responsibility to do their homework. If a woman says to her husband, "I'm tired of being kept ignorant," she may not get very far. But if she says, "I realize I haven't been your partner. I want to become better informed. I'd like to go with you to the accountant the next time we do the taxes," she has a real prospect of changing the household's financial environment.

Less Is More

We Americans are finally becoming aware that the accumulation of things need not be the focus and purpose of life. There are throwbacks, however. Here's a strategy for dealing with a spouse who's spending more than you think she should:

- Diffuse your anger. Ask yourself whether the problem exists, at least in part, because you've played Big Daddy all these years and kept her in the dark about family finances.
- Make an appointment to discuss the matter, and set an agenda that includes a time line ("We've got to have our finances under control within a month") and a bottom line ("If we can't manage to do that, we'll have to close our charge accounts").
- Be prepared for tears and abuse in your first discussion ("I'm not overdrawn. You're underdeposited").
- Do a cost-benefit analysis together to see what you can jointly give up as a first step. Focus on luxuries, not necessities.
- Come up with some new options. For example, figure out with your wife precisely what she needs to run the household. Then withdraw that exact amount from the bank. Make a collaboration of the endeavor by asking her to maintain an account of all expenditures.
- Be prepared for negotiating cripplers in the form of guilt and self-pity.

Overspending is scarcely confined to women. Several of my successful women clients are married to chronic spenders who can't come to terms with the fact that their wives make more money than they do. If you're ever in such a situation with a chronic overspending husband, follow the advice I give my clients:

- Stop rescuing. Let your mate experience the consequences of financial mismanagement.
- Set up separate credit.
- Set up a system whereby priority bills such as rent and utilities are paid by you.
- Establish a deadline for balancing the books.

- Offer options such as a joint system of tending to the family books.
- If your mate refuses to participate in the auditing, insist that he assume some of your other household duties so that you'll have time to balance the books.
- If the problem continues, insist that it be referred to a money manager.
- As a last resort, cut up his credit cards.

Negotiating with Your Landlord

The end of the year is approaching, and your landlord has asked for a rent increase. If your landlord is a:

JUNGLE FIGHTER: Expect to do some fencing. Know the law, because he will probably ask for a greater increase than other or similar property is getting or the law permits. Offer less, knowing that some increase is inevitable, and you'll have to compromise. Don't threaten. If you do, start packing.

DICTATOR: Do your homework. Get information on rents in comparable buildings, and show him the comparisons if they help your cause. Find out if there are vacancies in your own building; if so, point this out to him. If you've been a good tenant, point out the benefits to him of your staying on in the building. Avoid emotionalism, because it won't do any good. Anticipate that the landlord will probably remain rigid; be prepared to accept the increase or leave.

SILHOUETTE: Your rent increase notice will arrive in the mail. If you telephone, you'll just get his secretary. If you have anything to say, say it by mail.

BIG DADDY OR BIG MAMMA: Spending time with this landlord could pay off. He or she might listen sympathetically to your financial predicament. If the landlord remains firm on the money, negotiate for time; the landlord may be willing to defer the increase until you receive your expected raise or your tax refund. Tie the rent increase to needed repairs on the apartment.

SOOTHER: Use silence. Let it be known you're so upset by the prospect of a rent increase that you don't even want to discuss it at the moment. Suggest time to think about it. Let the Soother make the next move. In the meanwhile, make a contingency plan; look at other apartments. If you decide you want to remain in your present apartment, expect the Soother to offer a compromise figure at your next "discussion." Even then, maintain silence. Ask for more time. The chances are that the Soother will finally tell you that you can stay on, either at no extra cost or a minimal increase.

Know What You Want

Earlier we said that there was no person more formidable than one who knows exactly what he or she wants and what he or she is willing to pay for it. Carry that principle with you when you're shopping, and you'll be hundreds, even thousands, of dollars ahead.

You can't bargain in a department store or supermarket, but there are dozens of other places where you can—automobile agencies, antique markets, art galleries. You can negotiate the price of a home, a sailboat, jewelry. Whatever you're buying that *is* negotiable can be bought at a price you can afford *provided* you determine in advance what that price is and then vow not to exceed it.

You have to do your homework so that the price you settle on is realistic. And then you have to time your purchase with practiced mastery. That time is normally at the end of a sale. Watch how Terry, a client of mine and a creative money saver, bought a ring she wanted at a price she could afford.

She found the ring at a sale of antiques. Earlier, she had checked the reputation of the sellers and the quality of their merchandise. When she saw the ring, she knew at once that she wanted it, but showed no enthusiasm. She simply asked the price. "Too much," she replied after the price had been quoted. The dealer immediately dropped the price by $25. "No," Terry said.

Then Terry changed the subject, as though the thought of purchasing the ring had passed from her mind. She began to interview the dealer—about how he'd gotten into the business, what kind of training he'd had, where his work had taken him, where he got his merchandise. Before long, a palpable bond had formed: Terry was no longer a walk-in customer; she was a person who cared.

By this point, the day was almost at an end, and the ring had still not been sold. Just before closing, Terry offered to buy the ring at thirty percent below the asking price—the figure she'd had in mind all along. The dealer not only accepted Terry's offer, but her personal check as well.

When Trust Is Your Joint Account

How people who live together but don't marry divide financial responsibilities is a subject presently being tested and defined in courts of law. In the meanwhile, hundreds of thousands of couples are working the ground rules out for themselves, and some of them are doing an extraordinary job. Here's one situation that could serve as anyone's model:

Tim is a Win-Win/Silhouette. Sally's a Win-Win/Big Mamma. They decided to live together but not marry—not, at least, until they'd experienced one another for several years. Tim was a skilled carpenter with higher ambitions he could realize only by returning to school. Sally was a professional dancer. She wanted to start a dance studio. Splitting all household expenses was just the start of their agreement. Tim agreed to finance Sally's venture while she was getting started. He set a time line of one year. Sally agreed that, once the studio began to show a profit, she would finance Tim's return to school. Within a few years, they had greatly increased one another's earning power through their mutual support.

Tim and Sally maintained separate bank accounts, which they used to pay professional expenses, buy gifts for one another, and take an occasional separate vacation. Eventually, they bought property together and built their own home, forming a legal partnership to protect the child they decided to have. No hidden agendas in this relationship!

When You Think You've Got It Made:
A Time for Special Care

Wealth can inhibit creativity. The wealthy person no longer has to be creative himself; he can buy it. Once that starts to happen, however, let the buyer beware.

A young man I know grew up in a big, no-nonsense blue collar family. He learned early on to fend for himself. When he was eight years old, he sold one of his brothers the steak off his plate for a dollar. In his family, his father turned his paycheck over to his mother, and his mother guarded every penny. There was never any money for art or ballet or music. But Earl, as we'll call him, had talent. He wanted to act. He was an instinctual actor. He could sell himself to anyone. His talent earned him a scholarship to college. When he graduated, he met a wealthy young man, and they went into business together, buying land and building condominiums. "I don't have time for a lot of this," the wealthy partner said. "I'll let you buy in by working." That was fine with Earl. He took a small draw, learned the business, and hired the help. His wealthy partner pulled the business in, because he had that special verve, but it was always Earl who closed the deal. When Earl's contribution to their success became totally disproportionate, he left his partner—and took the nucleus of their organization with him.

What Earl's partner forgot was that human interaction is absolutely vital to any and all negotiations. He had no human connection with his own organization. For employees, it's equivalent to thinking in terms of the next raise, and nothing more. Unless people build the kind of human network that makes them invaluable, they become expendable.

Negotiating for Less

We've been talking a lot about ways to get more money. It's time now to deal with the other side of the coin: how to negotiate for less. More specifically, it's how to negotiate for a life on a less demanding financial scale. To say that this is a life-and-death issue is not to exaggerate at all. Countless men in their forties and fifties have been raised in a culture that expected them not only to be breadwinners, but constantly to increase the size and quality of the loaf. Their pressures are compounded when they marry wives who have great expectations of their husbands—far greater than their physical or psychological capacities to produce. These are the men who, if they're lucky, wind up only with heart attacks. There follow the loss of their job and the subsequent loss of self-esteem. Wives can't be satisfied, children can't be educated. They are unable any longer to perform to society's expectations. I have known many men who died and many others who court death each day via overwork.

We'll assume that you're such a person (or are married to one, in which case the scenario is just as important). You've paused, taken stock, and decided that accumulating things isn't a fulfilling goal. You want to change your life-style, because you're aware that life has become a routine of work to make money to accumulate things and maintain your image.

Attend and observe: Is your body telling you that you're burned out? If so, don't wait. Act.

Do your homework. Find out about other career possibilities, possible investments.

Do a series of probes to learn how your wife sees the relationship or life-style. If she doesn't respond, recognize that she wants life to continue as it is—and that you live with an ambitious and dependent person.

Know your bottom line: You're not willing to kill yourself by continuing at this pace.

Make an appointment with family and friends to discuss your situation. Announce the agenda.

When the negotiation begins, use warm-ups that deal with facts about your health and fatigue, the heart attacks of others in similar situations, about the need to come up with options and to discover how you can live more rationally and economically in some other mode. Your opening statement might go something like this: "I need to talk to you about an issue of deep concern to me. I no longer want to keep up the pace. I'd like to explore some options with you."

Leave time to listen to any fears that may come through: "How will we live?"

"Do we have to move?"

"What about college for the children?"

Express the benefits to all: your life and health, as opposed to your illness and possible death.

A negotiation of this importance may take many sessions. Expect to spend time, and to allow others time. Remember that you've been negotiating with yourself for quite a while in order to surface this issue.

If it's been your style to "make nice" and protect your family, be careful about making weak statements like, "Let's think about it for a while." Instead, be emphatic and believable. Say, "Let's explore our options."

Do a cost-benefit analysis together to see what you might jointly give up as a first step. But don't ask for critical trade-offs.

Watch your time line. Make a small amount of progress in your discussions and decisions each day, or you won't be believed. Tell your family that you'll eventually have to face this negotiation when you're sixty-five, so why not do it now so that you can *live* to be sixty-five?

Listen carefully to all their thoughts and arguments, and satisfy them to the extent that you can. But don't move or stretch that bottom line. This is one negotiation you can't afford to lose.

17

Negotiating for Sex, Love, and Romance

If you want love, be loving.

If you want romance, be romantic.

If you want sex, be sexy.

If sex, love, and romance don't flow your way, it's time to negotiate.

Negotiate? For *sex?* For *love?* For *romance?*

Absolutely.

Serious sexual problems need outside help. When businesses find themselves with troubles they can't resolve through their own resources, they call in consultants before the damage becomes irreparable. If you even suspect you're in that kind of predicament with a loved one, find someone skilled to advise you.

But let me repeat what I said at the outset: Many of the problems we experience in our dealings with others, many of the emotional binds in which we find ourselves, don't require long-term therapy and the expense of hundreds of hours and thousands of dollars in order to be resolved. They can be dealt with through the simple process of negotiation.

Nowhere has this truth been borne out more frequently or dramatically in my experience than in my clients' negotiations for sex, love, and romance.

If you approached negotiations for sex, love, and romance

as you approach a business negotiation, you would soon find yourself making better "deals." In business, when you want something, you make an offer. You say, "This is what I want, and this is what it's worth to me." In sex, love, and romance, you seldom make an offer. You wait for the other person to make it. This passive approach rarely works.

When you don't ask for what you want, your partner doesn't know what to give you. When you don't get it, you become hurt, then angry—and even less able to negotiate for what you want than before.

If you want sex, love, or romance, don't wait for your partner to make an offer. Make the offer yourself.

Skill in any negotiation depends on your ability to deal with causes and not indulge your emotions. But because the problems associated with sex, love, and romance are the most freighted with emotion of any we confront, the skill is more imperative here than anywhere. Fear of being alone, anger at neglect, feelings of exploitation and domination, hostility toward sexual competitors—these and other fears and anxieties, all of them negotiating cripplers, crop up again and again in the stories of my clients and workshop participants.

In recent years, the causes of these fears have become decidedly more complex; let's, first, have a look at them, and then get down to cases.

The Sexual Transition

The changes in sexual attitudes in recent years have been so vast it sometimes seems that sex itself has been reinvented. What was once unmentionable is now common talk. Children have knowledge today that many adults died never knowing. Openness and candor about sex have created expectations that have never before existed. These expectations, in turn, have created strains and tensions that make negotiation for sex, love, and romance imperative. For this negotiation to succeed, it must be conducted with an awareness of the transition under way with respect to the roles of men and women.

We are all in transition. The fallout of the sexual revolution is inescapable. It permeates life. Rules are changing, roles are changing, control is changing. Women—those who have been liberated, at least—aren't as frightened as they once were. They've found more options—work, school, politics, fun. They're more aware of their needs and their drives. They have more information. They can have children when and if they want them. And they have the reinforcing tradition of sexual freedom that has taken hold in the United States in the last ten years.

The days when most of a family's decisions were made primarily to further the breadwinner's career are all but gone. It is not simply a consequence of the women's movement and the rise of feminine consciousness; it's that more and more households include a working female whose needs for attention and support may be every bit as vital as her mate's. By 1990, two-thirds of the adult women in the United States will be in the labor market. The impact of that eventuality on sex, love, and romance will be enormous. A majority of women won't be as sexually available as they once were; they simply won't have the time, let alone the energy or, in some cases, the desire. Creative interest often drains off sexual energy. "I'm no longer willing to accept the rage of the boardroom in the bedroom," a career woman I know states. "And I'm not so attuned to my husband's moods. In the past, I would get hooked into going to bed with him because he was upset or worried or depressed, and I felt that the sexual reward was the payoff to his long day. I now have my own long days."

But when they do want sex, women are allowing themselves to be more assertive, a development that has placed a new and often uncomfortable burden on men. In the old days when women didn't ask for sex, male performance was an issue primarily among competitive males. Today, male performance is an issue among women, as well. They expect to receive as much pleasure as they give. Formerly, sex occurred primarily when the man wanted to have it. Nowadays, it occurs when both partners want it.

The male in a two-career family must be aware of the transition that women are going through if he proposes to negotiate for sex. He must recognize that the energy of the woman in his life is no longer consecrated to his needs.

Many men are simply unprepared to cope with this challenge to the dominance they had always taken for granted.

They had "signed up" for working and risking on the outside, and resting and being cared for at home. Women "signed up" for just the opposite; now not only must they deal with the anxieties any new adventure creates, they must deal with the strains their new identities impose on their relationships with men.

As a consequence of this revolution of roles, both men and women find themselves caught in a double bind. Men who persist in their old competitive roles find themselves typed as chauvinists. Yet if they seek to become more sensitive, caring, and responsive they are often perceived as weak. Women who remain traditionally submissive and passive are often consumed by the feeling that they have sold themselves short. Yet when they seek new expression through assertion and strong decision-making roles, they are typed as unfeminine and bitchy.

The best way for men and women to extricate themselves from this double bind is to negotiate openly with one another for sex, love, and romance. But openness doesn't come easily for men; they've been conditioned not to cry or express grief or ask for affection. Women, always more emotionally open, now guard their responses lest they seem weak. Today, instead of participating in dialogues, men and women are speaking parallel monologues.

For all the above reasons, negotiating for sex, love, and romance is more complex today than it has ever been. It's imperative, therefore, that you know not only how to negotiate, but with whom you're negotiating. So let's look next at the styles, and the strategies for dealing with each of them.

Dictators

Dictators work hard. They're used to issuing orders. They operate from a stern inner discipline. The one place they sometimes feel that they can let down is in bed. But few of them are sexy or romantic lovers, because they don't take the time to explore, or to find out what the other person needs or wants. They make love with the same kind of control they exhibit at the office. They will choose the time and manner, and give only what they're programmed to give. They lack the grace and charm so essential to the opening ceremonies that are such a vital prelude to sex. "The only time I receive affection is in bed," one woman I interviewed observed. Most Dictators are just as casual about closing ceremonies; after sex, it's as though nothing had happened.

Strategy:

- *Address the issue.* Example: "It's difficult for me to be loving in bed when you never show me kindness at any other time." If your partner asks you what you want, be ready with options: a telephone call during the day just to touch base; time alone without having asked for it; expressions of regard in the living room as well as in the bedroom.
- *Renegotiate the relationship by stating what you want changed.* "I would like to spend two nights a week alone and one night a week not being responsible for dinner." Brainstorm options—more of those times together when you do enjoy one another. If you both love the ocean or football, go where the juices flow.
- *Evaluate your trade-offs.* You may not be getting emotional expression or touching, but you may be getting other things such as fun, intellect, money, or physical privacy if you yourself don't like touching all that much.
- *Address the obvious.* "We make love every Thursday at nine o'clock whether we want to or not." If you want, negotiate for a time variation.

Jungle Fighters

Big on romance but short on love, they are, if anything, even more destructive as lovers than Dictators. You will be intrigued by their charismatic sexuality, which you think they'll share with you. However, they're almost totally committed to their own satisfaction, without regard for the other person. The typical male Jungle Fighter is almost more interested in the pursuit than in the sexual event itself. He likes variety and plays to win. Challenge, conquest, and performance are his criteria. A woman who isn't "good in bed" is dropped without a second chance.

Female Jungle Fighters are no better. "I had a blind date

last night and went to bed with him and that's it, no more," a woman Jungle Fighter told me.

"You knew that fast?" I said, "Wasn't there anything about him you liked?"

"Oh, he was pleasant, and we had a nice time, but he didn't perform. If we don't connect sexually, I don't want to waste my time."

A Jungle Fighter may not perform very well, either. Anyone geared to win-lose outcomes will not be concerned with his or her partner's satisfaction.

Strategy:

It hinges on your initial decision not to accept more abuse.

- *Ask yourself, "What's my payoff?"* And make sure you give an honest answer. Your reward or trade-off had better be a powerful one, because your ultimate fate may be rejection.
- *Stop rewarding abusive behavior.* If your Jungle Fighter partner is abusive, stop making love until he or she changes and takes you seriously. This isn't sexual blackmail. It's an option—one that, in many cases, stops abusive behavior.
- *Don't take abuse in public, either.* If your partner consistently embarrasses you, take your own car to the party or restaurant so that you can leave if you have to. Or call a taxi. Or ask a friend to drive you home.
- *Make an appointment out of the bedroom and name the agenda.* "I want to discuss how we talk to each other in public."
- *Be firm.* Don't be compromised by your fear of retaliation.
- *Follow through.* When you announce, "I won't be going to the party with you Saturday"—don't go!

Silhouettes

They give you little. Little time, little affection, little consideration, no clues to their desires, and no indication of whether they are pleased. They are rigid, mechanistic, and without spontaneity. Sex is a task to accomplish; it should be accomplished with the utmost efficiency—that's the Silhouette's approach. There is a minimum of tenderness during intercourse, and none otherwise.

Creative Silhouettes can be exciting telephone lovers. They can tease and play, send funny cards and intrigue you with their presentation. But when they're with you, they're rarely, if ever, as loving or tender. "What do you mean, I'm not tender?" the Silhouette says as he unpacks his suitcase instead of holding you in a long-awaited embrace.

Never embrace Silhouettes in public; they don't like public demonstrations. Remember that they hide everything, including their feelings. Consider the aggressive Silhouette who could be loving and tender only when she was stoned. It drove her dependent Soother mate to distraction. "Look," he told her one day, "when you're stoned and we make love, I never know whether I'm experiencing you or the drugs. So when we make love, can it be without liquor or marijuana?"

"You look," she replied. "The only time I'm able to release my feelings is when I'm stoned. You'll have to take it that way or not at all." Because he was terrified of being alone, he accepted the Silhouette's terms.

Capitulation was not his only option—nor is it yours if you're dealing with a Silhouette.

Strategy:

- *Pay attention to how you respond to your Silhouette partner's responses in other situations.*
- *Pay attention to yourself.* If you're coming on too strongly in other situations, your Silhouette mate may not be able to let down his or her guard in a romantic situation.
- *Don't accept blame that isn't yours.* Don't think that the Silhouette is failing to respond because of something wrong with you.
- *Pay attention to your partner.* Ask, "How can I help you feel more comfortable?" But make him or her contribute to the solution, rather than making the entire effort yourself.
- *Take the initiative.* Create a romantic environment. Invite your partner to share it. Be willing to ask for what you want. Ask, lightly, "What are you going to buy for Valentine's Day?" Tell your Silhouette it means something to you to be remembered. Give suggestions—and, above all, recognition.
- *Tap into your support network—your web.* If you're not getting

the affection you need from your Silhouette, spend time with friends and family.

- *Do a cost-benefit analysis.* Ask yourself what benefits there are in living by yourself when you live with a Silhouette. If the costs exceed the benefits, look for other options.

Big Daddies and Big Mammas

They may seem, for a time, like conscientious lovers, but the moment you begin to show some independence they become calculating and unsympathetic. In sex, love, and romance, as in any other endeavor, they want partners they can mentor. Big Daddies who marry much younger women do so in the expectation that they will teach and lead them. But they rarely marry for long. Most little girls, after all, do finally grow up to be women. Conversely, most "little boys" do grow up to be men, at which point they may leave their Big Mamma wives.

A relationship with a Big Daddy or Big Mamma can be extremely loving, with a lot of touching and feeling and stroking, as well as attention to your needs. After a while you begin to suspect that you're involved with a parent, not a lover. "I think you may be too tired tonight," or "It may not be comfortable for you to do this," or "I don't think this would be good for you." Sometimes you feel as though you'd like the Big Daddy or Big Mamma to remove their arms from around you, because they're crushing you to death.

Strategy:

- *Pay attention to yourself.* Ask what you're doing to create the dependency you so resent. If you want your lover to stop being your Big Daddy, you should first stop being his little girl. The same goes for little boys married to Big Mammas. As you become more adult, your partner can be freer to express the child in him or her. Play together.
- *Become an active partner.* Don't wait for invitations; issue them yourself. Create your own romantic environment.

If you find that your relationship is fulfilling on multiple levels but that you live like loving roommates—renegotiate. If you choose a secondary relationship, set ground rules based on respect.

Negotiate for discussions outside the bedroom (parity, shifting roles, growing up or growing young).

Soothers

They display enormous amounts of affection, but how genuine is it? They put on a great performance to satisfy your needs and ignore their own—on the surface. Inside, Soothers often seethe with anger. One way they get even is to use the oldest negotiating tactic of all: "I have a headache . . . I'm tired . . . I'm depressed." Eventually, their partners recognize that they're living with good and kind and loving persons who no longer turn them on.

Because Soothers are so obliging, they have a difficult time saying "no." They say "yes" in order to be liked. "If I were a woman, I'd be pregnant every ten months," a male Soother once told me. Women Soothers, in particular, find themselves in fast and frequent sexual relationships. They rationalize their behavior by telling themselves that they don't want to hurt the other person. But they often get hurt themselves. There's no phone call the next day, and so the affair goes nowhere because many Soothers are reluctant to assert themselves by calling the other person to say, "I had a nice time. I'd like to see you again."

Passive negotiators wait for others to create a romantic environment for them. Many Soothers are attracted to Jungle Fighters, whose flare and pizzazz are magnets for the needy. The Soothers' lack of self-love pulls them toward debilitating relationships. They expect love and romance and find only sex, but they proceed anyway, hoping it will convert to the other two. Passive negotiators will sell out anything in the hope that a love that has died can be resurrected. They recognize only the hopes they've invested in another person, not the reality of that person.

How can anyone degrade himself or herself to such an extent? If you're a stylist who's frightened of loss, you will hang on to what you have, be unwilling to make trade-offs with

yourself, dip below your bottom line, eliminate options and opt for the status quo—anything to alleviate your disaster fantasies.
Strategy:

- *Be specific.* Ask your Soother partner for exactly what you want. "I want you to be ardent . . . passionate . . . slow . . . fast . . ."
- *Be prepared for a lack of follow through.* Persist until you get satisfaction, or look to your other options.
- *Monitor your style.* Do you assume the dominant role, thereby perpetuating your partner's dependency and passivity? Are you too aggressive? Consuming? Demanding?

Ask your partner what you could do, and in what kind of way, that would make him or her feel it was safe to respond.

Use small talk and verbal probes to find out what your partner likes.

Do a cost-benefit analysis regarding your rewards for staying with the Soother. Set a time line for creating a "profitable" relationship.

If you have both been Soothers, explore together—massages, porno films, discussion groups.

Win-Win Negotiators

It's in negotiating for sex, love, and romance that Win-Win Negotiators most often ask the question that distinguishes them most sharply from win-lose negotiators: "How much will the loss affect the other person?" Two young people were wrestling with the classic problem of career versus marriage. The young woman, a Win-Win Negotiator, wanted to go to medical school. Her lover, a Dictator, was against it. "If you love me," he said, "you won't go." The Win-Win Negotiator thought about that for a few minutes. "You know, you're right," she said. "The husband of a doctor would lead a very difficult life. You'd feel cheated by the amount of time I couldn't give you. I love you enough to let you go."

As lovers, Win-Win Negotiators are spontaneous, responsive, and open. As romancers, they're not afraid to make their desires known. They know how to create a romantic environment. They encourage you to share. Women, in particular, will say, "Dinner was on you last time. I had a wonderful evening. Next time I cook." Or else they'll invite the man out to dinner at their expense. Knowing that this can be a sensitive point for some men, they'll arrange in advance to be given the bill.

Win-Win Negotiators show their appreciation. A card, a telegram, a phone call, or flowers follow in the aftermath of an enjoyable evening, and keep romance alive.

Strategy: No great strategies needed here.

- *Be forthcoming.* Tell them what you want.
- *Attend.* Listen to what they want.

Negotiating for Conversation

Many men aren't aware of how to negotiate for sex because they don't understand that, for most women, the trade-off for sex is talk. This point has been validated over and over again by Sharon Goldsmith, codirector of Seminars on Sexuality, a Los Angeles–based sexual reeducation group. Numbers of male bedroom negotiators lose because they haven't attended to the opening ceremonies and warm-ups that should have been conducted before they reached the bedroom.

But it's not just males. Women absorbed in careers are often just as forgetful of the need for conversation as a prelude to sex.

If you find that your partner has time for sex but none for talk and you want both, negotiate.

- *Address the issue.* "It's difficult for me to be loving when I'm angry, and I'm angry because we don't have time to talk."
- *State what you want.* "I want the first forty-five minutes alone with you when you come home from work."
- *Make a trade-off.* Accept your partner's counteroffer to give you part of that forty-five minutes to hear what you have to say and the rest for his or her concerns.
- *Follow through.* If you've asked for talking time, don't schedule something else. Be there, and willing to talk.

Once you're talking freely together, you can try this sexual Icebreaker.

Step One: "Tell me three things that you most like that I do with you." Ask your partner to be specific— not "I like the way you touch me," but when, where, and how. Reverse the question and ask: "What three things do you most like to do with me?" Again, ask for specifics. Discuss his answers.

Step Two: Ask, then, "What is one thing I do with you that you don't like?" Reverse the question: "What is one thing you do that you do not like doing?" Ask for specifics and discuss.

Step Three: "What was the most exciting or satisfying experience for you we have recently had?"

Step Four: "What was the least exciting or satisfying for you?"

Step Five: "What is the one thing that you would like me most to change?" Again, ask for specifics and discuss.

This adapted Icebreaker is meant to get the other person talking with you about your sexual needs, desires, and problems. It's important to continue the dialogue once started.

Negotiating for Better Sex

What follows applies particularly to relationships with nontouching Dictators and Silhouettes, but the principles are valid for all styles.

1. ADDRESS THE ISSUE. Say, "We only touch when we make love. I would like you to touch me at other times, too, to hold me and nothing else."

2. BE WILLING TO DEMONSTRATE FIRST. Do to your partner what you want your partner to do to you; then ask him or her to do it back. Then ask for it back. Avoid indirect messages, such as leaving the massage book on the dresser. Better to demonstrate how nice it can be. If you still don't get a turn, do a mid-course correction. Ask, "What are you willing to give me?" If the answer is, "What more do you want?" be prepared to answer; your partner may not have known. And then demonstrate, be it hand or foot or face massage, or whatever. Many nontouchers don't practice and thus don't have the skills. The next day, follow through; move to a neutral zone—not the bedroom—and renegotiate your wants.

3. MAKE TRADE-OFFS. Trade-offs are easy if you communicate openly and understand that you don't always have to perform, but you can participate:

"You want to make love, I want a back rub—let's negotiate. I'll be willing to go along with what you want but as a trade-off, I'd like a back rub."

4. INFORM YOURSELF. Find creative options for pleasuring one another. Then demonstrate them on or discuss them with your partner. And don't be so grim and serious and by-the-book about it. Sex and humor are soul mates:

"The latest research shows sex helps strengthen the heart muscle."

"You always consider sex a joke. Make me laugh!"

"How can I convince you to spend three hours behind locked doors with me? Haven't you ever been curious about what happens to a prisoner of love?"

5. ATTEND AND OBSERVE. Is it that your partner can't touch people, but can touch objects or pets that don't threaten him or her? Some people just aren't touchers; if your mate isn't, you knew this going into the relationship. If it's developed since your courtship, when did it start? What happened? Is there a hidden agenda? Listen for your partner's bedroom anger. Address the issue: "Are you angry? What do you really want—holding, touching, time?"

6. DO A COST-BENEFIT ANALYSIS. You're not being touched the way you want to be. There are no romantic opening ceremonies, or tender closing ones. Against those costs, balance the benefits. Security? Proximity to power? Freedom from decisions? If those are benefits to you, they may outweigh the costs. If they don't, explore other options and develop a contingency plan. You've made a good try at reaching agreement; it may be time to move on.

Sweetening Your Offer

To get another person to cooperate with you, you have to provide a payoff. If you aren't aware of the rewards that turn your partner on, you can't expect collaboration. I call these rewards "reinforcers."

One way to identify your partner's reinforcer is to ask. "What delights you?" You'll get a straight answer from a Win-Win Negotiator. You'll get assorted curve balls from the other stylists. You'll get a balk from a Silhouette.

Negotiating for Time Together

If your partner refuses to give you time, attend and observe. What happens when you spend time together? Is it fun and pleasant, or tense and hostile? Try to emphasize those ingredients that are present when the time together is joyful.

If both of you want to spend more time together, explore your options:

Do time pies (Carve your day into slices proportionate to the amount of time you spend on each activity), and compare them.

Evaluate what each of you is willing to give up in order to make time for one another.

Identify your priorities and shift the minor ones.

Plan a weekend to be off by yourselves and devoted exclusively to one another. Take turns making the arrangements. Better yet, make it a surprise. "Kidnap" your spouse or live-in. One Friday morning, a woman I know casually suggested to her husband, "Let me pick you up at the office after work. I want to show you a gift I'm thinking of buying you for your birthday." That afternoon, by prearrangement, their children went to her parents, she packed two suitcases, picked up her husband, and to his utter astonishment, drove him to the airport, where they boarded a plane for Lake Tahoe, his favorite gambling spa and her favorite retreat. En route, she handed him an envelope with his "gambling money." The following Monday, she could hardly wait to call me. "It was," she said, "a win-win weekend."

Now let's consider what to do when you've asked for partner time and you don't receive it.

- *Attend and observe.* When was the last time you received it? Was it in public or private? If public, it was probably for show, and you may be involved with a Dictator.
- *Check your hidden agenda.* Is what you asked for what you wanted? Did you ask for attention when you really wanted touching? Did you ask for time without asking for attention?
- *Be specific.* Offer a program: "I want to spend one night alone with you in a fabulous hotel."

If your partner says he's busy, ask when he's free during the next month. If he's not free at all, it's possible that he's really too busy. It's just as possible that you're with the wrong partner. It's time to negotiate with yourself to stay, leave, or modify.

"No" in the Evening. "No" in the Morning

You've just finished dressing for work—and your partner wants to have sex.

You're ready to retire after an exhausting day—and your partner wants to have sex.

How do you say "no" without injuring feelings and impairing the prospect of future invitations?

Offer options:

"Let's plan to get up earlier."

"Let's plan to go to bed earlier."

"Let's plan a day just for sex."

Or how about this solution from a Win-Winner:

"I'm a morning person. I think best and feel best and even make love best in the morning. But my wife's a night person. My wife make love in the morning? Never. Me make love at night? Hardly ever. What did we do? We negotiated for high noon."

The Night That Failed— and How to Cope

Suppose your lover makes promises, promises of "tonight's the night." You prepare dinner and anticipate an evening of intimacy. Your agenda blows up as your partner, sated by your gourmet meal, falls asleep on the couch. Negotiate! Pay attention to timing. Enjoy each other first, dinner second. If your partner protests that he's hungry, be prepared (you know his style). Have champagne, Perrier, cheese and crackers in a tray next to the bed.

When the Sex Isn't Good

If you've found your lovemaking has become mere mechanics and you are treated like a service station, plan an evening together of only touching and holding. Consider it a negotiating tune-up.

If you want to explore a new technique and your partner doesn't, proceed in small steps and avoid any critical whammies. If your partner tries and doesn't like it, you have to accept that. Negotiate for a substitute action.

If your partner happens to be a Silhouette/Dictator, and he stands firm in his refusal to explore, pause. Recognize your own style. Have you been making excuses for his age, pressures, stress, and fatigue? Monitor your own Big Mamma tendencies, and your possible lack of willingness to satisfy your own needs.

Acknowledge your partner's nontalking style by using nonverbal gestures. Instead of putting the latest sex manual next to the bed, be playful.

Sexual rejection is not a typical response. Before you assume a relationship is over, collect your data. Is the rejection temporary? Situational? Who stopped what and when? Reflect upon your own patterns.

In interpreting the data, you're in a position to make some choices: to stay, leave, or modify. You can stay if the rejection is a temporary problem due to nonsexual circumstances. Don't make assumptions or leave without reflection. Test out your feelings by observing the other person and then talking about the problem. Discussion should be simple and nonaccusatory. Use probes to find out what's really happening. For instance:

"I care about you and this relationship. I feel it's not working. How can *we* make it work?"

Set a private time line to see if your partner's behavior changes. Calculate your R.O.I. If you're willing to make the investment, hang in there. But not forever.

When Your Partner Cuts Off from the World

We all have periods when we prefer to be unsocial. Frequently, we neglect to consider that, in opting for solitude, we're isolating our partner as well. The condition is magnified a hundredfold when our partner is a Silhouette.

He'll beg off from social contacts on the excuse that he's got work to do. He probably has a hidden agenda, to protect himself against the embarrassment of not having anything to say to others. The overt message is: "I don't like people." The hidden message is: "Small talk is difficult for me, and I can't compete with a dazzling partner." Make no mistake, the fear is a real one. He may have no friends outside his business pursuits and be unable to talk about anything but business.

Here's one way to break the impasse:

YOU: I understand it's important to you to be alone. It's equally important to me to have friends over. We can divide our week up: for three days of the week we'll be alone, doing whatever each of us wants to do. On three days we can have friends in. On the seventh day, we'll be with one another, doing things together. Let's try it.

If your partner is agreeable, it's critical that you follow the ground rules of the agreement. Don't invite friends in or encourage drop-ins on the days you have agreed not to. Don't plan to be away when friends drop in. Avoid negative hehavior.

Negotiating for Private Time

Very often, one partner drops everything in his or her life in behalf of the other person. How do you find that in-between area, in which you support your partner but still have private time for friends and favorite pursuits?

- *Do a "time pie"*. Find out exactly how much of your day or week or month is given to the support of your partner, and how much is left for you.
- *Evaluate the result.* Come up with some options. Dig into your dreams. Ask yourself, "What would I like to be doing?"
- *Draw a "fantasy pie"*. Give a slice to each of the activities that aren't presently part of your life, and larger slices to those activities that are presently undernourished.
- *Make your trade-offs.* Many of them will be within yourself. Some will be with your partner or family.

Gladys is a young manufacturer's representative at the top of her field. She has one young daughter by her first husband. Recently, she remarried. Her new husband has a son and daughter by his first wife; both children seem to need more attention than Gladys' own daughter. The moment she enters the house, she is barraged with questions and complaints. Gladys needs to negotiate with her family for thirty minutes of "alone" time when she comes home from work, and she needs to do so promptly, before she begins to resent their presence, particularly the presence of her newest family members. In our seminar, Gladys has learned about the importance of timing; she picks a time when emotions will be subdued— immediately after dinner. She invites everyone to a neutral setting, the living room.

> GLADYS (*addressing the issue*): I'm feeling overwhelmed when I come home each night. I understand (*acknowledging the others' point of view*) that you all need my time and attention, and I'm willing to give it to you. But I need thirty minutes in my bedroom alone, and then I'll be ready to be with you.
> PAUL, *Gladys' husband:* There's no need for you to work at all.
> GLADYS (*recognizing Paul's hidden agenda*): I'm willing to discuss your feelings about my work when we're alone, but that's not the issue right now. The issue is whether I can have "private time" when I come home each evening. If we continue this way, I won't be much use to anyone.

I intend to take that time (*clear statement of desire and intent*), but I will make all of you this offer. If you don't see any improvement in my behavior in three weeks, I'll renegotiate.

Because she chose her time with care, stated the problem clearly, offered a plan, allowed time for the plan to work, remained open to negotiation, and refused to be diverted from the main issue, Gladys gained her private time.

The Case of the Suffocated Husband and the Overdependent Wife

A Soother/Silhouette came into one of my negotiating seminars with a problem that should ring some bells, because it's one that almost all of us confront. He wanted, and desperately needed, time for himself. For twenty-seven years, he'd been married to a Soother/Big Mamma who believed that sharing life together meant living in one another's skins. She wanted to be with her husband at every possible moment—eating, drinking, sleeping, working. At the slightest suggestion from him that he wanted to be by himself, she became ill with a variety of ailments ranging from backaches to sinusitis.

The husband was a simple man. All he wanted was a Saturday morning on which to work on his book, in a place where he didn't have to interact with another human being. Not once in their marriage, however, had his wife granted him such time. She was a completely dependent woman who read into any separation the prospect of abandonment.

At last there came that moment when the husband said to himself, "Enough!" He picked a quiet time when his wife was in good health, no crisis was looming, and they'd just enjoyed some time together. "I'm planning to take Saturday mornings to work on my book," he began. (Note that he announced his plan; he didn't ask her permission.) "This is something I need to do."

"Well, why can't I be with you?" his wife asked.

"Because on Saturday mornings I need to be by myself."

At that point, his wife began to cry. But the husband did not get detoured. He stuck to the issue. "I understand that this is going to be a change for you, but we need to do some things separately. What are some things *you* would like to do alone?"

"I don't like to do anything alone. I just want to be with you. Why can't we just be together?"

Rather than answer her question and risk the prospect of being sidetracked, the husband stuck to the issue once more. "I understand that it's important for you to be with me. I'm prepared to make a trade-off. On Saturdays, I'll work on my book by myself. On Sundays, we'll be together the entire day."

The woman frowned. "But we're already together on Sundays."

"And we have a miserable time. I become angry, and I withdraw. What I'm promising is that we'll really be together. I won't be angry, and we'll enjoy each other."

Which is just how it worked out.

When You've Been Away from the Dating Game

You've just dissolved a traditional marriage after fifteen years, and you'd like some new relationships. But you're unnerved by the pace of the new dating game. No one said "My place or yours?" on the first date in the old days. Don't panic. Take heart from the experience of one of my seminar clients, who learned how to negotiate with a Jungle Fighter. After their first dinner together, he asked her to spend the night with him. She refused.

"I bought dinner," he said. "Do you mean you're not going to bed with me?"

"Look," she said. "Let's negotiate. I feel sex is fun. You may also be fun. Let's have dinner again and see how we enjoy ourselves. I'll treat. If it works, I'll *make* dinner the next time, and you can bring the wine."

They did see each other again, and when the relationship became intimate it was on her terms as well as his.

Negotiating with a "Dazzler"

You like this person. He or she is charming and interesting and fun. What you don't like is that these attributes are focused too much on others, and not enough on you. At parties, he or she plays to an audience. In restaurants, attention is given to waiters and people at adjoining tables. This isn't a new agenda; it's been discussed several times before. This time you're determined to come to terms with the problem.

1. Write a script that reflects your disappointment but doesn't begin with your bottom line.
2. Do a warm-up: "I know you like to mix with people. Tonight, I'd like the attention."
3. Arrange a quiet setting. Don't sabotage the encounter by going to a favorite haunt where you'll surely meet friends and every waiter will slap your partner's back.
4. Prepare a contingency plan in the event that your dazzler fails to focus on you. Suppose you're to have dinner out. Tell the dazzler that you'd prefer to meet at the restaurant. That way, you'll have your own car, and can leave when you wish.
5. Address the issue. If the dazzler does his number, say, "I don't enjoy going to dinner with four other strangers. I'd like to spend it with you. If you aren't able to share the evening, let's make a date for another time."
6. Have your bottom line ready, and don't wait too long to invoke it. Leave.

There's one other special stratagem, which I call Carr's Theory of Role Appropriation, after a special friend, but you have to have the dramatic flair to carry it off. Instead of—or in addition to—asking for attention from the dazzler, *you* be the dazzler. *You* play to the audience. Your dazzler partner will become so confused he'll not only never take you for granted again, you'll be the audience he'll play to.

Endings

You can't negotiate successfully with someone about whom you're indifferent. If yours is a relationship of convenience or a long marriage that lost its verve years ago, you may not care that much about striking an equitable bargain. It's when you love, admire, value, or respect the other person that you can negotiate successfully for sex, love, and romance, because then, and only then, does the other person have something that you want—himself or herself. It is a respect for the other's uniqueness that allows for a collaboration.

On the other hand, when you're committed to the relationship and the other person isn't, you can't negotiate a win-win outcome, either. You'll give more than your share; you'll have fewer options to play with, you'll be dealing with an empty bucket.

The time does come when having made a hundred percent effort to negotiate, both with yourself and the other person, you just can't reach agreement. That's the point at which you want to have the self-confidence to say, "This relationship must end." Not all personal problems are soluble, not even by the most competent Win-Win Negotiators. And points are no longer rewarded by society for self-styled martyrs who seek to gain esteem by "putting up with a lot."

An ending needn't be tragic. Two people discover they may not be meant for one another after all. A win-win attitude in such an instance can ease a couple through their transition to independence and help them find an acceptable new level on which to relate.

Here is how two people who have developed doubts about their relationship can negotiate a "win-win" separation:

> WOMAN: We've spent a lot of time with each other. I care for you a great deal. But right now, I need to be alone. I want to see you, but I don't want to live with you.
> MAN: I'm not happy with your decision but I can understand your need to be alone. I care about you. I don't want to lose contact with you.

Together, they negotiate the ground rules:

> To see one another when they both feel like it.
> To avoid questioning one another about others they are seeing.
> To maintain regular contact by phone.

Negotiating for sex, love, and romance is possible only when both partners are willing to trust. You know you have a relationship of trust when sex, love, and romance have become so blended they are indivisible.

Negotiating with Your Family

However restrained we may be with our emotions in other areas of life, most of us perceive the family arena as the one in which we can really let go. Where office conflicts usually focus on issues, family conflicts, by and large, get mired in feelings. They are much more threatening to our sense of emotional security. The intensity derives from the fact that family members exist in the same space and know one another intimately. They identify one another's "hot buttons," and know when and where to push them.

Today the major issues in the family revolve around questions of equity or fairness. As families increasingly have two wage earners, the problems of dividing up and sharing responsibilities and tasks comes in for major attention. Added on to this new constellation of issues are the old conflicts over power and control. Who will have the power? Who will control whom? As with everything else, the answers to these questions are radically different from what they were just a generation ago. Then, it was the father who generally held and exercised the power. Today, power is much more evenly distributed, in many cases, among all members of the family.

And the children! What forces they are exposed to before they reach their teens! It is not simply a widespread permissiveness that makes them precociously aware of sex. It is a sense

236

of expectations about society that translates into premature experimentation, raising all sorts of questions about the duration and extent of the authority that parents once took for granted in their relationships with their children. How can a mother negotiate with her fourteen-year-old daughter to be in the house at 10 P.M. each night, when six months earlier she put her on the pill? What can parents teach about moderation to children who are already taking drugs?

Changing roles and rules have created confusion among parents and children both as to who really holds the power. In many cases, confusion has turned to resentment and resentment to scapegoating, with children the targets of the parents' frustrations.

If conflict is inevitable, it's also normal and healthy—or can be, provided the persons in conflict have the tools with which to negotiate their differences. The sad reality is that the tools are employed least in the arena in which they're most needed. Not only tools, but the attitude or orientation that makes satisfying, enduring agreements possible.

Parenting Styles

In the home, as elsewhere, negotiation techniques are founded on an appreciation of the styles of the people involved. You've seen throughout how complex styles can be—how office Dictators can be household Soothers, and so forth. So bear in mind that whatever style family members assume with one another, the capacities to express styles they use in other arenas are always there.

Jungle Fighter parents are a good example.

All Jungle Fighters at work aren't Jungle Fighter parents. But if the strain exists, there is a tendency even in the home to threaten, intimidate, or punish in order to obtain the kind of behavior they want. As much as they may love their children, they do have a tendency to ridicule—"Dummy, can't you do anything right?"—until such rhetorical questions become self-fulfilling.

"The unfortunate thing with such child rearing techniques," says Dr. Ron Mann, "is that the parents do not realize the damage they are doing. They often only see the desired goal, i.e., higher grades, better manners, or more swimming trophies. The love, support and joy that could permeate the family environment is overshadowed by the demands and pressures for performance."

The best defense against Jungle Fighters is not to be intimidated by their bullying, as we've previously noted, but that can be very tough for a child to do with a parent. If you're a child in such a predicament, seek an ally in your non-Jungle Fighter parent. If you're that parent, support your child.

DICTATORS: They're often more imperious in the home than anywhere else. The idea of putting up with anything from children is one they often can't support. They frequently make decisions without including the children, however much the decisions affect the children's lives. If this situation is allowed to continue, the children *can* grow up believing that that there's no way they can control their own lives.

But even Dictator parents can be handled. When you deal with them, it's generally a good idea to begin with a probe. "What are your ideas about my going away to college next year?" You can be sure that the Dictator has some; he or she has probably already picked out the college. The next step is to prepare your own case in support of what you want. The research must be extensive, and the logic overwhelming. Your argument should be made without a drop of emotion. The argument itself should be delivered at a scheduled time, when you're certain you have the Dictator's attention. Preferably, the appointment should take place outside the home, so that the Dictator can't hide behind a book or a newspaper, or beg off because of a television program. Give your parent an idea of the agenda at the time you make your appointment; if, on the other hand, he or she might use the information as a means of blocking you off, try not to reveal the agenda. Simply say, "It's about a matter that's important to me." When you make your presentation, don't bother with opening ceremonies. Be direct. Stress the advantage to the Dictator of your idea. If the answer is no, don't give up; try again when his or her mood is better.

If you're so intimidated by the Dictator that you can't make an effective case, use an intermediary.

SILHOUETTES: The boy was fourteen, quiet, thoughtful, tender, vulnerable, and yet extraordinarily articulate. His mother was dead. His father, a Silhouette, had never remarried. Well, yes, he had. With his wife gone, he'd committed himself totally to his first love, his research in oceanography. When his son asked for time, Dad always said, "Tomorrow." But tomorrow never came. The boy esteemed his father, nonetheless. He recognized his brilliance—"worshipped" is a better word. He wanted only one thing in life, recognition from his father. But none of the elaborate hints he offered—the excursions he dreamed up, the attempts to interest his father in the local teams, the requests for help on his homework—seemed to do the trick. In desperation, the boy sent his father a tape recording in which he set forth his feelings of loneliness and need and love. If his father ever listened to the tape, the boy never knew; his father never acknowledged receipt of it.

Why do Silhouettes have children when all they want is to be left alone?

BIG DADDIES AND MAMMAS: Compared to Jungle Fighters, Dictators, and Silhouettes, Big Daddies and Mammas would appear to be much better parents. At least they are solicitous and caring; at least they offer attention; at least their manner of parenting does not scare their children half to death.

And yet, Big Daddies and Mammas are often much more difficult to deal with. Their concern may be more purposeful than heartfelt, and their manner of control may be much more insidious and wearing.

The advice proffered by Big Daddies and Mammas usually comes in the form of a talk dedicated to the child's welfare. With voices full of warmth and tenderness, they remind children what to do and how to do it and when to do it. They will coax rather than coerce, using a lot of "You should's . . ." or "I know you will want to's. . . ."

But they, too, can be dealt with. Firmness with affection is the rule. Watch what happens when it's applied.

One young woman was asked by her Big Daddy/Big Mamma parents to suggest a present she'd like to receive for her graduation from high school. "I'd like a car," she replied.

"Not an expensive car. Just a beat-up jalopy." Instead of a car, the parents bought her an expensive set of luggage. "I'll never use this luggage," the daughter said. "My life-style's much too laid-back." But she didn't end it there. She said, "I intend to return the luggage and apply the money toward a car." Which she did.

SOOTHERS: They need their children's love and will do anything to get it, nurture it, and hang on to it. A Soother mother dealing with a misbehaving child will defer the matter until Father comes home. Then Father must play the role of punisher.

Soother parents will promise everything to children and then deliver nothing. They know why they make such promises—to gain and hold affection. Some Soothers resent having to make them; "forgetting" to deliver is their way of getting even.

Rather than rely on a Soother parent who promises to do something for you, do it yourself.

Be specific. "I would like to meet you at four o'clock under the clock at the Biltmore. I would appreciate your being on time." For good emphasis, add, "If at three o'clock it looks like you're running late, please call me." Many Soothers will express their anger by being late; unless you're this specific, you can expect to be kept waiting.

Deal with one issue at a time. Even if your Soother parent volunteers to perform several tasks for you, confine him or her to one.

Summarize conclusions after all discussions. Point up the items the Soother parent has agreed to be responsible for and those you've agreed to handle together. Or ask the Soother to summarize his or her understanding of your discussion.

Offer specific options. "Dad, you said you'd get me some new soccer shoes. I've got a game on Saturday. I can meet you at your office after school, or go get them myself."

WIN-WIN NEGOTIATORS: They aren't perfect parents. They do become angry at times. They do argue. They aren't always right. Which only means they're human. But any child raised by Win-Win Negotiators is very lucky. Win-Win parents are firm, but also kind. They are acute and reflective listeners, attested to by the thoughtful questions your own statements provoke. They will encourage you to deal innovatively with problems and to try out many options. They will encourage you to work toward your own goal rather than impose goals on you.

Here's a perfect example of a win-win negotiation with children:

Lettie Campos is a single parent with a limited education who turned a few thousand dollars of inherited money into a means of support for her children. Because her work as a caterer took her away from home each day, she gave each of her children money as they requested it. Then, one day, she calculated how much she'd been giving them—and promptly called a family conference. "I added up how much money we've been spending for movies and pizzas and so forth, and it comes to two hundred dollars a month."

"Wow!" the children chorused.

"I just want to ask you one question: Are you getting your money's worth?"

"No!"

Then began a concerted effort by all members of the family to establish a reasonable budget and to determine how the money should be spent. It was the children, more than Lettie, who came up with the most creative ideas. One of them proposed that they give up eating in restaurants. At first Lettie rejected that idea entirely because of the extra demands on her time. "I'm not willing to do that additional cooking, too," she said. But the children, between them, volunteered to prepare dinner and do the cleanup three times a week. In this manner, they cut the family food bill by 35 percent.

The fallout from Lettie's first discussion of the problem with her children was serendipitous. The family joined the neighborhood "Y" and partook of dozens of free activities. Instead of buying all their books, they made greater use of the neighborhood library. When it came to entertainment, they voted for quality over quantity, electing to save their money for orchestra seats to *Annie,* rather than spending it on a series of inferior movies.

Lettie Campos is a Win-Win Negotiator, perhaps the most consummate one I have ever known. She paid attention to her feelings when she was overwhelmed by her children's money demands, she laid out the problem for their consideration, she listened attentively to their options, she agreed to experiment— and won a bounty in the process.

Money and the Family

It may be extremely difficult for men to fathom what's involved emotionally for women who want to move from a position of dependence to one of equality or independence. Perhaps the dilemma of one of my clients will help. She was a woman in her early sixties who had been married for forty years. She came to see me in a state of high emotional distress because, after all these years, she was on the verge of leaving her husband. It was obvious that she preferred not to do that, but just as obvious that she could not remain with him in their present state. "What would make it possible for you to stay in that relationship?" I asked her.

"I need to become independent," she said.

"In what ways do you feel you're not independent now?"

"Well, for one thing, I have a job, but I give my husband my paycheck."

Not only did the woman give all of her earnings to her husband, she did not know how much money they had, or where he kept their money—half of which was legally hers. They did not even have a joint checking account. Although she earned an excellent salary, she was totally dependent on her husband for her needs. He was a Dictator, very charming and generous when he wanted to be, but he needed above all to maintain control over his wife. So he would dole out money to her, $20 at a time.

To a certain extent, the problems are rooted in the traditional unwillingness of men to share control in this most primary area. But to suggest that this is the sole cause is much too easy. Women share the blame with men for failing to inform themselves sufficiently.

Money conveys hidden messages between parents and

children as often as it does between husband and wife. Jungle Fighters, Dictators, and Silhouettes, in particular, often use money as a substitute for time with their children, because they are driven to give time to their work. But money given in lieu of attention and affection may wind up buying little but grief, because the children are rarely deceived. One sixteen-year-old I know, the son of a wealthy attorney, cracked up an expensive sports car his Dictator father had given him. The father bought him a new car. A month later, the boy cracked that one up, too. A third car, a third crackup. "If you want your son to kill himself," I told the father, "then give him the fourth car."

"Are you trying to tell me that I'm the cause of these accidents?" the father said incredulously.

"Three crackups in a row ought to tell you something. Your son doesn't want your gifts. He's trying to get your attention."

Career vs. Marriage—How to Handle It

You're middle-aged, thrilled with life, overflowing with energy and enthusiasm. You've got a loving husband and daughter and an engrossing job. The single flaw in your existence is your husband's qualified support for your career. A benevolent Dictator, he has encouraged you to work so long as it doesn't interfere with your life together, and particularly with his own career. Thus far, you've avoided the issue, but now it must be confronted because there's a promotion pending for you that would mean more professional responsibility and less time for your family.

That, in short, is the challenge that faced Dottie, one of my seminar students. It is an all but classic description of the challenge facing thousands of women trying to combine career and marriage. Sometimes the problem is rooted in traditional notions about the responsibilities of men and women—i.e., men are in charge, and women care for the family. Sometimes, when extra schooling and an increased need for help are involved, it's simply a matter of money. Often it's a combination of the two—as it was in Dottie's case.

If you find yourself in Dottie's predicament, consider her strategy:

1. *Explore the options.* To find time for her classes, Dottie knew she would have to hire a housekeeper two days a week instead of one. To maintain their entertainment commitments, she knew she would have to enlist her husband, Roberto's help. She could also ask their daughter, Celia, a ten-year-old with the self-assurance of a Dictator and the efficiency of a Silhouette, to cook one evening a week.

2. *Look at the trade-offs.* Although money was tight, Dottie was willing to invest a portion of the family's savings toward her advancement and the extra income that would accrue (R.O.I.). She would entertain at home rather than in a restaurant. She would lose time with Celia, but make their time together count for more.

3. *Do a cost-benefit analysis.* Dottie's analysis confirmed that the increase in the family's economic base and in her own skills more than offset the discomfort that might be caused during the transition period.

4. *Recruit allies.* Dottie asked Celia if she would like to repeat the hot dogs–and–salad meal she had prepared for her tenth birthday party. Celia agreed to cook this and other meals once a week.

5. *Watch the timing.* Dottie called a family meeting for a time when all three of them were relaxed and no other activities were pressing.

6. *Do a warm-up.* Dottie told Roberto about her dissatisfaction with her present position, about the prospect of her promotion, about her feeling that the time was right for her. She also expressed her feeling that an expanded role in the family would make Celia feel more mature.

7. *Address the issue.* Briefly, clearly, and assertively, Dottie told Roberto what she wanted.

8. *Attend and observe.* Dottie watched Roberto sink into the couch, saw him squint, noted that the small muscle on his jawbone had begun to twitch. She listened to his counterarguments—Celia would be neglected, they would spend more money, his own life would suffer. She recorded her own shock at his attitude.

9. *Keep focused.* Despite her dismay, Dottie kept to the agenda: assistance and time to achieve her objectives.

10. *Be alert for hidden agendas.* "I count on your being here," Roberto said. That was the real issue.

11. *Try a contingency plan.* Said Dottie: "I can't advance without the additional training. I want the advancement. The first class begins Tuesday. I'm willing to take one class instead of the two I'd planned. Let's try it for a quarter, and see how it works. If it doesn't work, we'll make an adjustment."

Dottie took her class. Roberto was unwilling to hire a housekeeper for an extra day until he saw his own weekends being absorbed by domestic work. Eventually, he helped with the shopping and barbecued for their parties. Several months later, Dottie received her promotion—and a big increase in salary.

The Man Who Came to Spend the Night

Before the 1960's a woman who lived with a man out of wedlock was whispered about in society. Today, living together is so common that almost no one remarks it. Yet there are men and women—women, especially—who still hear echoes of the past. One woman I know, a mother of three children in her forties, insisted that her fifty-year-old lover leave at three o'clock each morning so that he wouldn't be there when the children awakened. The man was so distressed that he finally abandoned the relationship.

The presence of children compounds in still other ways the lives of persons trying to make new relationships. There is the problem of finding time to be alone. There is the problem of authority—children not wanting to be told what to do by other than a natural parent. There is the problem of emotions— the anger and resentment and bewilderment children feel in dealing with a surrogate parent. All of these problems impinge on the basic purpose of the relationship, the attempt by two people to find harmony together.

Let's consider how the man who was pushed from the house at three in the morning might have avoided going to his bottom line.

First, he could have inventoried his feelings. He knew that

he felt rejected and lonely after the warmth and intimacy of the night. He also knew that he had a tendency to let things ride; while he had hinted at his displeasure, he hadn't followed through.

Second, he could have considered what he knew about his lover's feelings. He knew she'd recently left a traditional marriage and wasn't comfortable with the present-day custom of "overnight dating." He knew she felt her relationship with him might add to her problems with the children. He knew she cared for him, in spite of the problems, and that, while she wouldn't respond to a "full thrust" ultimatum, she would negotiate.

Under those circumstances, here's the strategy he might have used:

1. Planned a negotiation on neutral turf—certainly not in her bedroom.
2. Acknowledged her concerns about her recent separation, "modern" dating, fear of the future, and the adjustment of her children not simply to the absence of their father but to the presence of a new man in the house.
3. Addressed the issue: "I resent being kicked out at three A.M."
4. Brainstormed together in order to develop options, but had options of his own to consider in case she hadn't any.

- He could have stayed over on nights the children were with their father, so that she could get used to his presence.
- She could have spent some nights at his place, in which case he would have paid for the sitter.
- They could have taken a weekend vacation together.
- He could have helped her develop and rehearse a script for negotiating with her children.

A man entering a relationship with a woman who's recently separated should anticipate a negotiation with the woman's comfort in mind, particularly if children are involved. It's a time when women are exceedingly vulnerable, and it calls for uncommon awareness on the part of their new partners. If it's the man who has the children and the woman who moves in, the responsibility shifts to the woman. When both partners have children, both must be sensitive to the children's developmental needs, confusion, and insecurities.

When Your Child Threatens to Drop Out

The teens are a time when many a child, even those who have previously been loving and gregarious, adopts the reclusiveness of Silhouettes. It may be weeks before you discover that your child has been ditching classes or has dropped out altogether.

Rapid action is vital. If your child is out of school too long, the academic problems he or she encounters on returning will only reinforce the initial dissatisfaction.

1. Pick a setting that's familiar and comfortable to both of you for a family conference.
2. Do a series of probes. Find out what he or she is unhappy about. Peer pressure? Academic pressure? Failed to make the team? Doesn't like the school?
3. Try to keep the dialogue going by signaling your availability. Don't invade his or her room; just walk by and make your presence known.
4. Don't threaten or command, like a Jungle Fighter. It won't get you anywhere.
5. Do set a time line. "It seems to me that if we can't come up with some options by Friday . . ."
6. Gather information from teachers, counselors, your child's trusted friends.
7. If you can't solve the problem yourself, call in outside help, just as business does when in a tough spot.

When Your Child Begins to Swear

You may laugh when your four-year-old suddenly erupts with some cuss words, but it's important to deal with the matter at once, and not encourage swearing at any age. Even if cursing doesn't offend you, it will offend others with whom your child associates.

1. Do your homework: Try to discover who the child's model is. It could be you!
2. Call a meeting. Make sure it's private, and that no friends are present. If other members of family are to be involved, do a warm-up with the child alone.
3. Watch your timing. It's impossible to communicate when your child is angry—or when you are.
4. Address the issue. Say, "I want to talk to you about the language you use. Let's talk about what you feel when you're swearing."
5. Listen for a hidden agenda. Swearing may be your child's way to get attention or evoke a response from a Silhouette parent.
6. Explore options—other ways to express anger, such as pounding pillows or clay, tearing paper, drawing; a "graffiti wall" on the inside of the closet door. Ask the child to suggest options.
7. Set up a monitoring system, particularly if you've been the model, with provisions for extra chores for whoever swears.

Negotiating with Small Children

Small children are powerful negotiators. What parent hasn't felt his or her resolve dissolving in the tears of a three-year-old? Men are particularly vulnerable in this regard. "Where's the negotiation with a three-year-old?" one of my male students observed. "Whatever he wants I give to him." What a mistaken attitude that is! The parent's task is to help the child develop into a mature, self-directed, responsible individual, not one interested solely in self-gratification.

This is not to suggest that the child's entreaties should be ignored. It's your job to find creative options that will satisfy both of you. Examples:

- Your children are upset that you're going out. Calm them with this offer: "I'll be going out some nights during the week. But each of you will also have a night with me alone. Think about things you would like to do." If at all possible, follow their suggestions.

- You find your weekend totally preempted by your children, and without creative focus. Give them this option: "I'll take Saturday for myself. But on Sunday, we'll be together the entire day, and do something special."

Small children can be eminently reasonable. The key is to include them in the decision. One client tells how she took her two visiting nephews, ages six and eight, to the supermarket and all but fainted from humiliation as they raced, screaming, through the aisles, pulling goods off the shelves. Later, she realized that her nephews might not know what she was doing in a supermarket; seeing her pick cans and boxes off the shelves, they thought they could do that, too. Before their next trip to the supermarket, she sat them down and asked them to help her plan their meals for the next few days. When they had finished the shopping list, she assigned articles to each of them. When they next went to the supermarket, each child took a shopping cart and silently and purposefully went on his appointed rounds. Each returned to the checkout counter fifteen minutes later, chest heaving with pride. "They couldn't have been happier," my client reported. "Did we ever celebrate!"

When You're the Referee

Every night is a battle royal between the two children whose chore it is to do the dishes. You've had it. Confront the issue and use a whammie.

"I don't want to listen to this every night. Either the two of you decide which jobs you're going to do and do them without all this fuss, or I'm going to be a dictator and tell you exactly what to do. Now, negotiate!"

Negotiating A Family Crisis

Grandmother's been seriously ill, and now Mother must go to care for her for the next month while she's convalescing. The rest of the family will have to assume responsibility for the household. How do you handle the situation without creating tension and anxiety?

1. Set a family meeting before Mother leaves, and at a normally tranquil time.
2. Set an agenda. Do warm-ups, so that the children will expect what's coming and be disposed to cooperate. Talk about the fact that life will be different.
3. Be brief and direct. "We won't have Mom around to do all the things she normally does—the cooking, the cleaning, the laundry, even the shopping. What can we do to help one another?" Brainstorm.
4. Identify times of day when tensions are high, and schedule activities that will disperse those tensions.
5. Attend. Respond to the children's concerns about how their lives will function. If children are apprehensive about being alone, set up a support system with neighbors and friends.
6. Apportion new responsibilities among family members.
7. Reserve any prospective argument with your spouse for private discussion and resolution, so that the family meeting will not lose its focus.

Bridging the Other Generation Gap

I have a win-win relationship with my mother. The reason is due, in no small part, to her fabulous sense of humor. "Hello, Doctor?" she'll say. "This is your mother. Is this Senior Citizen's Day?" Meaning, do I have time for her?

How many thousands, indeed, hundreds of thousands of middle-aged persons don't have time for their parents? How many elderly parents are spending their last years with bitterness as their only companion? In many respects, the lonely parents have only themselves to blame. They are paying for the years in which they ruled, rather than raised, their children. "My dad never listens to my point of view," one forty-year-old man laments. "He's always right. Nothing I do pleases him, so I tell him nothing about my life." Or, the son of a Silhouette: "My father never talked to me. Now, I don't know what to say to him."

What I consistently tell parents who wish to become part of their children's lives is this: *Address the issue—and without blame.* The important issue is not the twenty years of missed opportunities. It's *now*. Accept at least part of the responsibility for whatever frictions developed between you. Ask: How can I become a part of your life?

If you're an elderly parent, you have power to trade off. You not only know your child's likes and dislikes, you know how to deal with all the daily administrivia that gums up his or her life. Make an offer of specific help. Come up with a plan and some options. A concert? Museum visit? A film? A ball game? Be specific. You know your child has a morning meeting near the museum. Suggest: "I'll meet you for lunch on Thursday, across the street from the museum. Afterward, we can see the Modigliani exhibit."

If you're the child of an aging parent, you may well have the problem of making money available without humiliating your parent or increasing his or her sense of dependency. Win-Win Negotiators will make certain that their parents' self-respect is preserved. Here's how to do it:

1. Recall the past. Remind your parent how he or she—or they—helped you through college, or to get started.
2. Speak with candor about your own present circumstances. If you're attempting to help them out, you're probably in good shape. It will mean a great deal to them to hear that assessment from you.
3. Don't suggest that your parents need your help. Stress, instead, that you want to share your good fortune, just as they shared theirs with you.

Negotiating with Friends

You find drugs in your son's dresser drawer. You need someone to talk to, to help you figure out what to do. Your partner's in Europe on business. You call your best friend.

Your mother's moved into her new apartment, where she's seated now, crying inconsolably because the difference between being the cherished wife she was until a few months ago and the widow she is today has been brought home to her, literally, in an ineradicable way. Your brother's living in Seattle, your sister in New York, and you're in Phoenix, alone. Whom do you call? Your best friend.

Families break up, drift apart, move on. Fissures develop that can't be breached. Into the gap come friends, whose loyalty and love, unencumbered by history, seem better—and in many cases are better—than what you obtained from parents. Very often when an emergency develops, summoning your family might evoke all kinds of compromising emotions. You know your friends won't ask any questions.

Careful. Close friends require the same care and attention and negotiating skills on your part as do members of your family.

Negotiating with Professionals and Other Intimidators

Why is it that intelligent, perceptive, successful men and women, poised and adept in all other circumstances, suddenly behave like insecure children when they walk into a doctor's office?

This same bewildering problem crops up over and over again in dealing with other "intimidators"—salespersons and service people, as well as lawyers, stockbrokers, and bankers— even though they are performing a service for *us*. "The rougher I treat them, the better they like it," one service person confided to me.

Let's be fair. There are countless professionals who are not intimidators. There is a tendency in all of us to deify The Professional. Some professionals try to discourage this tendency. Others exploit it.

The basic technique of these intimidators is to make us feel they know something we don't, and assign us to a childlike role. The means are sometimes so adroit we're not consciously aware of the power jockeying that's going on. Consider this simple greeting: "Hello, Brad, I'm Dr. Laurence." If Brad were fourteen and Dr. Laurence were fifty, nothing would be wrong. But Brad is in his late forties, and the doctor is ten years younger. If the doctor wishes to place the relationship on an informal footing, he should drop his title in favor of his own first name. But he doesn't do that.

The same subtle power play exists in all the professions and even many of the services. The lawyer says, "I don't want to throw a lot of legal theory at you." The stockbroker says, "Listen, sweetie, let me take care of it." The realtor says, "I know the market." Translation, in all cases: "You couldn't possibly understand." And often, in fact, you can't, because the language they speak—medicalese, legalese, what I call "psychoese," or any other kind of esoteric patter—is deliberately designed to perpetuate the mystery of their craft. So long as they alone remain privy to the mystery, they alone retain control.

And, oh, how beautifully it has worked! By accepting that they do, in fact, know more than we do about our interests, our bodies, our money, our happiness, we have perpetuated the glorification syndrome.

All of us, at one time or another, have been poorly treated by people we pay for service. In the following pages, we'll consider some techniques for achieving parity with professionals and other intimidators.

Priority One: Style

Before you negotiate with any professional, you have to be certain you've chosen one appropriate to your need. To do this, employ step one of the four-step process (see Chapter 12). Ask yourself, "What's the problem?"

Do you really need a professional, or can you solve the problem in whole or in part by yourself? Do you have a hidden agenda? Is it help you want, or is it affirmation and validation—someone to tell you you're on the right track?

Once you've decided you need professional help, you must then determine your role in the relationship.

Do you want a professional who works *with* you?

Do you want a professional who works *for* you?

Do you want a professional who *tells* you what to do?

These questions pertain to style—yours and the professionals'. Make certain your own style and purpose fit well with the style of the professional you're choosing. If you're a Soother who prefers to avoid responsibility, choosing another Soother to represent you could result in stagnation. Your preference, in business matters, could be a Dictator, who will make all your decisions for you. If you're seriously ill, you'd be most comforted by a Big Daddy or Big Mamma doctor who would reduce your anxiety with lots of strokes and love.

Suppose you're a writer, musician, or artist who needs an agent. You may want a Jungle Fighter to represent you. He or she will make all the nasty phone calls and threats at the bargaining table, and may well get you top dollar.

You may not need just a doctor or lawyer; your hidden agenda may call for a Big Daddy or Mamma who will take care of you. Or you may not want comforting so much as you want low-key, efficient, meticulous attention to detail as only a withdrawn Silhouette can give.

Preparing for Your Meeting

Before any meeting with a professional, remember that you are paying for a service, and (that payment depends on the quality of service given).

Do your homework in advance of your meeting. Explore your options, and gather information. When you're ready, call for an appointment. If possible, set your agenda at that time, and definitely inquire about the fee. Explain to the professional's secretary or receptionist that you're looking for someone to represent you, and you'd like five minutes of the professional's time. If the professional's "gatekeeper" tries to finesse you, explain that you'll be happy to pay the charge, if there is one. (A charge for such a call already tells you something about the professional.) It may be that the gatekeeper can answer your questions, in which case you won't need to speak to the professional directly. But be alert, in either case, to the manner in which you're treated.

Whenever I receive a referral, I say "Bravo!" to myself if the person begins to ask me questions. "It sounds as if you're interviewing me," I tell the caller. "I think that's a good idea. Instead of talking to me on the phone, why don't you make an appointment? I'll give you twenty minutes of my time at no charge."

When you arrive at the professional's office, bring an attitude and your experience. Promise yourself you won't be intimidated by the professional's status or possible contempt for others. Hopefully, you've arrived before your situation has become desperate, so that panic doesn't impinge on clarity and focus.

Part of your preparation should be to write out all of your questions. Bring that list with you to your appointment. By all means, make notes during your appointment.

It's your job to inquire about fees, to note working habits and amount of time spent with you. It's your job to determine if you're well received, if the office is clean and comfortable, if your comfort is uppermost in the minds of the staff or if you're made to wait an unconscionable amount of time, if the professional puts you at ease or makes you nervous, if he or she is perfunctory or thorough.

All of this information is available to you, much of it simply by observing, the rest by asking questions either of the professional or of his or her staff.

How to Interview a Professional

To me, the key moment in any relationship with a professional is the first encounter. You not only learn what you want to know about that person, you make known to him or her what you want to know about yourself—that you're alert, concerned, informed, and determined to participate in all decisions affecting your life.

Not long ago, I had occasion to shop for a new attorney. My first objective, when I called him, was to establish that when I eventually saw him it would be for purposes of exploration and not necessarily commitment. I began with a probe. "Mr. Bart," I said, "you've been referred by a friend. I'd like to come in and talk to you for an hour [specifying time] about a problem I've been having. [No details of the problem at this point. No full thrust.] I'd like you to understand that this is merely a preliminary meeting [setting the agenda for exploration, not action], and I'd like to know what you charge."

"I'd be delighted to see you," he said. "My fee for the hour will be seventy-five dollars. If we go over a few minutes, don't worry, and I certainly won't be charging for this phone call."

(Had his reply been, "Don't worry about the fee," I would have persisted: "I really must know before coming to see you. It might be a barrier to our working together." I'm thereby also planting the seed that I intend to be a partner in this endeavor.)

When I went to the attorney's office for my initial visit, I observed how the receptionist was treated by the various partners in the firm, and how she treated me. She was well treated, and so was I. I also observed that the office waiting room wasn't crowded, a sign of consideration for clients. The office had a conservative look; there was no razzle-dazzle or expensive chic that the clients would ultimately pay for. And I was well prepared for my hour; I had gone over my problem, done my homework, readied my questions, inventoried my needs. An hour is not a long time when you have a major problem, and $75 is a lot of money.

My questions were listed on a piece of paper. I also had paper with which to make notes during our interview. I can't stress strongly enough how important that piece of paper is. When you're in pressured situations, feeling fear, anxiety, or anger, you tend to forget what you came for. You're afraid, believe it or not, to waste the doctor's or lawyer's time. Listing your questions will make certain that you don't forget them.

When I met the attorney, I noted that his desk was filled with papers, but not in a disorganized way. Everything was in folders. There were no piles of papers or folders in which my particular paper might one day get lost. I could surmise that this attorney was a busy man—a good sign—but not a harried one.

The exploratory meeting is just that—a time to evaluate how the professional treats you and how he or she thinks. You want to get past the superficial trappings of the office and the professional's veneer of brilliance. You want to know what options he or she would consider in handling your problem.

You do a full thrust in laying out your problem, but you shouldn't ask for or expect any detailed planning of strategy in this preliminary visit. What you're after is some insight into the workings of the professional's mind, knowledge of his or her orientation and philosophy and how it matches up with yours.

Since we had talked on the phone and agreed to the purpose of our meeting and its cost, I came right to the point. I described the problem and told him what I wanted. Then I asked him a question I always ask of professionals in such circumstances, and one I recommend to you: *"Inasmuch as I'm inexperienced in your field, tell me the questions I ought to be asking you."*

His reception could not have been more cordial. He laughed with delight at my question. He then enumerated the questions I should be asking. I carefully wrote the questions down—and later asked these questions of two other attorneys before finally settling on Mr. Bart.

Devious? Not at all. *Caveat emptor*—let the buyer beware. You're shopping, and the seller must pass inspection.

When you're interviewing a professional, be alert to little ploys such as too familiar address, and to bigger ploys like, "If you don't go along with my decisions there's no way I can help you." Be sure that the professional does most of the talking. You won't learn enough about him or her if you spend your hour talking about yourself. If you're confused about an answer to your question, ask for clarification. Men, in particular, are often too embarrassed to confess to an expert that they don't understand what he or she is talking about. What he or she is talking about pertains to your life.

Leave the interview certain you've learned what you need to know. No matter how pleasing the chemistry between you, don't make a commitment until you've had an opportunity to put some time and distance into the mix. First impressions can change overnight.

It was clear to me, after interviewing my three candidates and thinking about their responses, that I wanted Mr. Bart to represent me. When I informed him of my decision, I said, "There's a very easy way to negotiate with me. Keep me informed, and return my phone calls." At the same time, I let

him know what was in it for him. "I won't bother you unless it's important, and I'll pay my bills on time."

Negotiating with Your Doctor

For a doctor, I want a Win-Win Negotiator who accepts me as a partner in my health care. Such doctors are hard to find. Most of them are still caught up in what I call the "awe concept."

Doctors differ in their training, their skills, their dispositions, and their psychological preparedness. Some of them simply can't handle what happens when, at the age of twenty-four, they're given a white coat and sent on rounds, when persons old enough to be their parents or even grandparents call them "Doctor" and look to them for salvation. There are doctors who are inattentive, who don't keep up on the latest treatments, who make wrong diagnoses, who drink too much and stay out too late, who overload their practices, who are impatient and make snap decisions, who are in business more for the money than for the healing they are supposed to give. There are thousands of splendid doctors. There are other thousands who embody one or more of these problem characteristics. Surely the worst of these problems is the doctor's unwavering belief in his own wisdom.

A young woman I know visited a prestigious gynecologist complaining of severe abdominal pain. The gynecologist gave her a perfunctory examination and assured her that nothing was wrong. "You look terrific, sweetie." But the pain persisted. She returned to the doctor; again he assured her that everything was normal. Several days passed. One night, she awakened with pain so severe that she had to crawl to the telephone to summon help. A friend raced her to an emergency hospital where a hysterectomy was performed. The postoperative analysis disclosed that something had gone wrong with her intrauterine device, and that gangrene had set in. It was a miracle that she hadn't died.

Who was the responsible party? The doctor? Perhaps. But what that young woman needed to say and didn't was, "The fact that I look terrific is not relevant to my pain. I want to be thoroughly checked out."

When people have unnecessary surgery, I have to ask, "Who's the culprit, the doctor who knows that surgery is his safest course, or the patient who failed to ask whether the operation was truly necessary?"

I know of a plastic surgeon who walks into an examining room, glances briefly at a woman patient, says, "All right, we're going to do your eyes, but your boobs need doing too. Make an appointment at the desk," and then disappears. What is almost more appalling is that the woman patient then goes to the desk and says, "Doctor says I should make an appointment to do two things."

What she—or you—should do is run to the nearest exit. The surgeon is patently a Jungle Fighter, the worst possible choice for a doctor. But if he is a brilliant surgeon whose services you require, don't let him bully you. Respond with a *full thrust*. "No, that's not what I wish." Ask about the diagnostic procedures, the possible consequences of the surgery, and the rationale for his suggestion. Demand answers. *Address the issue* at all times. Tell him, "I feel you're pressing me." Unless he can convince you of the benefits of surgery, don't let him perform it.

"I'm Hardly a Piece of Meat"

We come now to that matter patients are most loathe to discuss, and the one that most needs discussing—the doctor's fee.

Like other professionals, doctors all have fee schedules. They are, or should be, yours for the asking. It's imperative that you inform yourself about these fees before you undertake treatment.

A young woman who had recently moved to Los Angeles asked a friend to recommend a physician after experiencing a sore throat that persisted an undue length of time. The doctor was a kind, fatherly man, a prototypic Big Daddy, who put his arm around her, called her "Judy," and assured her that everything would be all right. Judy's first visit lasted twenty minutes, during which time he listened intently to her story, and then told her that she needed to schedule another appointment for a more complete workup, a request to which she acquiesced. After her second examination, he prescribed some extremely expensive medication. Judy bought the medicine without question, then suffered severe side effects. After reporting these, she asked if there wasn't some cheaper medication he could recommend. He prescribed a medication that was one-fifth the price. Two weeks later, Judy received her bill from the doctor—for $430.

Now some of this was her fault. She had not been specific. She had not announced to the doctor that she did not want a complete workup, that she was not enlisting him as her physician, that she specifically wanted treatment only for her sore throat. She did not inquire about the doctor's fees in advance of her appointment. She should have used the appropriate tactics and done her homework. If she had used a mid-course correction, in which she stopped, asked questions (How much should these services have cost? What are the prevailing rates? What will the insurance company pay?), prepared to communicate her message without hostility, and admitted to herself that she had participated in creating the problem, and then took steps to fix the situation, she could have saved herself a lot of misery. But she atoned for her mistakes. She promptly called the offices of several other doctors and asked what their fees were for a complete physical. The answer was $150 to $250. Then she called the original doctor and objected to her bill. "That's my fee," the doctor replied. "No one's ever questioned it before." He invited her to come in to discuss the matter. "No thanks," she said, "I'm a little short on cash." "This one's on me," he said—at which point Judy recognized that she was in control. Her confidence shot up. She went to see the doctor. "I'm sorry you feel the way you do, Judith," the doctor said, "but look at how the price of meat has risen." "I'm hardly a piece of meat," Judy said. She wrote out a check for $230, the amount she had ascertained that the insurance company would allow, marked the check "paid in full," handed it to the doctor, and left his office.

Judy did well. Her story proves that you don't have to acquiesce to a gouging. But consider how much misery she could have saved herself had she used the appropriate tactics from the outset—the ones she eventually used.

Negotiating with Your Stockbroker

Why on earth you should have to negotiate with a stock-broker when the money he's using is yours defies all logic. Nonetheless, you do. Otherwise, you'll find decisions being taken that are often contrary to your interest. This is not a book on investing, but just bear this incontrovertible fact in mind: your interests and your broker's interests are inherently contradictory. He makes money only when he buys and sells your securities—but it's often in your best interest to do nothing. It's from this conflict that your most basic problem flows.

A while back, I tried an experiment. On successive days, I went into two different brokerage houses in Beverly Hills, California, as two different people. My objective was to determine how the style I broadcast would affect the treatment I received.

First Day: I wore mousy clothing, sensible shoes, and a bland face, and affected the slouch of a Soother who knows the world has passed her by. I hemmed and hawed to the receptionist about how I might want to invest a little money in the market because I'd heard it was the thing to do. Result: "Help yourself to some pamphlets, honey," the receptionist said. That I might want to discuss investments with a broker was not even considered.

Second Day: I walked determinedly up to the receptionist and waited just long enough to let her take a good look at me— my quiet but coordinated outfit, carried on an erect but relaxed body, the in-fashion styling of my hair and makeup, the thin briefcase in my hand. "Hello," I said, "I'm Dr. Warschaw. I'd like to make an appointment to see your manager. I'd like to discuss some investments." Five minutes later, I was seated in the manager's office, he was listening respectfully to my ideas about how I wanted my money invested, and it was evident that he was prepared to give me as much time as I wished.

Before you visit a broker, *do your homework.* Read books on investing, newspapers and periodicals about the stock market. Sit in a brokerage house, just to absorb the atmosphere and acquire the feeling of belonging. When you find yourself face to face with a broker, *attend and observe.* What kind of person is this? The stock market attracts more than its share of aggressive people, not simply because there's money to be made but because the manner of making the money is downright intoxicating. So you can expect to encounter Jungle Fighters, Dictators, Silhouettes, and Big Daddies and Mammas. I'd choose a Silhouette; he or she will approach the market most clinically, pay greater attention to detail, and in an arena highly charged with emotion, react with clinical detachment.

Many stockbrokers attempt, almost by reflex, to dominate their women customers. I won't accept such treatment. I've trained my women clients not to accept it, either. "I liked you when you were stupid and didn't ask so many questions," a Jungle Fighter stockbroker said to one of my clients.

"I have one last question," she replied. "When can I pick up my portfolio?"

You have options galore when you make investments. There are hundreds of firms and thousands of stockbrokers to choose from. You can keep choosing until you find a broker who will *want* you to participate in all decisions. You have the most potent trade-off imaginable—your business in exchange for his or her deference to your wishes.

If your broker tells you he or she is too busy to consult you on all decisions, you have a simple remedy—a cost-benefit analysis. Are the profits he or she is making you enough to compensate for a lack of regard for your wishes?

Have a contingency plan ready—another broker to go to if this one proves unsuccessful. Pull on your web. Find out which of your friends have successful relationships with their brokers. Interview those brokers before you need one. Tell them you might want to transfer your account. Ask them to outline their market strategies.

Your return-on-investment can't always be measured in dollars and cents. If the value of your portfolio diminishes, but your investment strategy is sound, don't fault your broker.

Negotiating with Your Agent

"Agents," a famous television writer once observed, "are people we hire to say the things in our behalf that we're afraid to say ourselves." While most people don't have agents to represent them, the problem that their representation creates is one everyone can learn from.

That problem has to do with dependency.

We've dealt repeatedly throughout this book with the difficulties involved in determining what you want and then confronting the choices and decisions that will lead you to it. Can you imagine paying someone ten percent of your earnings to perpetuate this dependency and to intimidate you as well?

The greatest mistake people who hire agents make is to assume that the agents will then charge off to conquer the world in their behalf, with no further effort on their own part.

You must work for your agent at least as hard as he or she works for you, and probably a good bit harder. If you're in a profession in which agents are used—writing, acting, composing, painting, sports, and so forth—it may mean you have time. Use that time to train, to put your sound out, to cultivate contacts, and to monitor your agent's activities in your behalf.

Don't assume that your agent knows what's best for you and don't, whatever you do, consign all of the decision making about your career to him or her. Before you know it, the agent, not you, will be in control of your destiny. Remember that your agent's function is to recommend, not to make decisions. Until he or she has earned your trust through performance, you should subject those recommendations to more than normal scrutiny. Agents aren't always the best judges of what the market will bear. I have a client who was sought by a studio to produce a film. She suggested to her agent that he ask the studio for a profit-sharing provision in the contract.

"They'll never do it," he said.

"Try," she insisted.

The agent tried, and failed.

"Go back and ask them for a royalty on each run of the film," she said.

"They'll never do it," he said again.

But the producer was adamant, which compelled her agent to act. He did, and was dumbfounded when the studio agreed.

Don't wait for your agent to do it all. You've got to be a partner in efforts to secure benefits for yourself. You've got to come up with creative ideas with which your agent can promote your work.

Set a time line. Just about all creative people have experienced that most baffling of initial problems: You can't get work until you have an agent—and you can't get an agent until you have work. Once you miraculously resolve that paradox and have an agent, it's assumed by one and all that you're talented and have something to offer. If nothing's happened after a year or two or three—whatever deadline you've set—move on. Before you do, however, make a contingency plan. Find another agent. *Then* fire the old one.

Divorcing Your Doctor, Lawyer, Agent, Etc.

No professional is right for you, no matter how talented he or she is, if you don't get the service you need. Don't jump to conclusions; if your calls aren't being returned, your professional may really be busy, or out of town; he or she may really not have received your message. But if he or she repeatedly shows you lack of courtesy or respect, or won't listen attentively, it's time to remember who's working for whom.

Attempt a mid-course correction: "I think we're on the wrong track. If we can't work together any better than this, I might have to look elsewhere."

Before you're forced to your bottom line, try some warm-ups: "What progress do you think we've made in the last three months?" Or: "I feel our relationship isn't working. How do you feel about it?"

Be sure that a hidden agenda isn't making you stay on long after it's time to leave.

If you're put down and ignored, if your judgment is not considered, if what *you* want isn't uppermost in the professional's mind, it's time to move on. Fire your professional, using a full thrust: "I'd like my statement and my records."

Negotiating with Your Banker

One day I came upon a friend of mine as he was walking down the street. "Stumbling" is closer to the truth. His eyes were on the pavement, his head was forward, his shoulders were stooped. I thought, my God, someone's died.

No one had, it developed. My friend was on his way to see his banker—not because he was in trouble, simply to borrow some money.

Few people realize what power they represent when they

walk into a bank. Believe it or not, bankers need *you*. Without you, they couldn't stay in business. They can be picky only to a point; ultimately, they *have* to lend money. More than that, they're in competition with hundreds of other banks for your business.

So, when you walk into your bank, look your banker in the eye. Use small talk and probes to gather information. "I'm thinking of expanding. A lot would depend on how much the capital would cost me." It's up to the banker now to come at you with terms that would make that expansion attractive.

Be sure you've done your homework. No matter how well disposed toward your request, your banker will still need facts and figures.

Be sure, too, that you ask for enough money. Few people do that. I once asked a banker if there was any difference between men and women in the way they negotiated for a loan. "No," he said, "neither men nor women ask for as much as they really need."

When you've made your presentation, *pause*. Give your banker time to study your proposal.

If the loan is refused, you have the right to know why. You're bridging here; you may want to come back.

Once your loan is approved, keep your contact informed on the progress of your venture.

Negotiating with Contractors

Some of your best friends may be contractors. Some of mine are, too. But I would never do business with them without a contract, no matter what calls on loyalty they mustered or what inducements they offered.

Anyone who has ever built or remodeled a home knows that reality is no match for fantasy. Unless you take precautions, your dreams can overwhelm your judgment.

If the contractor gives you promises, pressure, and razzle-dazzle, the chances are he's a Jungle Fighter. Make him be specific. When he says he'll finish in April, make him specify the completion date in the contract.

Demand references. Ask, especially, for a record of the jobs he's done within the last year. Follow up those references.

Beware of the contractor who won't give you a fixed-price contract, but insists, instead, on a "cost-plus-ten" deal. He can't possibly get hurt on that basis, but you can go broke. If "cost-plus" is the only way you can get the job done, insist on a "not-to-exceed" clause that states the most he can possibly charge. If the contractor refuses, don't proceed unless you're prepared for financial ruin.

Whatever agreement you reach, get it in writing, and then show the contract to your attorney before you sign. The attorney's fee is the best $50–$100 you'll ever spend.

Sink your bottom line in concrete. Don't let it stretch by making noncontracted modifications. That opens the door to mischief.

Know your resources—the city and county building inspectors whose job it is to protect you. They make regular inspections, but call them if you even think that something's gone wrong.

Negotiating a Crisis

Rain has flooded the carpets, soaked the ceiling, ruined the drapes, and damaged the electrical wiring. You need a roofer, the drapers, carpet repair, insurance assessor, and an electrician.

Don't panic. Reduce your anxiety (jog, meditate, or eat a Godiva chocolate). Don't make a major decision on the day you gather your information unless the crisis compels it—i.e., water still pouring through the ceiling.

Do your homework. List the damage item by item and next to each item the type of service needed and the name of a referral. If you've no referrals, pull on your web by calling friends, associates, and relatives.

Do comparative shopping. Call at least three numbers from the "yellow pages." Remember: you're still the buyer even in an emergency. If you don't like the price, don't buy.

Suppose the electrician's the first to arrive. He's in a hurry, offers no opening ceremonies, and assumes he'll begin work immediately. You spot his Jungle Fighter style, so you're specific about what you want. You ask him his price per hour, and his estimate for this particular job. He replies, Jungle Fighter style, "I'll let you know when I'm finished with the job." You stay focused on your agenda and repeat your request, using the broken record technique if necessary. You curb your own **Big Daddy/Big Mamma** tendencies to offer him coffee and a chat, because it will cost you money.

When you obtain his estimate, it's outrageous. You say to him: "I'd like you to do the work because you come so highly recommended. However, you're five-hundred dollars over the average for this type of work." (Your homework is paying off.)

He replies: "Take my estimate or leave it."

You reply: "I'd like to take it, since I know that I'll have work for you after this crisis [a benefit for him]. I would be willing to pay two-hundred dollars over the average price for your quality services."

You win by not responding to his intimidation. The work has quality potential, and you're willing to pay for quality work. He wins a customer, future business, and referrals.

Negotiating with a Conglomerate

Customers can't talk to computers. Only programmers do that. So don't waste your letterhead when you develop a problem with one of the great conglomerates. Pick up the phone and call.

Here are some giveaway characteristics to help you identify the party on the other end of the line:

Jungle Fighters will keep putting you on hold.

Dictators will cite company policy.

Silhouettes will cut you off.

Big Mammas and Daddies will commiserate and tell you what you should have done.

Soothers will commiserate and tell you they can't help you.

Win-Win Negotiators will ask for pertinent information and promise to follow through.

Suppose you're calling to discuss a bill that seems far out of line:

Have paper and pen or pencil ready. Note the date and time of your call.

Listen carefully for the name of the service representative. If he or she doesn't give it, ask for it.

Give the person you're calling a deadline for gathering the necessary information and getting back to you. If he or she hasn't called by then, you call.

If you can't get satisfaction from this representative, ask to speak to his or her supervisor. Say to the supervisor, "These are the steps I've taken. The problem hasn't been solved. How can we solve it?"

If you have to write instead of calling, end your letter with the statement that you will call on a certain date to find out what action has been taken.

Negotiating in a Department Store

You have two opponents to deal with when you're shopping. The first is that salesperson coming your way, with shrewd, testing eyes sizing you up as a looker or buyer, a smile that says, "Well, you're probably not good enough for our lines, dearie, but let's give it a try." The second opponent is yourself. Unfortunately, you can't take these opponents on one at a time. That salesperson knows all about those "wants" you've carefully tried to disguise.

Negotiate with yourself. Is that ski equipment essential to your life? Or are you playing out a fantasy?

Do a quick cost-benefit analysis. If the benefits exceed the costs, the purchase is a reasonable one. If costs exceed benefits, and you still want the items, consider what you're willing to trade off.

What you don't need at this moment is the counsel of a self-interested stranger.

If you feel you're being pressed, say to the salesperson, "I'd like to think about it. I'll let you know." Then do think about it—at least overnight.

Jungle Fighter salespersons, in particular, may try to disrupt your thinking with incessant patter. There are two ways to handle that. Either use the broken record technique, repeating, "I'll get back to you," over and over again, or else address the issue: "I feel you're pressing me, I'm taking time to think about it."

Negotiating with Hairdressers

They'll shape your image, validate your body, make you appealing. You'll trade off a lot for their best effort; you'll acquiesce, accept their abuse, flatter their ego. The supposed trade-off: your own uncertainty about how you should look in exchange for their all-knowing wisdom.

If such Soother-like tactics only paid off! They don't. Not only does the abuse continue, and even increase, the domination of the stylists results in work that flatters them, not you.

I've seen Soothers in beauty salons wait and wait for the Jungle Fighter stylist who abuses, humilitates, and manipulates them. "I'm two hours behind. Go get lunch or something," one stylist said to a woman who arrived on time for her appointment. And she did!

If you're being intimidated by a hairdresser, don't accept the abuse, because it will only continue.

Address the issue. "This is the third time you've made me wait."

Announce your limits. "I'll be back in one hour, at which time I expect to be taken. If it happens the next time, I won't return."

Prepare a contingency plan. Interview other stylists. Note hair styles you admire; ask who did them.

Do it. If you're made to wait once more, leave.

Gaining Parity with Headwaiters

I walked into the restaurant ahead of my escort, who was parking the car. I walked up to the captain and said, "Reservation for Doctor Warschaw." The captain consulted his list, but did nothing more. I supposed that, seeing the reservation was for two, he was waiting for my escort. The moment my escort arrived, the captain beamed, "Right this way, Doctor," he said.

"I'm not the doctor. She's the doctor," my escort said.

The captain stopped, turned, looked at me, then at my escort, then back at me. "You're kidding!" he said.

I've told this story many times to large audiences, and it always hits a nerve. Many of us are "bull-dozed" by headwaiters. Somehow they manipulate us into seeking their approval, even though it's we who are buying the service.

They do have power. They can make your experience memorable or disagreeable. But you have power too—the power of your patronage and that all important word-of-mouth endorsement by which restaurants live or die.

Insist on courtesy and efficiency, and complain if you don't get it. A Win-Win Negotiator observed his Soother dinner companion being abused by a Jungle Fighter waiter, who impatiently tapped his pencil against his pad. As he waited for the Soother to order, she asked, "Which is better—the lamb or the fish?" "Make your own decisions," the Jungle Fighter replied. Then he turned to the Win-Winner. "What do you want?"

"Another waiter," he said in a determined voice.

There are those who believe that service persons must be dealt with harshly. I couldn't disagree more. I believe strongly in courtesy and openness, and in responding to good service not simply with a tip but with a smile and a thank you.

If you're dissatisfied with the service you've been given, you have to make that known. People won't know what to offer you if you don't tell them what you want. You'll get what you want most often by making them want to give it to you. Jungle Fighter tactics—loud curses at the waiters, caresses for the waitresses, ostentatious tipping—rarely do the job; even if you get the attention you want, you'll mortify those who are with you. If you get a poor waiter, ask the manager for another one. If the service continues to be bad, call for the owner. In a calm, firm, quiet voice say, "This is my first experience in your restaurant. So far it hasn't been a good one. How can you help me?" Your question is open-ended, there's been no abusiveness, and you've put the responsibility on the owner.

Seating and service can be negotiated; just remember that you're the buyer and be a courteous one. That's the key to your dealing with all service people.

When All Else Has Failed

There are a few problems that can't be well resolved if you will remain calmly focused on the issues and your objective. One of my clients gave a parking lot attendant a $20 bill; he gave her change for $10. An hour later she noticed the discrepancy. Before returning to negotiate, she made certain that she hadn't spent the money elsewhere. She decided that the best strategy was to assume an honest error had been made. But he told her everything had come out "even." Instead of losing her composure, she said, "Well, the money may not be in your drawer, but it isn't in my pocket, either, so we have to find out where it went." At her request, the attendant called his supervisor, who then talked to my client. He told her the money couldn't be returned because the attendant had come out even. However, they would give her $10 worth of parking validations free.

But there are those times when reason and regard for the other person can't do the job. Your last recourse—your bottom line—if you don't get satisfaction from any commercial entity, be it Consolidated Edison or A–Number One Used Cars, is to go public.

Lodge a complaint with the Better Business Bureau.

Tell your story to a newspaper or television station with a consumer advocate program. Most business people abhor the prospect of adverse publicity, but you must use this bottom line with discretion, and only after you've made absolutely sure of your case. One of my clients, stuck with a $600 repair bill on a used car she'd been pressured into buying by a Jungle Fighter salesman, wrote the president of the agency, demanding reimbursement within forty-eight hours, and threatening disclosure to the action reporter of the local television station if she didn't get it. She got it.

Remember: you need service, but the people who offer service need you. That goes for everyone from the biggest conglomerates to the person who waits on your table. If you'll keep this mutual dependency in mind *and* do your homework, you should never have to feel inadequate or manipulated.

Your Negotiating Checklist

Whether you're dealing with doctors, lawyers, stockbrokers, service persons, or anyone else you hire to help you, the following commandments apply:

DO

Ask the fee, and when necessary, negotiate a fee reduction or time to pay.

Gather information before your interview. Ask specific open-ended questions.

Write down your questions before the interview.

Ask for clarification of any statement you don't understand.

Trust your instincts.

Remember that the subject of concern is your money or body or life.

Stay on the track and focused on your agenda.

Focus on the positive but maintain clarity about the negatives.

Be cautious and stop, reflect, and then respond.

Get a second opinion, or even a third.

Be wary of a negotiator who doesn't give you an option.

Remember that you are the buyer.

DON'T

Give in if the facts prove you're right.

Be seduced by another person's status, license, or credentials.

Become angry, unless anger is appropriate to your objective, and then be sure it's diffused.

Let others make your decision for you.

Be easy just to make people like you. They won't.

Believe that you haven't a right to know. You do!

Closing
Ceremonies

You've just taken one giant step toward a livelier, fuller life. You've learned how to negotiate for power, for money, for sex, love, and romance, with members of your family, with friends, with doctors, lawyers, even headwaiters and hairdressers—all the people, in effect, who populate your life and contribute to its tensions. But in order to negotiate to your maximum in any of these categories, you must ultimately learn to negotiate with the most formidable adversary of all—yourself.

Most people pass through large portions of their lives as though they were on automatic pilot. Life, itself, is unfelt and unobserved. It takes an external event of great magnitude to shake them from their torpor—loss of a job, a divorce, an illness, a death in the family. For Jungle Fighters, the event must be truly calamitous. Dictators respond only when the overwhelming responsibilities they've heaped upon themselves produce heart attacks or nervous breakdowns. Silhouettes finally recognize that time alone means loneliness. Big Daddies and Mammas finally acknowledge that they're taking care of everyone except themselves. Soothers look with horror at the cost of being nice to everyone, regardless of the circumstances—

a life without passion, a feeling of emptiness. Even Win-Win Negotiators are sometimes brought up short by the realization that their priorities are askew.

It's at this point that we PAUSE.

The pause is the beginning of awareness. It's the moment when all the clues have come together into the irresistible prospect that your life—and your style—aren't working for you. At last, you are willing to look, in a systematic way, at how your life is spent.

However it happens, the shock alerts you to the realization that life is not being experienced as it ought to be, and that it is you who must do something about it. At that point, the recognition that the responsibility for change is yours becomes clear and visceral and unchallengeable. Under these circumstances, even a Soother will become aroused.

Negotiating with yourself reduces to a single question: *How do I want to live my life?* If you know that answer, everything else falls readily into place; if you don't, you can't begin to find a place for yourself.

Rather than answer that question, many people prefer to let others answer it for them. They often play roles that others either expect them to play or allow them to play. If one person in a relationship is extremely passive and allows the other person to rule his or her life, setting all the criteria for performance, the other person will do it. That, in effect, makes the other person a Dictator or Big Daddy or Mamma, even though he or she might not have elected that role. Not only is the passive person allowing this dominance, he or she is saying, "I need it."

If you've been a Soother all your life, you can't be a Win-Win Negotiator tomorrow morning. Nor is the transition any easier or swifter if your dominant style has been that of a Jungle Fighter, Dictator, Silhouette, or Big Daddy or Mamma. You may not even need or want to make a complete transition; it bears repeating that the magic, energy, and verve of the Jungle Fighter, the prowess and decisiveness of the Dictator, the creativity of the Silhouette, the empathy of the Big Daddy/ Big Mamma, and the loyalty and generosity of the Soother are qualities worth preserving.

Yet the Win-Winners I have met in the course of my

research and interviews possessed much more health and vitality than exponents of Win-Lose, Lose-Lose, and Lose-Win styles. It struck me that they were practicing a form of preventive medicine; by forgoing acts of personal destruction so typical of the abusive stylists, they were eliminating one major cause of the ulcers, heart trouble, and weight problems so prevalent among the other stylists and their victims. I found Win-Winners to be mostly successful in their businesses, to be experiencing a balanced life filled with the love of family and friends and commitment to the world around them. While they respected work and money and power, they had incorporated all three into a well-balanced life. If they weren't rich, they felt rich.

In the old way of winning, one person garnered all the rewards—power, control, presidency, and Gold Cup. It was old-style winning that nurtured the Dictator/Jungle Fighter style. It worked for a long time—for the winners, at least. But it doesn't work well any longer.

The new Win-Win philosophy in a personal negotiation is based on one simple, demonstrable fact: we need one another. Once you declare for Win-Win, it changes your style of behavior. You're no longer self-absorbed, but self-enlightened. You put energy into achieving your goals, but save enough to help others achieve theirs. Nowhere is the conversion to Win-Win more dramatically perceived, perhaps, than in the relationships between parents and children.

Every child is a future negotiator. He or she will negotiate to a great extent in terms of the imprint you give. Children who grow up with Win-Win persons as models learn mutuality, sharing, love, and respect. They discover that personal power derives not from the exercise of abusive control over others but from competence and self-esteem. Because they, themselves, were not abused, they will not need to abuse others.

Such learning isn't automatic. It takes effort on the part of both parents and children, particularly in making certain that old, habitual attitudes don't seep into the relationship.

We've seen that women have been raised to believe that there is some man out there who will take care of them. If you want your daughter to grow up with a more independent frame of mind, don't say to her when she asks about needs, "That's something you needn't worry about." Encourage her to work for something, just as you would encourage your son. If you reward assertiveness in your son, be sure you also reward it in your daughter.

We've seen that men have been raised to focus on the skills and attitudes necessary to getting ahead in their work and in life. What they also need is to develop the compassion and tenderness that has for so long been typed as feminine. If you want your son to grow up with a more humanistic frame of mind, you can help him develop compassion by sitting and talking to him and giving him opportunities to assist and help others in a loving and caring way. Teach him to listen to the emotional as well as the intellectual content of experience.

Nurturing your children on the positive new ideas at large in society will produce in them the equilibrium, fairness of judgment, and self-esteem that make a Win-Win Negotiator. What better tribute to your parenting can there be than to build confident negotiators who have courage, are willing to take risks, and have the compassion to understand that a win in which the other person is left empty is no win at all?

The best possible negotiator is really an amalgam of the best in men and women. By blending the traits that society has always encouraged in each sex together with those qualities you've always cherished in yourself, you become not a reflection of another's image, but something new and unique.

At no previous time in history have men and women been presented with such freedom to choose behavior patterns, goals, and expectations that are not sex-typed. Certainly each sex brings a different life history to the negotiating table. But both are able to make choices without reference to the old societal mandate to "act like a man" or "act like a woman." The Win-Win women negotiators I've interviewed are well-informed, decisive, and tough when toughness is needed. But they can also be nurturing, feminine, and responsive. Men can be tender and sensitive without being accused of weakness.

We no longer need to live as though we were products of the economy of scarcity. We all have the capacity to love, share, and enjoy a diversity of people and experiences.

We have gone through a revolution in human relationships with respect to marriage and the family. Yet, in my practice and with my groups, I can see a return to some of the stabilities of older relationships. I see growing understanding that both men and women should actualize themselves in careers as well as marriage. I see more open, cooperative relationships, without one person needing to be up and the other down. I see people merging the best of the old and new. I see the fruits of "Win-Win."

Index